WILLIAM THOMAS
& family

The 300 year history of 12 generations of the
THOMAS family of Devon and New Zealand.

by T N Price

First published 2001 (in hardback) by the author.
ISBN # 0-473-07735-3

This paperback edition published 2011 by:
Starting Gun Books, Auckland, New Zealand

National Library of New Zealand Cataloguing-in-Publication Data

Price, Trevor N. (Trevor Nelson), 1937-
William Thomas & family : the 300 year history of 12 generations
of the Thomas family of Devon and New Zealand / T.N. Price. Pbk. ed.
Previous ed.: Auckland [N.Z.] : T.N. Price, 2001.
Includes bibliographical references and index.
ISBN 978-0-473-18748-4
1. Thomas, William, fl. 1710-1732—Family. 2. Thomas family.
3. New Zealand—Genealogy. 4. Devon (England)—Genealogy.
I. Title.
929.20993 —dc 22

Cover by Mary-Ann Attree
Printed by Lightning Source

This book is dedicated to all those family members who assisted
willingly to provide the contents of this book.

"Not to know what happened before we were born,
Is to remain perpetually a child,
Unless it is woven into the life of our ancestors. "
Cicero… Roman Orator 106-43 BC

APOLOGY:

We offer an apology to all descendants of William and Eliza Thomas.
When we produced *"The THOMAS family"* book in 1993 we had not at that time found a living descendant of <u>William and Eliza Thomas</u> and that book mainly contained the life history and family tree detail for William's <u>brother John Thomas and family</u>, plus <u>Uncle George Thomas and family</u>.

The detail contained in that book, of William and Eliza and son Jack, is in the main accurate, but is very much short of detail. For instance, without the help of a living descendant we had found only one child, when in fact there were 14 children. So, we have spent a lot of the past eight years gathering information for this book, to put the matter right.

Trevor.

CONTENTS:

AUTHOR'S NOTE:

The following pages have been compiled from information received from many Thomas descendants, historical books and official documents. We acknowledge most of these on page 312, however, we thank all of you for your general interest and encouragement.

The LIFE STORIES run from that person's birth to their death, and we show as many photos as we could place.

The 'New Zealand FAMILY TREES'. We apologise for any spaces.

--oo0Ooo--

A brief explanation of the 'New Zealand Family Tree' layout…
There were two brothers who came to New Zealand……
JOHN AND GEORGE THOMAS
with John's wife Jane and their two sons William and John.
We have nominated John, Jane and George as lst generation New Zealanders and their children as 2nd generation, and this continues on down to today's 8th generation in the year 2001.

lst, 2nd and 3rd New Zealand generations are shown in the
BRIEF FAMILY TREE on pages 8 and 9.

The TREE detail is printed in vertical columns, starting with the first born and completing their children's and grandchildren's details before moving onto the next oldest's details.

b	=	Birth date.	at =	Town of Birth or Marriage.
m	=	Marriage date.	d =	Death date.
Bur at	=	Town where buried, not town where died.		

A look at your own immediate family will show you
how easy to read this system is.

The **FAMILY INDEX** at the rear of the book contains your name.

CHAPTER ONE

THE THOMAS FAMILY:

This book is about the Thomas Family of Devon and New Zealand.
In fact it covers nearly 300 years.....
from 1700 through to the present day... 2001.

TWELVE GENERATIONS altogether are followed and we have divided these up into 4 Devon and 8 New Zealand generations.

Two brothers, **JOHN THOMAS** (Chapter Three) & **GEORGE** of the 5th Devon generation, came to New Zealand and we have made them the first New Zealand generation.

John and George left behind in Devon, two brothers and two sisters. We follow their sister **ELIZABETH's** family (starting page 24) whom we have met and who still lives in Devon.

In the main, this book details the lives of Chapter Three John's son **William and wife Eliza** (Chapter Four) and their 14 children.

For the life story and family trees of William's <u>brother John and Phebe Thomas</u> plus William's <u>Uncle George and Polly Thomas</u> please refer to the book, by the same author....
"The THOMAS Family of Devon and New Zealand."

BRIEF FAMILY TREE and INDEX.
Due to there being a large number of people named......
William, John, Elizabeth and George Thomas,
we follow this page with a Brief Family Tree starting in
1700 and depicting the first seven of the twelve generations.

Chapter Two provides more details of the Devon families.

THOMAS FAMILY TREE

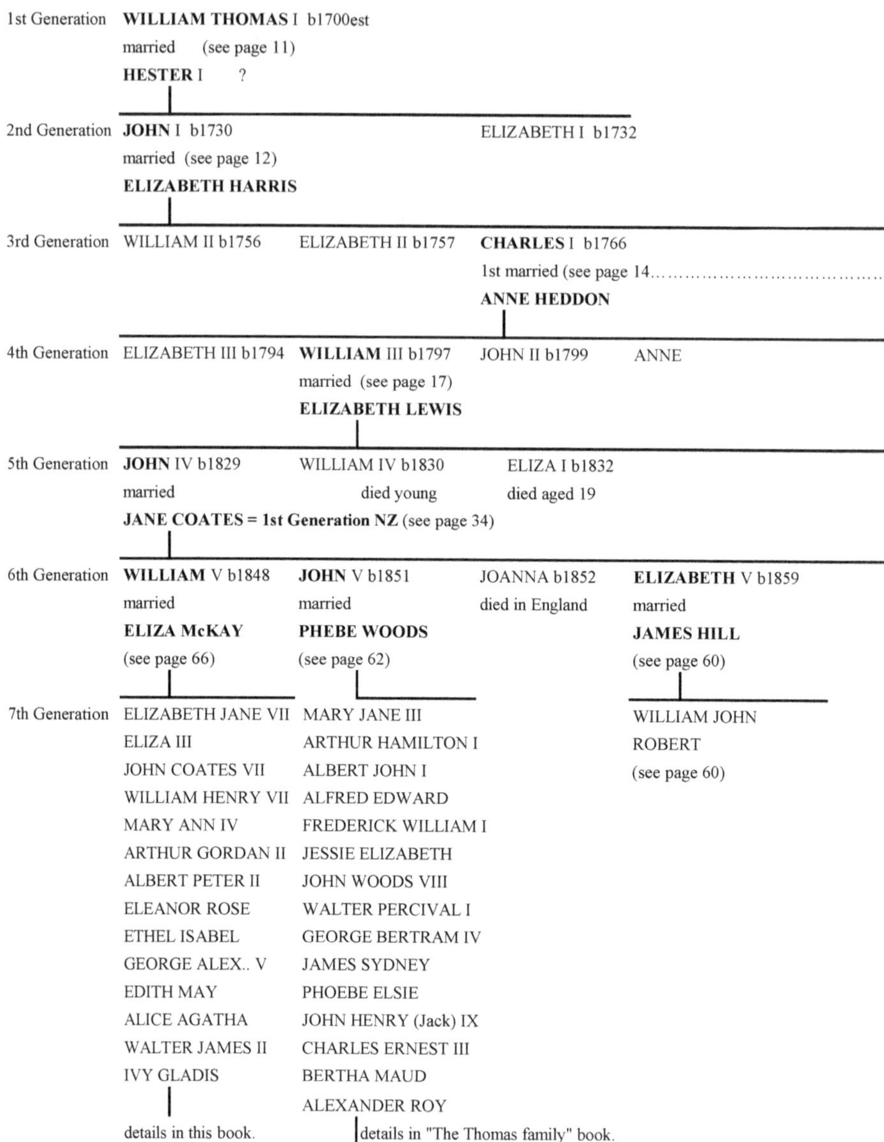

1st Generation **WILLIAM THOMAS** I b1700est

married (see page 11)

HESTER I   ?

2nd Generation **JOHN** I b1730   ELIZABETH I b1732

married (see page 12)

ELIZABETH HARRIS

3rd Generation WILLIAM II b1756   ELIZABETH II b1757   **CHARLES** I b1766

1st married (see page 14...

ANNE HEDDON

4th Generation ELIZABETH III b1794   **WILLIAM** III b1797   JOHN II b1799   ANNE

married (see page 17)

ELIZABETH LEWIS

5th Generation **JOHN** IV b1829   WILLIAM IV b1830   ELIZA I b1832

married   died young   died aged 19

JANE COATES = 1st Generation NZ (see page 34)

6th Generation **WILLIAM** V b1848   **JOHN** V b1851   JOANNA b1852   **ELIZABETH** V b1859

married   married   died in England   married

ELIZA McKAY   **PHEBE WOODS**   **JAMES HILL**

(see page 66)   (see page 62)   (see page 60)

7th Generation

ELIZABETH JANE VII	MARY JANE III	WILLIAM JOHN
ELIZA III	ARTHUR HAMILTON I	ROBERT
JOHN COATES VII	ALBERT JOHN I	(see page 60)
WILLIAM HENRY VII	ALFRED EDWARD	
MARY ANN IV	FREDERICK WILLIAM I	
ARTHUR GORDAN II	JESSIE ELIZABETH	
ALBERT PETER II	JOHN WOODS VIII	
ELEANOR ROSE	WALTER PERCIVAL I	
ETHEL ISABEL	GEORGE BERTRAM IV	
GEORGE ALEX.. V	JAMES SYDNEY	
EDITH MAY	PHOEBE ELSIE	
ALICE AGATHA	JOHN HENRY (Jack) IX	
WALTER JAMES II	CHARLES ERNEST III	
IVY GLADIS	BERTHA MAUD	
	ALEXANDER ROY	
details in this book.	details in "The Thomas family" book.	

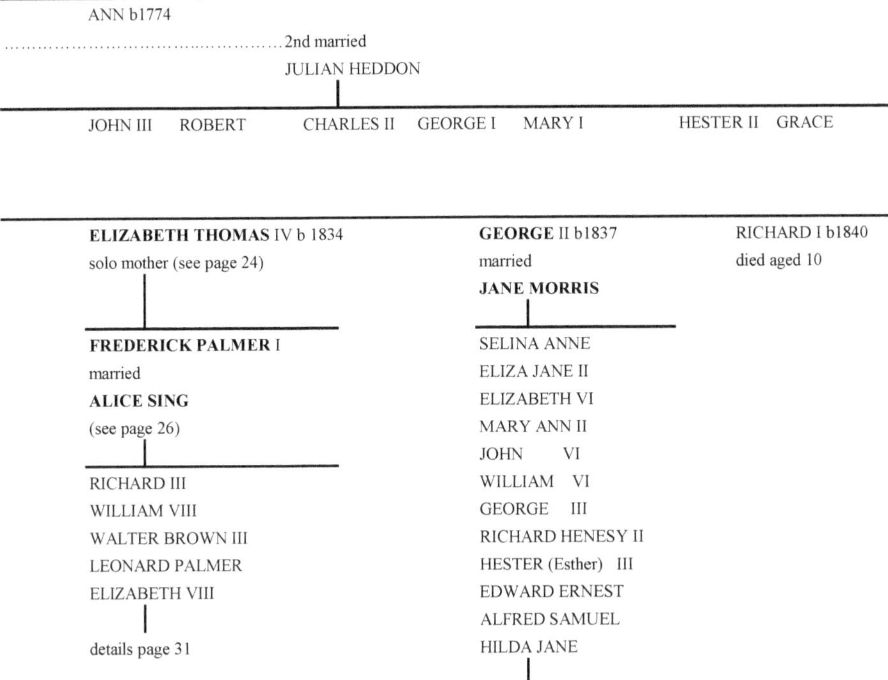

ANN b1774

....2nd married

JULIAN HEDDON

JOHN III   ROBERT   CHARLES II   GEORGE I   MARY I   HESTER II   GRACE

ELIZABETH THOMAS IV b 1834	**GEORGE** II b1837	RICHARD I b1840
solo mother (see page 24)	married	died aged 10
	JANE MORRIS	

FREDERICK PALMER I	SELINA ANNE
married	ELIZA JANE II
ALICE SING	ELIZABETH VI
(see page 26)	MARY ANN II
	JOHN VI
RICHARD III	WILLIAM VI
WILLIAM VIII	GEORGE III
WALTER BROWN III	RICHARD HENESY II
LEONARD PALMER	HESTER (Esther) III
ELIZABETH VIII	EDWARD ERNEST
	ALFRED SAMUEL
details page 31	HILDA JANE

details in "The Thomas family" book

DEVON.

The THOMAS FAMILY BEGINNINGS.

In Chapter One we provided a brief family tree to show the generations at a glance and follow the earliest known seven generations, starting from 1700.

In this Chapter we provide greater detail of the first six generations, and follow Elizabeth Thomas' Devon Family Tree down from the 5th to the 11th generation.

--oo0Ooo--

Situated in the north of Devon, England, are the small villages of BERRYNABOUR, BITTADON and WEST DOWN and the larger town of ILFRACOMBE. All are known to feature in our Thomas family beginnings but West Down is the village and district in which they spent the greatest amount of time...... from 1730 until 1991.

BERRYNABOUR: The 1887 "Gazetteer of the British Isles" describes this parish as *"a coastal Parish and Village in north Devon, 2.5 miles east of Ilfracombe, having 4982 acres and 534 population, a Post Office and Telegraph Office."*

BITTADON: The Gazetteer states *"this small Parish centres around the village and is situated 5.5 miles NW of Barnstaple"*. A population of 47 is recorded in it's 1841 Census. Unfortunately we have found that all Church of England records before 1812 were lost in a fire.

WEST DOWN: We do not know how large the village was in the early 1700's but by 1887 it was *"both a Parish and Village in Devonshire with a total population of 461 and has 4082 acres. The village is seven miles north west of Barnstaple* (and seven miles south of Ilfracombe) *and there is a Post Office and a Telegraph Office."*

In 1990 we found the district still contained a few hundred village residents and the surrounding rural population. Our inquiries at West Down revealed that the earliest built part of their St Calixtus, Church of England, was erected circa 1320.

1st Generation

WILLIAM THOMAS……. married……………. **HESTER ????**
b 1700-10   estimated 1729   b 1700-10
Both are possibly buried at Bittadon, without a headstone.

They had two children that we know of :-
* **JOHN THOMAS**   bapt 19 May 1730 at West Down.
   ELIZABETH THOMAS bapt 11 June 1732 at West Down.

We have researched nine parishes surrounding West Down, for William and Hester's baptisms and marriage. These were not found in records for West Down, Ilfracombe, Berrynabour, East Down, Marwood, Georgeham and Braunton. No records have survived for the parishes of Morthoe and Bittadon for the estimated time frame of 1690 - 1730.

As these events were not found in the other parishes, we believe they occurred at Bittadon. People did not travel very far in those days. We strongly think that the few miles covered by these four parishes of Berrynabour, Bittadon, West Down and Ilfracombe, were the 'home grounds' of our Thomas family beginnings.

An earlier generation ?
Purely speculative and not provable due to the fire, but……..

FACT: There was a John Thomas living at Berrynabour in the late 1600's. He had two daughters, Mary (baptised 10 February 1691) and Helena (baptised 16 June 1695). There were no further Thomas children baptised in this parish until 1730. There were no burial or marriage records found for these people.

GUESS: We think this John Thomas was ours, and with his family moved to work in nearby Bittadon circa 1696. Additional children would have followed, possibly including a son William (baptised at Bittadon 1700-10) who married Hester in that Church of England about the year 1729.

2nd Generation

JOHN THOMAS....... married.............. **ELIZABETH HARRIS**
bapt 19 May 1730   4 May 1755   bapt 20 March 1730
at West Down.   at Ilfracombe.   at Ilfracombe.
died. (buried poss 1802 at Ilfracombe)   died and buried ?

They had four children:-
WILLIAM   T. baptised 24 March 1756 at Ilfracombe C of E.
ELIZABETH T. baptised 3 August 1757 at West Down.
* **CHARLES THOMAS** baptised 26 May 1766 at West Down.
ANN   T. baptised 19 June   1774 at West Down.

We commenced our research of the West Down Church of England records at the year 1600 and found no baptisms or marriages in this church for people named Thomas, until our 2nd generation John was baptised in 1730. John and Elizabeth married in Elizabeth's hometown of Ilfracombe and John described himself as *"John Thomas of Berrynabour"* in the documents. They had their first child William baptised in 1756 at Ilfracombe, amongst many of Elizabeth's family.

In 1757 it would seem that they were living in Bittadon ... probably near to the West Down border. It is possible the West Down Church was closer to their home than the Bittadon one, as this is where their second child Elizabeth was baptised. When the third child Charles was baptised at the West Down Church in 1766 father John described himself as............. *"John Thomas of Bittadon"*. John did not record his residential address at any of the other three children's baptisms. Although there are large gaps between the children's baptisms we could find no record of additional children's baptisms or burials.

We have searched the Bittadon Land Tax records for the 50 year period 1780-1830 (the only years available). There were 9 properties in the Parish which paid tax and none of these were owned by, or occupied by any person named Thomas. John would have been unable to describe himself as 'Farmer'. There were three large farms and he and his family were probably living on one of these, where John would have been employed as a general farm-hand, known then as an 'Agricultural Labourer'.

ELIZABETH HARRIS:

2nd generation John Thomas' wife Elizabeth Harris was a twin.
Her parents THOMAS HARRIS and BEATRIX SOMERS were
married at Ilfracombe on 20 October 1718 and had eleven children,
baptised at Ilfracombe Church of England. Their children were….

John   H bapt 6 August 1719, died the same month.
Esther H bapt 17 July 1721, died on 15 Aug 1721.
Esther H bapt 16 August 1722.
Thomas H bapt 7 December 1724, died aged 10, 13 April 1734.
John   H bapt 2 August 1727, died aged 3 on 5 October 1730.
Sarah   H bapt 20 March 1730. (twin)
*** ELIZABETH HARRIS** (twin) bapt 20 March 1730.
Mary   H bapt 26 June 1732.
John   H bapt 5 June 1733, died on 11 June 1733.
William Thomas H   bapt 19 May 1734.
John   H bapt 27 October 1738.
Father.....   Thomas Harris died 22 July 1750 and was buried at Ilfracombe.
Mother....   Beatrix Harris died 7 May 1748 and was buried at Ilfracombe.

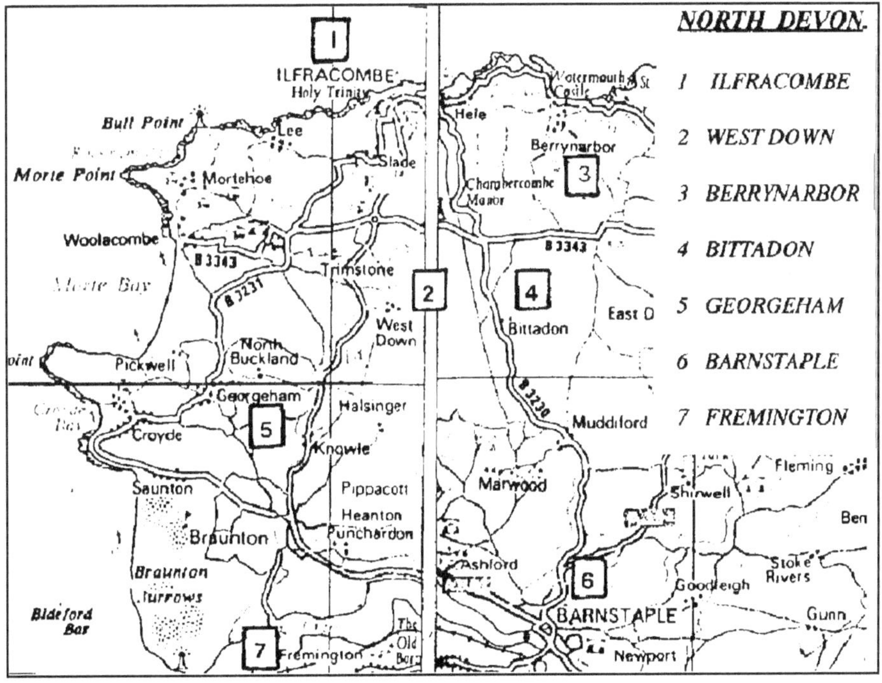

CHARLES THOMAS first married....... **ANNE HEDDON**

bapt 26 May 1766	10 January 1794	bapt 27 December 1772
at West Down.	at West Down.	at West Down.
died 28 August 1831 (65)		died 1 July 1799 (27)
Buried at West Down C of E. :		Buried at West Down.

                                        :

second marriage......**JULIAN HEDDON**

4 June 1800   bapt 15 June 1768

at Stoke Damerel.   at West Down.

                           died 6 June 1844 (76)

                           Buried at West Down.

CHARLES and ANNE had three children:-

    ELIZABETH T bapt 12 October 1794 at West Down.

    * **WILLIAM THOMAS** bapt 12 January 1797 at West Down.

    JOHN   T bapt 21 April 1799 at West Down but

                  died 27 April 1799 and buried at West Down.

CHARLES and JULIAN had eight children:-

Anne T bapt 22 March 1801.	John T bapt 8 August 1802.
Robert T bapt 2 January 1804.	Charles T bapt 9 August 1806.
George T bapt 2 April 1808.	Mary T bapt 7 January 1810.
Hester T bapt 16 June 1811.	Grace T bapt 3 January 1813.

    These children were all baptised at West Down, Church of England.

ANNE and **JULIAN** were sisters.

    Their parents, ROBERT HEDDON and MARY TUCKER were

    married 28 March 1762 at West Down and had six children......

    Mary   H bapt 5 March 1763. Elizabeth H bapt 4 August 1764.

    Robert H bapt 19 June   1766. * **JULIAN** H bapt 15 June 1768.

    John   H bapt 24 May   1770. * **ANNE** H bapt 27 December 1772.

Father Robert Heddon died 30 Mar 1806 and was buried at West Down.

Mother Mary Heddon died 14 Oct 1806 and was buried at West Down.

We have researched the West Down Land Tax records of 1780-1830 and
none of the large number of estates were owned by, or occupied by, any
person named Charles Thomas. We do not know his occupation ... he may

have followed his father and became an agricultural labourer or, like his son William, may have learnt the trade of a mason.

Mentioned on the headstone of this Thomas burial plot in the West Down Church grounds, is Charles, his two wives Anne and Julian, plus daughter Anne (wife of Thomas Hill) and daughter Hester (wife of Richard Collins). It also carries this phrase:-

They lived in Peace, They died in Love,
In hopes to live with God above.
No worldly wealth did they require,
To live with Christ was their desire.

WEST DOWN'S...... ST CALIXTUS CHURCH of ENGLAND.

This Church played a large part in the lives of our Thomas family,
for at least six generations and from at least 1730.

4th Generation

WILLIAM THOMAS married......... **ELIZABETH LEWIS**
bapt 12 February 1797   1 January 1821   bapt 1 June 1794
at West Down.   at Ilfracombe.   at Ilfracombe.
died 14 December 1866 (69)   died 29 November 1866 (72)
Buried at West Down.   Buried at West Down.

They had six children all baptised at West Down......

* **JOHN THOMAS** bapt 22 March 1829. (Came to New Zealand and full details of his life and descendants are in another book.)

WILLIAM T. bapt 26 December 1830 (thought to have died young.)

ELIZA T. bapt 29 April 1832, died aged 19 on 14 February 1851.

* **ELIZABETH THOMAS** bapt 16 March 1834. (She never left Devon. Full details of her life and descendants start page 24.)

* **GEORGE THOMAS** bapt 10 Sep 1837. (Came to New Zealand and full details of his life and descendants are in another book.)

RICHARD T. bapt 23 August 1840, died on 19 February 1850. (10)

We have searched many parish records for baptism and death details of children who may have been born during the eight years between their marriage in 1821 and John's birth in 1829, but have found none.

ELIZABETH LEWIS:

William's wedding details show his wife's name as Lewes but all other references found, use the spelling LEWIS.

Elizabeth Lewis' parents were JOHN LEWIS (Husbandman of Ilfracombe) and JOANNA RICHARDS (Spinster of West Down). Banns were called at the West Down Church of England on March 14 + 21 + 28 and records show that neither of them could sign their name. They married on 29 March 1784.

We have found four children mentioned in the registers:-

John Lewis   bapt 23 May 1784 at West Down.
Mary Lewis   bapt 13 April 1788 at Ilfracombe.
* **ELIZABETH LEWIS** bapt 1 June 1794 at Ilfracombe.
William Lewis bapt 12 September 1798 at Ilfracombe.

WILLIAM'S OCCUPATION:

The 1841 Census Returns have only one Thomas family at West Down.
William and Elizabeth Thomas and all 6 children detailed above, were living
at Bradwell Mill, West Down at that time.

Over the years William changed his occupation as the need arose, but we
believe he learnt the art of a mason first and probably worked around the
West Down town and district. At the age of 24 in 1821, no occupation was
listed on his wedding records. When he baptised his children John, William
and Eliza (1829 to 1832) he gave his occupation as *'Mason'*. When he
baptised his children Elizabeth, George and Richard (1834 to 1840) he gave
his occupation as *'Miller'*. In 1841 he described himself as a *'Farmer'*.

BRADWELL MILL:

The two storey building in the centre with a chimney is the family home.
Hiding part of it's roof is a very old pear tree. At the right of this building
and attached to it, was the grain Mill. The long building to the left of the
home, was once a bake-house and the other two were general farm buildings.
On the extreme left of our photo is another farm complex ... originally part of
the Bradwell community.

BRADWELL MILL... 1990:

upper...   The main front entrance to the house. On the right
behind the pear tree, the steps up to the Mill room can be seen.

lower...   Standing at, and looking away from the house's front door,
the bake-house is on the right and the two farm buildings are on the left.

BRADWELL MILL and WILLIAM THOMAS:

The deeds of Bradwell Mill show that William Thomas bought the Bradwell Mill ruins in 1825 and this was his immediate family's home for the next 41 years until he died. Future generations lived there and even in 1990 (166 years later) when we arrived at West Down, we found it still owned and occupied by William's descendants.

William paid 65 pounds for the ruins, containing two cottages, one with the corn mill attached, and foundations of numerous other buildings, all on one third of an acre, a short distance from the West Down township.

Land Tax.

Our search of the West Down Land Tax records from 1780 to 1832 showed only one person by the name of Thomas in this entire Parish, who owned or occupied land and paid taxes during this 52 year period. Although William officially bought the property in 1825, it was not until June 1830 that he first paid tax of three shillings on this property. He was recorded as being both the 'Proprietor' and 'Occupier' and paid the same amount of tax in 1831 and 1832. No more records are available.

Over the 52 year period Bradwell was in three sections. The large Bradwell Barton (farm), Bradwell and Bradwell Mill, all being shown as three separate taxable units. Bradwell Barton was divided into five smaller units in 1810, but Bradwell Mill is the property we are interested in.

From 1780 to 1790 Phillip Challacombe rented the 'Bradwell Mill' property to William Kidwell. From 1791 to 1801 he rented it to John Harris. From 1802 to 1805 he rented it to John Coats of Willincott Estate. In 1806 he put himself down as 'Occupier'. From 1807 to 1826 he rented it to John Heddon, then the proprietorship changed to Avery Berry who continued to rent it to John Heddon until 1829.

The next year (1830) William Thomas became the proprietor / occupier.

History.

Mr John Longhurst of the Ilfracombe Museum was interested in the history of the district and in 1979 wrote to George Thomas of Auckland, (great great grandson of 1837 George, our John Thomas' brother.) In his letter he detailed some ancient history of Bradwell Mill that he had uncovered. In part he says:- *"There is no trace of Bradwell Barton* (a large farmyard... not let with the rest of the Manor) *which was situated about. 1.5 miles west of West*

Down Church. All that is now on the site are a few agricultural buildings however, the Mill situated about a quarter of a mile to the east, still stands. Prior to the Conquest this land had been in the King's hand.

Bradwell is mentioned in the Doomsday Book. The name is of Saxon origin meaning BROAD STREAM - Brade Wielle.
Ralph de Limesei, a nephew of William the Conqueror had, in 1086, four estates in the Braunton Hundred, one of which was Bradwell. At that date it was spelt Bradevilla and of 873 acres.

In the Book of Fees of 1242 it is recorded as Bradwill when Ralf de Pyn was the Lord and held it for a half fee for the honour of Gerard de Odingeseles. He was succeeded by Augustin de Pyn in 1303.
By 1316 the estate was called Bradewille Pyn. In 1346 William de Pyn held the estate for the honour of Braneys because both honours were then in the hands of the Prince of Wales (Richard) whose head manor in Devon was Bradninch. William Pyn's daughter Joan carried Bradwell to Robert Yoe the elder, of Heanton Satchvil, who died in 1409. It then passed to Robert Yoe the younger who died in 1428, it passed to his grandson William Yoe and when he died in 1481 it passed by a female heir to the Rolle family who held it for many generations.

Bradwell then passed to the Walpole family in 1810 and thence in 1822 to Lord Clinton by inheritance."

Described here is the property next to the Mill, but the Mill may have been part of the same title in earlier years and enjoyed a similar interesting background.

In 1825 William Thomas became the owner of Bradwell Mill.

From 1825 to about 1833, William Thomas the Mason, restored the ruined Bradwell Mill site and he and his wife moved into the cottage with the Mill attached. All their children seem to have been born here. On a beam inside the Mill is carved the date 1830 and we wonder if William Thomas did this to record for posterity, the year he got the Mill operating and grinding again. Further improvements were done to the Mill with the present overshot wheel installed in 1893 and a new pitwheel was cast by Raffels in 1900. The cogs of this mill were made in the old style out of apple tree wood. The remains of the crown wheel, pinion, hopper etc, were still there for Mr Longhurst in 1979 and he advises the building beside the road was the bake-house and the pear tree near the door to the Mill is over 100 years old. He aged the present house as being built in the early 1800's, possibly by William Thomas as he bought 'only ruins'.

This author is 6 feet tall and had to stoop to pass through all the doorways on the property. There is no sign today of the 'broad stream' but Mr Longhurst could still trace to the north of the Mill, the leat and millpond.

William was soon earning enough money from this Mill to replace his mason activities with those of a miller. It is believed he milled corn for his closest neighbours too. We are advised that the restored Mill was worked for a further hundred years but was not worked after William's grandson, Frederick P Thomas, died in 1938.

We know William taught his sons John and George, the milling trade, as this was the occupation that gained them both assisted passage to New Zealand.

After 10 years of Mill operation the 1841 Census was taken and William, described as a Farmer, employed a full time agricultural labourer named John Brown. This Census return seems to depict Bradwell Mill as a 'Hamlet' of seven residences, with eight families totalling fortysix people.

The KITCHEN AREA at BRADWELL MILL in 1990.
Jill Price (centre) with Elizabeth (nee Thomas) and Alfred Newcombe.

Included in the 1841 Census at Bradwell were, William and Ann Coates and 2 children, George and Sarah Lewis and 4 children, William and Mary Robins and 5 children, Elizabeth Kift and 4 children, George and Ann Guard and 2 children, Richard and Jane Edwards and 5 children, John and Mary Winser and 2 children and our William and Elizabeth Thomas and their 6 children. All but two of the men were described as agricultural labourers. William Robbins was a mason.

In 1990 there were only three houses left in the area and William Thomas descendants still had ownership of a few paddocks near the Mill upon which sheep roamed and orchards grew. It is thought that William gained access to some of these during the years prior to 1841 and that he continued with the milling as well.

William died two weeks after his wife in 1866 and the property was put up for auction early in 1867 at the West Down Public House .... but was not sold. By this time son Richard and daughter Eliza had died and it is thought young William had also died.

Sons John and George had emigrated to New Zealand and only daughter Elizabeth was left at West Down.

Soon after the auction failed, she became the owner, paying William's estate £ 265.

--oo0Ooo--

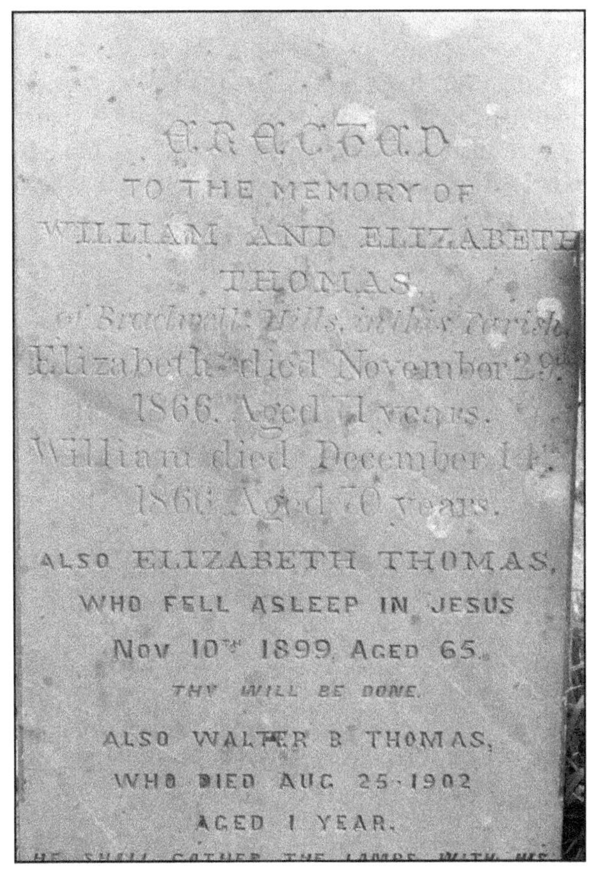

William & Elizabeth's
WEST DOWN HEADSTONE.

5th Generation

ELIZABETH THOMAS: (1834-1899)

Elizabeth was the fourth child of William and Elizabeth Thomas of Bradwell Mill, West Down. She was baptised 16 March 1834 and, as a solo parent raised three children. She died aged 65 on 10 November 1899 and was interred at the West Down Church of England cemetery.

The 1841 Census shows her at age 6, living with her parents and all five brothers and sisters at Bradwell Mill, West Down, Devon.

The 1851 Census shows that at age 16 she had left home and was living and working elsewhere. Only her younger brother George, then aged 13 was still at home with his parents. During the past 10 years, brother William is thought to have died. In 1850 her brother Richard died, and her sister Eliza died 2 months before the Census was taken. Now she only had two brothers, John and George. In 1848 brother John married Jane Coates and went to live and work in Ilfracombe.

The 1861 Census shows us that Elizabeth returned to live at Bradwell Mill and at age 26 was unmarried. During this 10 year period her elder brother John emigrated to New Zealand in 1854. The following year his wife Jane and their two children (William and John), together with Elizabeth's younger brother George emigrated to New Zealand also. Elizabeth was now the only surviving child of William and Elizabeth left in Devon.

The 10 years between the 1861 and 1871 Censuses were busy for Elizabeth.
A story passed down the generations starts around the New Year of 1865 when a man named Frederick managed to get two local girls pregnant. Unfortunately for Elizabeth he decided to marry the other young woman. This appears to have hardened Elizabeth's attitude and although she continued to have male companionship and two more children, she never married. The Thomas name therefore continued for two more generations after her at Bradwell Mill.

1865… October 18: Elizabeth's first child Frederick Palmer Thomas was baptised at the West Down Church of England.

1866... November 26: Elizabeth's mother Elizabeth died aged 72.
1866... December 14: Elizabeth's father William died aged 69.

In 1867 Bradwell Mill and lands went up for auction but were not sold.
Later that year Elizabeth became the owner. Mortgages were held over the
property most of the time she and her parents owned the Mill and land.

1868-69 Bessie Thirza Tucker Thomas was born. She appears to have
married a gentleman named Legg, and died 19 November 1905 aged about 37
without children. She possibly lived in Wales.

The 1871 Census shows Elizabeth aged 35 and her two children (Frederick 6
and Bessie 2) living at Bradwell Mill with a gentleman named William
Tucker aged 38. His occupation was stated as 'Miller'.

The 1881 Census still shows these four people living at Bradwell Mill.
Sometime after Bessie's arrival, another child was baptised Kently Sydney
William Tucker Thomas. The descendants of Frederick have been told that
his half-brother Kently was very upset when he heard his mother had
remained unmarried. It appears he changed his name ..... dropping the
Thomas ... and left Devon. They believe he travelled to Wales, married and
raised a family. We wonder if this Tucker family has any idea of their
connection to Bradwell Mill and this Thomas family of north Devon.

Elizabeth signed her Will on 7 May 1888 and it remained unchanged for the
next 11 years. Son Frederick was made sole Executor and Trustee and the
simply written Will left everything to the three children.
On 7 September her estate was valued at £ 286.

10 November 1899
Aged 65, Elizabeth died and was buried in the West Down Church grounds
along with her parents and her grandson Walter.

--oo0Ooo--

FREDERICK PALMER THOMAS: (1865-1938)

Frederick was born at Bradwell Mill and baptised at West Down Church of England on 18 October 1865. His mother Elizabeth remained unmarried and raised him on her own. Both his grandparents William and Elizabeth Thomas died soon after his first birthday. We assume he was educated at West Down and believe he later worked with his 'foster father' William Tucker at the Mill and on the farm paddocks owned by Bradwell Mill, as he was still there at age 16 for the 1881 Census.

Alice Sing became his wife in the early 1890's. Alice and Frederick had five children… Richard, William, Walter, Leonard and Elizabeth. Full personal details follow in the Family Tree page 31. Their children Richard and Leonard never married. Walter died at the tender age of one. Elizabeth married but there were no children, and son William married and had one child named Beatrice May Thomas known as May. (She told me she was supposed to be called April but arrived a bit late. T) William never saw his daughter May as she arrived after he had departed to take part in World War One. He was killed 3 December 1917 at Folka, only six miles from Jerusalem. May was just 7 months old.

Alice had been a school teacher before she married Frederick and later became the organist in the Wesleyan Chapel on the other side of the road near Bradwell Mill in 1890. This Chapel was erected in 1861 (complete with burial ground) and Alice's son Richard recalled attending Sunday School there before it was closed and demolished in the early 1900's.

In April 1938 Frederick wrote and signed his Will. He divided his property and stock up into five parts for his wife, three surviving children and daughter-in-law. When Frederick died in October 1938 the estate comprised Bradwell Mill, house and other buildings, over 34 acres of land and some stock. It was then valued at £ 1,943.

In 1990 we visited Bradwell Mill. It was a thrill to find Frederick's daughter Elizabeth (aged 81) still living in the old house with her husband Alfred Newcombe. We toured the grounds, looked at the now disused Mill and sat in the kitchen where the author's great great grandfather John (who brought his family to New Zealand) must have sat and eaten meals as a little boy and young man, nearly 150 years ago.

1992... Ownership of Bradwell Mill buildings and land has changed again since Frederick's Will was executed, but is still in family hands with May Verney. Until 1991, her aunt Elizabeth and husband Alfred lived in the old Mill house but soon moved to Ilfracombe. Expenses are high these days and May had the building complex up for sale as none of her children were able, financially or physically, to take over the property themselves.

2000... May has recently advised us that seven acres of the farm land is still theirs but the house, Mill and other farm buildings have now been sold.

So after 170 years and 6 generations of Thomas occupancy....... Bradwell Mill has left the family.

We acknowledge gratefully the assistance provided by Elizabeth Newcombe and May Verney of Devon, and George Albert Thomas of Auckland, New Zealand in gathering these facts.

1990 ... TREVOR PRICE with PAMELA MORGAN,
ELIZABETH NEWCOMBE & MAY VERNEY in DEVON.

FREDERICK PALMER THOMAS
and wife ALICE nee SING
at BRADWELL MILL.

1918
ELIZABETH THOMAS
(Newcombe) age 9
and
MAY THOMAS
(Verney) age 1

4 GENERATIONS.
JENNIFER, GWEN, MAY and
HELENA THOMAS.

ELIZABETH THOMAS
FAMILY TREE of descendants of her first son

6th Generation FREDERICK PALMER THOMAS:

+++

FREDERICK PALMER THOMAS...... married............... **ALICE SING**

bapt 18 October 1865	(date)	b
at West Down, Devon.	(town)	at Landcross, Bideford, Devon.
died 13 October 1938 (73)		died 13 November 1950
buried at West Down.		buried at West Down.

Alice was the daughter of Richard Walter SING and Ann BROWN.

Frederick and Alice had 5 children, Richard, William, Walter, Leonard and Elizabeth.

+++

7th Generation	8th Generation	9th Generation	10th Generation
RICHARD THOMAS b 8 June 1894 at West Down, Devon. d 30 March 1983 (89) Bur West Down, Devon.	remained single.		
WILLIAM FREDERICK THOMAS b 6 October 1895 at West Down, Devon. d 3 Dec 1917 (22) Bur Jerusalem, Israel. Killed ... WW1. m ===== at Barnstable, Devon. **HELENA BADDICK** b 1888 at Stratton, Cornwall. d August Bur Morthoe, Devon. (She was daughter of Elizabeth Baddick.) William & Helena had one child, May.	**BEATRICE MAY THOMAS** b 14 May 1917 at West Down, Devon. m ===== at Barnstable, Devon. **FREDERICK GEORGE VERNEY** b 1 February 1916 at Ilfracombe, Devon. d 30 June 1997 (81) Bur Ilfracombe, Devon. (He was the son of George Verney and nee) They had 7 children.	**GWEN VERNEY** b 13 December 1934 at m ===== at **ROGER AVERY** b at Marwood, Devon. **PATRICIA VERNEY** b 16 October 1935 at Ilfracombe, Devon. m ===== at **ALAN ROY WHITELOCK** b 11 December 1933 at Stoke Cannon, Exeter.	**JENNIFER ANN AVERY** b at **NICKOLAS WHITELOCK** **ELIZABETH WHITELOCK** **REBECCA WHITELOCK**

7th Generation	8th Generation	9th Generation	10th Generation
William & Helena cont..	May & Fred continued	**SHEILA VERNEY** b 26 March 1936 at West Down, Devon. m ===== at Stoke Cannon, Exeter. **MICHAEL TOM SMITH** (Mick) b November 1930 at Exeter, Devon. d June 1997 (67) Bur	**RICHARD SMITH** b at m at **CATHRYN** They have twin boys of 11th Generation born in January 1992…… Phillip &
		WILLIAM FREDERICK THOMAS VERNEY b 28 February 1942 at West Down, Devon. m ===== at **PAULINE ADAMS** b at Newton Abbott,	**FIONA VERNEY** b at
		PAMELA VERNEY b 31 May 1943 at West Down, Devon. m 23 Oct ===== at **DAVID MORGAN** b 1 January 1942 at Exeter, Devon.	**?** **MORGAN** **?** **MORGAN**
		ANDREW VERNEY b 16 June 1944 at West Down, Devon. m ===== at **JILL**	**JAMES VERNEY** **SARA LOUISA VERNEY**

7th Generation	8th Generation	9th Generation	10th Generation
William & Helena cont	May & Fred continue	**KENTLEY VERNEY** b 1 January 1951 at West Down, Devon. m ===== at Ilfracombe, Devon. **PAT COLES** b 18 May 1952 at Ilfracombe, Devon.	**PAUL VERNEY** b **TONY VERNEY** b **JOHN VERNEY** b

WALTER BROWN
THOMAS
b August 1901
at West Down, Devon.
d 25 August 1902 (1)

LEONARD PALMER
THOMAS
b 2 December 1904
at West Down, Devon. remained single.
d 25 June 1981 (76)
Bur West Down, Devon.

ELIZABETH THOMAS
b April 1909
at West Down, Devon.
d 6 June 1995
Cremated
m July 1934
at West Down, Devon. no issue
ALFRED JAMES
NEWCOMBE
b 13 January 1912
at Bickington, Devon.
d 16 June 1995
Cremated. *("Both sets of ashes scattered at Bradwell Mill,*
just along the road from the house, in the field
around the Christling Tree." BMV)
  We are sorry there are so many gaps in this tree.   These families still live in Devon.

We believe this to be a photo of **JOHN THOMAS born 1829** at West Down. We were given this photo during our visit to Bradwell Mill in 1990 by descendant Elizabeth Newcombe nee Thomas. She had been told that this was a photo of one of the two brothers that went to New Zealand..... that is, either John aged 25 or George aged 17. To the author this is a photo of a man much closer to 25 than to 17.

The photo was taken in London, we presume just before he departed from England in 1853, and was left with his parents. We wonder if the long side-burns and moustache were fashionable at that time, or, whether he grew these so as to appear older and closer to his wife's age.

CHAPTER THREE

5th Generation.

JOHN THOMAS and JANE

1829... BIRTH:

JOHN THOMAS was baptised 22 March 1829, the first child of William Thomas (a 'Mason') and Elizabeth nee Lewis. He was named after his maternal grandfather and was baptised in the Church of England at West Down, Devon, England. 'John' was a popular Thomas family name.

1841... CENSUS:

John lived all his childhood years at the family home known as Bradwell Mill in the Parish of West Down. He would have attended the School and Church in the West Down township. In 1841 during the Devonshire Census, he was aged 12 and recorded as the eldest child of six and had already left school and was working at home.

Lower photo, ***ILFRACOMBE........... 1990***
Looking across the inner harbour at St Nicholas Seaman's Chapel
and the Lighthouse built in 1320, on the hill.

ILFRACOMBE CHURCH OF ENGLAND
Exterior and Interior ... 1990.

1848... WEDDING:

In the township of Ilfracombe, Devonshire, on 16 March 1848 **JOHN THOMAS** aged 19 married **JANE COATES** aged 24. They were married at the Holy Trinity Church of England in Ilfracombe. John's occupation was shown as 'Miller'.

They had four children...... William, John, Joanna and Elizabeth.

Jane was born and baptised at Westdown on 19 October 1823, a daughter of farmer **PETER** and **ELIZABETH COATES.** Peter Coates is described as 'Yeoman' in our copy of Jane's baptismal record. According to Collin's Dictionary a Yeoman is *"A small landowner, a person of middle class engaged in Agriculture, a Farmer."* Jane's baptism and death certificates spelt the name 'Coats' and a New Zealand born child and a grand-child were given the name as Coates. It seems as if either form of spelling was acceptable.

More Coates family information on page 56.

The 1887 'Gazetteer of the British Isles' describes Ilfracombe as *"an urban District, Parish, Seaport and Market-town, with a Railway Station, and Lifeboat Station, on the Bristol Channel, 14 miles North West of Barnstaple, having 5627 acres and a population of 9275. It is an ecclesiastical district of Holy Trinity. It's Lighthouse of 29 feet height has a fixed light 127 feet above high water that can be seen from five miles."*

1850... The Directory "White's Devon of 1850" records on page 594...
'JOHN THOMAS--Flour Miller--of Fore Street.'

1851... CENSUS:

This Census shows our family had grown and that they had left West Down and were now living in the Ilfracombe Township.

Census District 29514 Ilfracombe, Page 25, Item 97 shows that living in rented rooms at Sea View House in Fore Street, Ilfracombe were:-

JOHN THOMAS Head of house. 29 years. Born at Westdown.
Occupation... Miller, employing one man.
JANE THOMAS Wife. 26 years. Born at Westdown.
WILLIAM THOMAS Son. 2 years. Born at Ilfracombe.

For some reason they lied about their ages.
John was actually aged 22 and Jane was then 27 and a half.

John and Jane had a second son born 1 May 1851, some four weeks after this Census was taken, whom they named JOHN THOMAS.
These four people... John, Jane, William and John, came to New Zealand.

At the beginning of the 1851 Census details, there was a description of the district. It reads:-- *"All that part of the town of Ilfracombe which lies between the Millhead and the Barnstaple Inn, including the north side of Fore Street, from the Millhead to the Bank."*

SEA VIEW HOUSE:
We visited Ilfracombe in 1990 and from this Census detail we were able to locate Sea View House which still existed. Above the Fore Street doorway was a small sign, **"SEA VIEW HOUSE ... erected 1700"**.
Our photo on page 40, shows this four storey, tall narrow building, which operated as a boarding house or series of small apartments in 1851. Modern road markings can also be seen. They lead to Millhead Lane. This was their home for six years from 1848 to 1854. John Thomas had only a short walk to his place of employment. The Mill was situated immediately below and behind Sea View House. In 1990 the present owner showed us a photo of the exterior of the Mill, as it was years ago, a round fronted building with "TOWN FLOUR MILLS" written above the windows of the milling-room. He showed us the location of the Water Race and Mill Pond, still partially visible. We stood in the circular milling-room where John would have ground grain 140 years ago, but now it is the present owner's lounge.

1852... JOANNA:
In 1990 whilst researching Church baptismal records at the Ilfracombe Museum, we found the third child born to John and Jane Thomas.

JOANNA LEWIS THOMAS was baptised 12 December 1852 by John and Jane Thomas, at the Church of England in Ilfracombe. She was named after her maternal grandmother, Joanna Lewis nee Richards.

What happened to Joanna ?
There are three possibilities as Joanna did not arrive in New Zealand.
We believe she died before she reached two years of age.
(a) We did not find burial details at Ilfracombe, West Down or Bittadon. London's Catherine House records show three possible Joanna Thomas deaths at Truro and Redruth in Cornwall (1852-1855) but no ages recorded.

We have no knowledge of any of our Thomas family living in Cornwall, so have not paid the high costs to gain these three death certificates.
(b) The ship's records for the family's emigration in 1855 are no longer available, so we can not determine whether Joanna boarded the boat or not. She may have died at sea, but once again those records are unavailable.

(c) Joanna may have died off the coast of New Zealand and been buried at sea. We do not think so and there is no record of Joanna's burial in Dunedin where the ship first berthed. When the ship finally arrived at Wellington, Joanna was not recorded in the local newspaper's Passenger List of those who had arrived, and which included the other members of her family.

1854... EMIGRATION:

JOHN and JANE THOMAS and family emigrated to New Zealand during the years 1854-5. They may have seen the New Zealand Company's advertisement we show on page 58. John Thomas (25) came first, arriving at Wellington on board the *'Duke of Portland'* on 12 February 1854. He obviously found work, liked the country and got word back to Devon, because his wife Jane (34), together with their children William (6) John (4) and John senior's younger brother George Thomas (17), arrived at Wellington on board the *'Sea Snake'* on 25 May 1855.

Unfortunately, both official sets of shipping papers have been lost to time, but passenger's names were recorded in the local newspaper.
"The New Zealand Spectator & Cook's Strait Guardian"

The **Duke of Portland** left London on 9 November 1853 and arrived at Wellington via Nelson 95 days later.

→

Skippered by Captain Seymour, she was an ash timbered ship of 600 tons and, as well as cargo, carried 48 passengers.

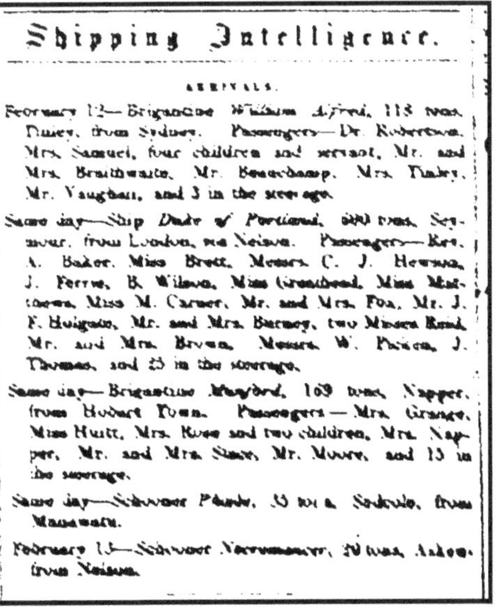

41

The Sea Snake left London on 6 January 1855 and arrived at Dunedin 21 April where a considerable amount of her cargo was unloaded.

→

The 19 passengers were all bound for Wellington and on 25 May 1855 they finally disembarked after a trip of 129 days. A metal sheathed ship of 500 tons, the *Sea Snake* was skippered by Captain Gilbert.

--oo0Ooo--

WELLINGTON:

1859... We do not know how long the family lived in Wellington or where else they lived and worked for the next four years.

We first find John and family living beside the Oakley Creek, Whau, in 1859. John bought Whau land in 1859. John and Jane's fourth child was born at Whau in 1859 and brother George was married at Whau in 1860.

John and Jane and brother George may have shifted to Auckland for employment, for better climatic conditions, or to escape the Wellington district's frequently occurring earthquakes of that period.

Maybe John and Jane went directly to Auckland, with George joining them in the area later.

--oo0Ooo--

AUCKLAND:

The WHAU District.

The Whau name changed between the elections of 1884 and 1887 to Avondale but it remained an independent borough until amalgamation with Auckland City in 1927.

In the 1860's the road from Auckland to the Whau Village was unmetalled and when travellers arrived they went there by foot or on horseback to the houses and farms. The Whau district of Auckland was described in the 1875/6 Wises NZ Directory and a reduced version follows...

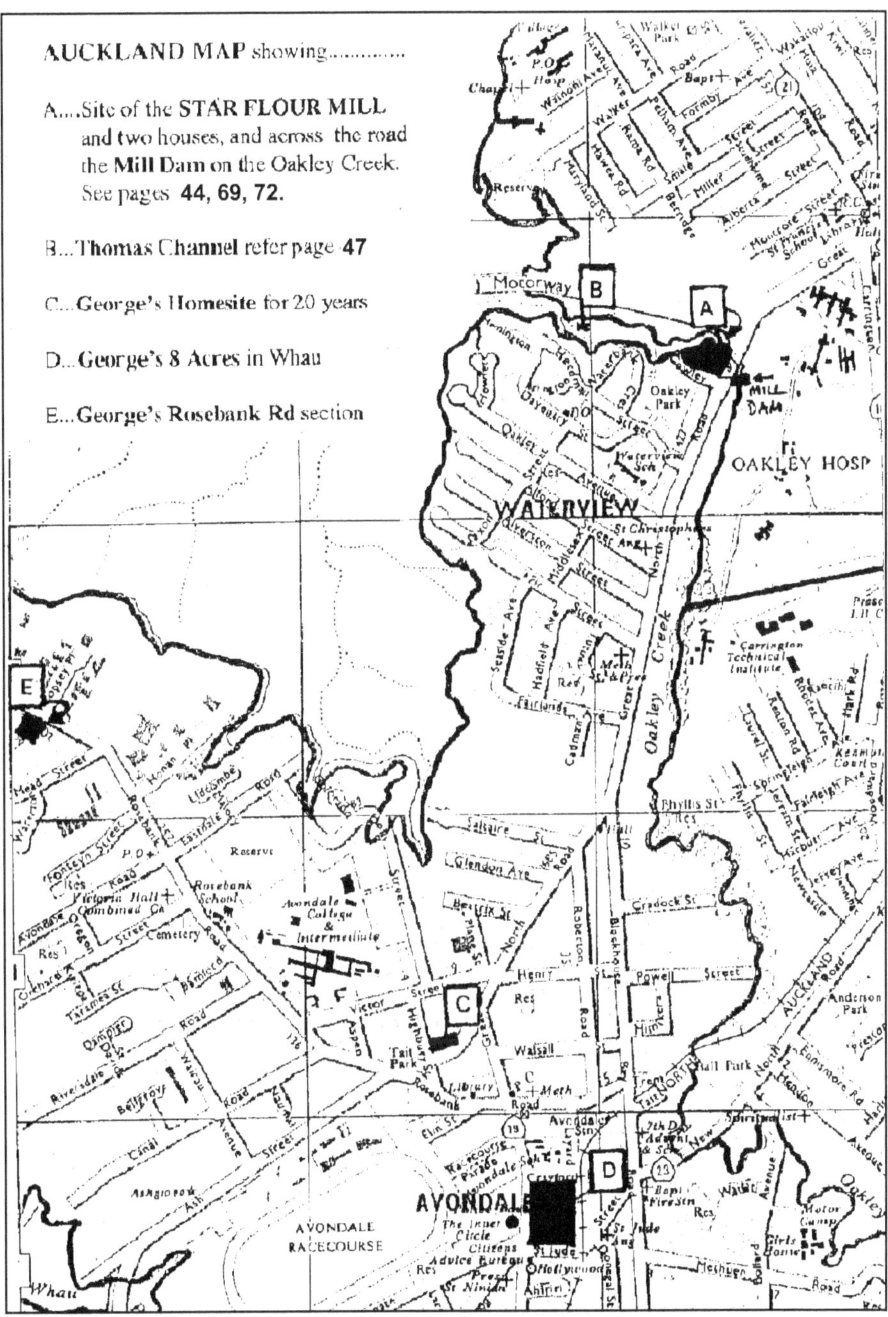

AUCKLAND MAP showing............

A....Site of the STAR FLOUR MILL and two houses, and across the road the Mill Dam on the Oakley Creek. See pages 44, 69, 72.

B...Thomas Channel refer page 47

C...George's Homesite for 20 years

D...George's 8 Acres in Whau

E...George's Rosebank Rd section

"The Whau Village is 6 miles from Auckland on the Great North Road. Another road via Mt Albert Highway connects it with the Mt Eden side of Auckland. A Presbyterian Church is in the centre of town and the Episcopalian Church meets in the Public Hall which was built in 1864. The school has a roll of fifty pupils and two teachers. There is a Hotel providing accommodation. The Whau Creek is navigable to small vessels and on it's banks the manufacture of bricks, tiles and pottery is carried on.
There are 3 stores, a Carpenter, two Smithy shops, Messrs Gitto's Tannery and the Star Flour Mills. A train does the Auckland to Whau trip once a day each way via Great North Road, and an omnibus twice each way via Mt Albert. The land provides large quantities of butter, potatoes and oaten hay and the view from the rising ground beyond the township is one of the sweetest English and homelike scenes."

1859... ELIZABETH

On 1 March 1859 John and Jane's fourth child was born, at Oakley Creek, a district near Auckland. Elizabeth was named after both her grand-mothers. Father John registered her birth and spelt Jane's maiden name as 'Coates'. He also recorded his occupation as 'Miller'.

1859... LAND PURCHASE... DEED 9D:389 #15423

Early in January 1859 John Thomas (a 'Miller') negotiated to buy some land in Auckland. He had registered in his name on 20 April 1858, the purchase of Part Lot 18A measuring 3 acres and 10 perches and, Part Lots 31, 32, 33 measuring 4 acres, 1 rood, 17 perches. (see pages 43 and 47)
He paid £ 195 for the nearly 8 acres of land situated beside the Oakley Creek and the Great North Road on the border of Whau and the Point Chevalier districts of Auckland.   (In 2001 the area is known as Waterview.)

John erected a home here for his family. He also erected a dam on the Oakley Creek, and down-stream and beside the creek he erected his grain / flour mill. He built it 4 storeys high and although much larger, it was of similar operating design as his father's mill in Devon, where he had learnt the milling trade.   He traded under the name **"STAR MILL"**.

We were advised in Devon in 1990 by descendants of the family still living at Bradwell Mill, that *"The brothers in New Zealand (or one of them) had sent out to New Zealand, a water wheel produced in Barnstaple of similar construction to that used at Bradwell Mill."*

1859... MORTGAGE... DEED 6M:400 #15424

On the same January date, John handed over £ 20-00 and signed a mortgage for £ 175, with Andrew Rooney, the land's seller. The document states *"...agree to pay the sum of £ 175 on the 1st January 1864 with interest thereon in the meantime commencing from 1st January last, at the rate of £ 8-10 shillings per centum per annum, (8.5 % pa) payable half yearly, the first payment to be made on the 1st July next."*

1860... 26 January ... DEED 6M:793 #16280

"The original Mortgage, principal and interest and costs due having been fully paid and satisfied..." the property was transferred into John's name.

However he immediately re-mortgaged the property.
We feel the £ 175 of the original mortgage was not enough to cover all the costs to erect the Star Mill building and the housing needs he had.

1860... MORTGAGE... DEED 6M:793 #16281

In part, this mortgage reads.... *"All land with all buildings thereon erected... also all the Machinery and Mill stones in and about the Mill erected upon the land hereby conveyed .... re-mortgaged for the sum of £ 450 until 25 January 1863 with interest of 12.5 % pa, paid quarterly."*
Another addition to the mortgage was that John would.......... *"during the continuance of this security keep the buildings comprised... insured against damage by fire to the amount of £ 300 at least, with the New Zealand Insurance Co or other ... and within 7 days after each premium shall become due, will deliver the receipt to Andrew Rooney."*

A H WALKER... Author.

In his book *"The Story of Pt Chevalier 1861-1961,"* A H Walker mentions John Thomas and the Star Mill quite a lot. Included here are excerpts for which we are most grateful that he recorded and also for his research time.

1860... OAKLEY CREEK

Oakley Creek was named after Mr Edwin Oakley, a civil engineer who advocated utilising the fresh water creek as a water supply source for Auckland. Mr Walker advises that... *"In 1860 a prize of £ 50 was offered by the Provincial Council for the best design of a water supply for the growing city. Four were submitted... and after considerable discussion and investigation the prize went to Mr Stewart for his Onehunga scheme.*

Both the Western Springs and the Oakley Creek schemes had almost equal merit, but the biggest obstacle to their acceptance was the amount of compensation which would have had to be paid to either Low & Motions or to John Thomas for the loss of power for their Mills."

This must have been an anxious time for John Thomas... wondering whether he would be able to continue his business or not.

THOMAS FLOUR MILL

In the *'New Zealander'* on 27 April 1861 an article written by J C Loch described all he saw on a trip from Queen St, Auckland, out the Great North Road to Henderson. On passing the flour mill of John Thomas he says....

"We then passed over the Oakley Creek with it's sparkling waters high on either bank and Thomas' Mill, for whose special use it's acqueous treasures have been hoarded up."

GRIST MILL:

In 1870, John Thomas' sons, who then owned and operated the mill, described the mill as a 'Grist Mill'. In fact they claimed in an advertisement that their mill was *"the only grist mill in Auckland."*

The term, 'Grist Mill', was explained in the Auckland Star 11 May 1887 as... *"...generally the first type of mill to be established, with local farmers having their flour ground by the mill, the Miller taking one tenth of the flour or charging about one shilling per bushel. These mills usually only worked during the harvesting season to satisfy the needs of the rural population. They were mostly small, water powered mills run by the Miller with one or two assistants."*

FIRST BORN:

At one point Mr Walker records that... *"In the middle 1860's residents of Pt Chevalier were the Walkers, Dignan, Blagrove, Thomas (Star Mill) and Josiah Dell."* He also felt that the first white children born in the district were Thomas, Richard and Elizabeth Walker.

However, the Walkers did not settle here until New Years day of 1861 and were not to know that John and Jane Thomas of the Star Flour Mill had enjoyed the arrival of their daughter Elizabeth on the 1 March 1859 and whose birth certificate clearly mentions her birth place...... Oakley Creek.

MILL SITE:

Walker described the position of the mill as...

"On the bank of the Oakley Creek John Thomas erected a flour mill, just to the right of the bridge which crosses the creek when travelling towards Waterview, using the water coming though the Mental Hospital grounds for driving the water wheels."

THOMAS CHANNEL:

The roads at the time were almost non-existent and Mr Walker mentions them as… *"no more than rough tracks"* and that *"during the middle 1860's and 1890's the upper harbour must have been a very busy sea lane. The many brickyards and lime kilns on the Whau and Henderson Creeks were all operated by sea transport. Thomas' Mill on the Oakley Creek was also worked in this way and hence the name Thomas Channel which runs past the end of the shell bank and which was sealed off when the northern motorway was formed a few years ago."* Thomas Channel allowed the Star Mill's boat and their customer's boats to enter the lower tidal waters of the Oakley Creek to deliver wheat and coal etc to the Mill, and to collect the Mill's finished product for delivery to its customers.

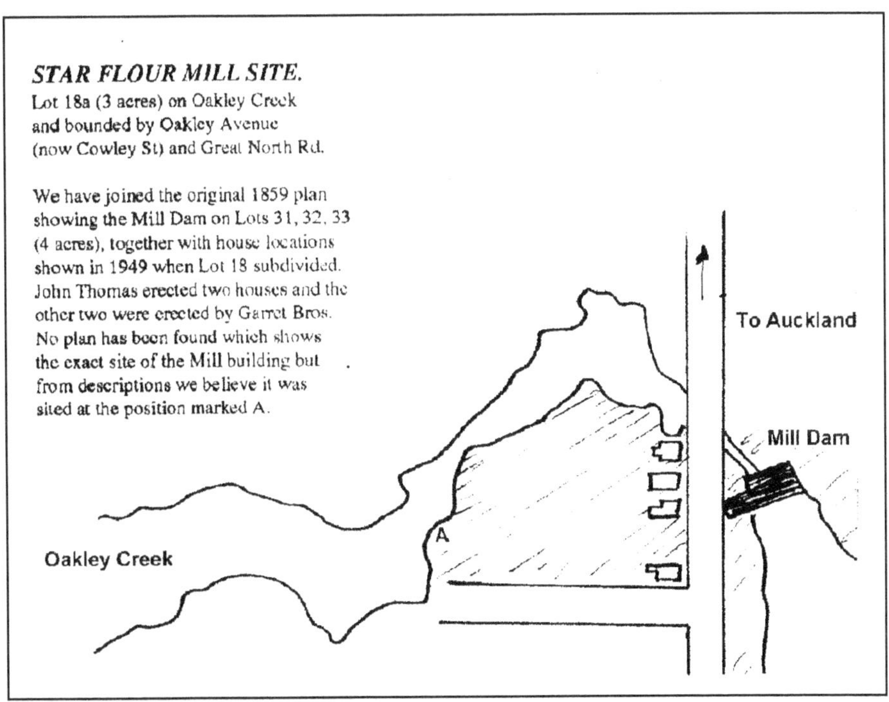

1865... DEED 11 M:72 #28831

On 21 February John fully paid off Andrew Rooney's mortgage and the land was once again debt free, but only for a few minutes, as John took out another mortgage that day.

1865... MORTGAGE... DEED 11M:72 #28832

A new mortgage from David Nathan, Auckland Merchant, of £ 350 until 21 February 1867 plus interest at 12.5 % pa, payable quarterly.

--ooOOoo—

BRICKS & MAORI WAR:

In his book *'The City of Auckland'* John Barr wrote...

"During the years 1863-64 the entire adult male population of Auckland was enlisted for compulsory service in the militia, volunteers or fire brigade, and had to undergo military training. ... On 22 July 1863 the Auckland First Class Militia and Volunteers joined the force and did duty on the Wairoa River. In February 1864 the Second Class of Militia, comprising business and trades-people were ordered onto active service."

In 1863 the Government set aside land for the Auckland Mental Hospital. Building of the hospital was completed in 1867.

During the non harvesting period, the flour milling business must have been too quiet for John Thomas for we found Mr A H Walker producing detail of our John making bricks.... *"In 1864 John Thomas successfully tendered for the making and supply of bricks for the erection of the new Mental Hospital,* (on the other side of Oakley Creek from Star Mill. T) *his price of £ 3- 16 shillings per thousand, being 18 shillings less than the next tender."*

Dulcie Twizell (nee Dove), John Thomas' great granddaughter, helped us locate four items referring to the brick contract, at the Auckland Library.   1.   A copy of John Thomas' Letter of Tender, dated 5 January 1864 and showing an address of *'Oakley's Creek'.* In it John states.....

"I have no bricks to deposit as sample but would guarantee them as good and suitable quality..."

2.   A copy of a letter from Robert Graham, Superintendent of the Auckland Provincial Council of 11 January 1864, which reads in part...

"I have the honour to inform you that your tender for supply of bricks for the new Lunatic Asylum has been accepted..."

3.   A copy of the Contract Bond document dated 20 January 1864 including a completion date of seven and a half months.

4.	A copy of the December 1863 detailed Brick Specification written by James Wrigley the Architect, which our John agreed to meet.

Mr Walker continues... *"Mr Thomas entered into a contract to supply 900,000 bricks at a rate of 180,000 per month for five months. The bricks were made at the present day (1961) entrance to the Northern motorway. He was under a penalty if he failed to fulfil his undertaking and this clause in the contract read... 'If the contractor fails to deliver the bricks as specified, the Superintendent of the Provincial Government, through Mr Wrigley the Architect, have the power to purchase bricks elsewhere and charge the difference to the contractor'."*

"Mr Thomas also ordered machinery for making bricks from Vickery, Masefield, prominent Auckland engineers at that time."

"The Maori War was at it's height... and after supplying the first monthly quota, Thomas, his foreman, and four workers were called for military service."

(A lot of time has been spent trying to find where our Thomas men served but with no result. **We think they probably qualified as Second Class Militia, called up in February 1864, but no proof can be found.** Unless they were required to mill or bake bread then sons William (aged 15) and John (aged 13) may not have been called up as the age limit was 18 to 60.

In *"Armed Settlers"* by HCM Norris we found this comment...

"The Militia of the Second Class were allotted duties in the town, but most of the other militia and the volunteers were sent on active service."

The 3 February 1864 *New Zealand Herald* issue states...

"100 Second Class Militia left that afternoon for duties at Otahuhu".

Did they carry guns? The Second Class Militia did not. It seems that had our men carried guns and gone in to battle, they would have been eligible for the New Zealand War Medal and none of our names appear on that list.

Did they work in the Ngaruawahia flour mills? John's brother George's descendants tell us that *"George set up a mill and bakery at the junction of the Waikato and Waipa Rivers at Ngaruawahia to bake bread for the Red Coat soldiers and the Maori they were fighting."* No Thomas mill was ever at Ngaruawahia, but brother George could well have set up and managed one of those mills at that site. T)

(Mr Walker continues...) *"When their term of service was completed, Mr Thomas found that the architect had purchased 500,000 bricks from Pollen's yard on the Whau Creek and 100,000 from Boyd's Grey Lynn works at a price of 18 shillings above his contract price. His guarantors, Messrs Macky and Thomas Milne Machattie, Merchants of Auckland, who had given bond of £ 500 had received payment for the first consignment, less the extra money that had been paid to the other suppliers. Messrs Vickery, Masefield had been unable to supply the brick making plant as they had to fulfil urgent Government orders for the steamers on the Waikato River, which were required to facilitate the movement of troops. This work could not therefore be postponed."*

"Mr Thomas petitioned the Provincial Government for some relief," (His Petition #44 was first heard in Session 18, October 1864 but all the documents are no longer available. T) Mr Walker continues… *"stating that the Superintendent Mr Robert Graham, had given him an undertaking to see that he and his workers would be exempt from militia duties."*

His petition stated… *"That owing to loss of time sustained by your Petitioner and his Servants on account of such Militia duties and the non supply of machinery as agreed upon by Vickery, Masefield, your petitioner lost the benefit of the fine weather, and was driven into the winter, before he was able to make any progress, whereby your Petitioner has been unable to fulfil his contract."*

The *New Zealand Herald* on 8 March 1967 produced an article written by E.W.G. Craig celebrating 100 years of existence for Oakley Hospital. (formerly known as the Auckland Asylum.) In part he wrote… *"Mr Thomas had to forfeit £ 497. He petitioned the Government, only to be told that the Government's needs had been a matter of life and death, while his problems effected only himself."*

Mr Walker continues… *"The hearing of the appeal was a long drawn out affair, several witnesses were called and just as the enquiry was terminating, John Thomas died suddenly at his mill on 5 April 1865. The strain and worry had taken its toll and he died at the age of 36, leaving a wife and young family.*

When finally the Auckland Provincial Government released its findings it granted £ 250 to the wife and family of the deceased, stating that the unfortunate Mr Thomas had met with unexpected and unavoidable difficulties in the execution of his contract."   (End of quote)

TIME AT WAR:
The contract to supply the bricks was signed 20 January 1864. John supplied the first 180,000 bricks. The Second Class Militia were called up early in February 1864. John petitioned the Government in October 1864. This leaves eight months, less time to supply the final 120,000 bricks, time to take advice from his guarantors, time to prepare his petition and time to await the date set down for the hearing of the petition. We believe John Thomas and his four men served time-at-war of five or maybe six months.

1864... The Whau Public Hall was opened on 14 November and there was a good account of the occasion recorded in the *Daily Southern Cross* newspaper. Our family probably attended but none were mentioned.

1865... JOHN THOMAS... Oakley Miller aged 36... died 5 April.
> The Weekly News dated 8 April, page 8, advises everyone of his death... *"...at his residence, Star Mills, Auckland."*
> Medically John died of dysentery and had lived 11 years in New Zealand. Son William was 16, son John nearly 14 and Elizabeth 6.
> His funeral costs included Dr Aickin's fee £ 9-15 shillings, 2 nurses for £ 5, his Undertakers Carson and McCulsky charged £ 32-5/-
> and £ 27 was spent on 'Mourning and Refreshments' at his funeral.

No Will was found, and John was declared Intestate. (see next page.) The family stayed on at Oakley Creek and milled flour for the next five years.
> The next record of property transfer occurred in 1870
> when son William turned 21 years of age.

John Thomas died during the course of Mortgage 11M:72 #28832.
Who ran the mill during this period?   Who was legally responsible?
With John's death, the Mortgagor, David Nathan would have reconsidered his mortgage. He seems to have taken a kind view to the family and extended his mortgage until 1870.

THOMAS BARRACLOUGH: Tom lived nearby and was a close friend of John and Jane's. We think that, whilst still operating his Oakley Creek Store he may have became an 'on site' financial and business adviser to Jane and her young sons William and John, until uncle George Thomas became available for the Mill's management. We found Thomas Barraclough ('Engine Fitter') married Jane in 1867 and, in 1870 he became a Miller and Mill Engineer and a one third shareholder in the business.

By July 1865 brother George seems to have moved from his home in Napier St, Auckland, to the Star Flour Mill site, as this is the address he gave at that time. We think the family must have decided that John's two sons would take over the mill when old enough, and that brother George supplied his labour and milling knowledge for the operation of the mill. He would have prepared his 16 and 14 year old nephews for ownership. We have found no evidence that George had any financial interest in the mill until much later ... until 1874 when he purchased the Star Mill from his nephews. The records show that he received wages and we feel he became the Manager of the Mill.

1865... JOHN's WILL: (Part 1)
25 April 1865. A statement signed by Jane Thomas to the Supreme Court of New Zealand, accompanied what Jane believed to be John's last Will dated 4 April 1865, (the day before he died,) which appointed her executrix of his estate, thought to have a value of not more than £ 2,800. On the same date a sworn statement from a merchant named Thomas Milne Machattie of Auckland, declared that he knew John Thomas when he was alive.

3 June 1865. Another sworn statement signed by Jane ……………..
accompanied an 'Inventory of Assets' and values seem to have been overstated at £ 1,800, covering debts owing to the company £ 400, machinery to make bricks £ 300, bricks £ 400, wheat and flour £ 450, third share of cargo boat £ 100, horses, drays etc £ 150.
Jane pleaded for authority to (a) collect the debts owed, (b) sell the bricks and (c) sell the wheat and flour… *"as I believe the same will sustain great damage and deterioration in value by keeping and that it would be greatly for the benefit of the estate that the same should immediately be sold and disposed of."* She advised the court that John has left her and *"three children surviving who are of the respective ages of 16, 14 and 6 years"*.

It appears the 25 April statement and Will were not proved to the court's satisfaction, as in this document Jane said she believed he left a Will in England and that she had done all in her power to obtain that Will and hoped *"it will be forwarded to New Zealand in the course of a few months."*

10 June 1865. Success at last. Another paper shows that Jane was given Court authority to administer John's estate (ie, collect the debts and sell the stock) until the Will of John Thomas could be produced and proven.
However, two sureties had to be sworn.

11 July 1865. An official Document of Bond shows that Jane, plus T M Machattie and George Thomas (John's brother) were bound to the Registrar of the Supreme Court for the sum of £ 5,600 (three times the estate value) as security for the administration of the estate. They had to produce an Inventory before 10 September 1865 when Jane would be eligible to commence the administration of the estate. She also agreed to supply the court with an account of actions taken for the estate, by 10 June 1866.
(Neither of these reports have survived to the year 2000.)

28 May 1870. See later entry… JOHN's WILL — part Two.

1867... FLOUR COSTS:
On 2 November 1867 the newspaper, *Daily Southern Cross* recorded the wholesale prices for flour...
"Imported flour from Adelaide £ 15 per ton, and from Chile and California £ 13 per ton. Local miller's price.. First quality £ 15 a ton, Seconds at £ 11 for one ton and Sharps ... £ 7 per ton. Baker's price per pound weight = 3 pence, baker's bread 2lb loaf = 4 pence."

1867... MARRIAGE:
On 29 August, Jane aged 44, a widow for two years and with children aged 18, 16 and 8, married Yorkshire man Thomas Barraclough aged 35, at the dwelling house of Rev. J Wallis in Newton, Auckland. They had a child.

At Oakley Creek, on 14 January 1869, Jane (now aged 45) and Tom had a son they named Thomas Coates Barraclough. Thanks to research by Carina Bowring, Joan Bridges and Linda Gomas, we have learnt that young T. C. Barraclough sadly died aged 6, during 1875 in Melbourne, Australia.

It seems Jane and Tom's marriage broke up in 1873.
Tom is said to have remarried in Onehunga on 23 December 1873 and shifted to Melbourne with a younger lady named Charlotte Cutter nee Kendall, taking his son Thomas and probably Jane's share of the Mill money. This will be one of the reasons why the Star Flour Mill was sold in September 1874 with Tom wanting out and wishing to sell his share of the property and business.
Charlotte, a coloured South African, born in Capetown, had given James Cutter three children and with Tom she had four more, the last in 1880.
Charlotte died aged 35 on 28 February 1882 at Euroa, Victoria, Australia.

Tom died at Euroa, aged 56 in August 1888 after a third marriage.

(Thomas Barraclough was mentioned in the Raglan Electoral Rolls for 1869/70 giving an address of 'Oakley's Creek' and in the Rates Assessment for the Whau district 1868 and again in 1869. He paid rates on two acres of Lot 18A at 12 pence per acre, a total of 2 Shillings (20 cents) each year.)

1870... Son WILLIAM married ELIZA McKAY in May in Auckland.

1870... JOHN's WILL: (Part 2)
There is no knowledge of the English Will ever being produced to the court. Three pages of Inventory and Final Account of the Assets and Disbursements of the £ 1,398 Estate of John Thomas were prepared for the Court on 28 May and signed by Jane Barraclough. They show the wheat and flour sold to I. S. Macfarlane & Co. Henderson & Macfarlane bought the third share in the cargo boat, George Thomas and the Workmen received wages, the Ironmonger and the Saddler were paid, and large debts due to I. S. Macfarlane, Henderson & Macfarlane and Alfred Buckland were paid.

1870... STAR MILL:
The story of the Star Flour Mill continues in son William Thomas' chapter starting on page 69. William must have worked at the mill in his late teenage years but developed a liking for carpentry. His son Jack told his son-in-law George Wright he worked for some time at the Wheelwright's Shop situated on Great North Rd opposite the Auckland Asylum. Most records show he took very little part in the Star Flour Mill's operation after his marriage but continued to hold his share of the investment until the mill was sold in 1874.

1871... FIRST GRANDCHILD: Elizabeth Jane (Lizzie) Thomas was born 14 February to William and Eliza at Oakley Creek, Auckland.
1872... Son JOHN married PHEBE WOODS in December at Whau.
1877... Son JOHN and family left Auckland for the South Island.
1878... Daughter ELIZABETH married James Hill in May at Auckland.

1893... JANE DIED:
Jane died in Auckland a widow on 25 July 1893 aged 72....
at the Costley Home in Epsom. Jane's death certificate is in the Thomas name and her Barraclough name is not mentioned on that document.
Costley Home was erected with funds bequeathed by Mr E Costley and was opened on 23 April 1890 for Auckland's 'Aged Poor' administered by the Auckland Hospital Board. It is possible that Jane was a 'founder inmate'

because at the National Archives in Auckland we found a set of minute books for Costley Home starting at July 1890. It seems the inmates gave the home everything they possessed (even rings) and the Hospital Board provided for them, for the rest of their lives. A committee met once a month to arrange staff hire, wages (the cook earned 30/- [£1.10/- or $3] a week in 1892), they reviewed inmate's eligibility to stay, and to approve expenditure. The only item that mentioned (Jane) Thomas was on 29 March 1893, four months before she died. The committee authorised *"the purchase of material for white washing and timber (?) for beds, as recommended by Sister King for inmates Thomas, Oates and Hurley."*

Jane Thomas was buried at Grafton Cemetery, Auckland.

We have not been able to locate either John or Jane's grave site due to the fact that around 1930 the Grafton Cemetery records were destroyed by fire. In recent years the Auckland motorway has carved through Grafton Gully and a lot of the graves had to be shifted. Before this happened the authorities had every grave site drawn in a plan and all legible names recorded from headstones still standing. Unfortunately less than one third of the sites were able to be recorded and John and Jane's names are not amongst them.

We have also searched records at 'Waikumete', 'Purewa' and 'Rosebank' Cemeteries operating at that time and unfortunately they are not there.

Jane died one year after sons William and John sold their Allenton Nursery. At that stage they were extremely short of cash and daughter Elizabeth was married with two children, somewhere on a farm. We do not think Jane's children abandoned her but it would appear she took poorly at a time when none of her children were able to assist her financially.

We continue with detail of…
wife **Jane's**……. **COATES** and **CHAPPELL** families on page 56,
then John and Jane Thomas' three surviving children……

ELIZABETH THOMAS   page 60.
JOHN THOMAS   page 62. A brief summary, as his life and descendants are fully documented in the book…   *"The THOMAS family"*.
WILLIAM THOMAS   Chapter Four starting page 66.

Information concerning the life and descendants of John's brother **GEORGE THOMAS** are fully detailed in... *"The THOMAS family."*

The COATES family of North Devon.

There always seems to have been people named Coats or Coates, living in the north Devon parishes of West Down, Ilfracombe and Georgeham. There are quite a lot of people named Peter, John and Elizabeth Coates and the records prior to 1700 are very faint and almost unreadable. We are still researching this name but feel confident that our lineage is as follows…

--oo00o--

PETER COATS, born in the late 1600's, had a son PETER in 1715.

--oo0Ooo--

PETER COATS junior, was baptised 18 January 1715 at Ilfracombe, he married **ELIZABETH FLEMING** on 11 December 1753 at West Down. Elizabeth was baptised 1 May 1725 at West Down, the daughter of Charles Fleming of West Down. She died 8 August 1792 and buried at West Down. Peter and Elizabeth Coates had four children that we have discovered…

    * **JOHN** baptised 31 July 1754 at West Down.
    ALICE   baptised 9 February 1758 at West Down.
    (She may have married Richard Chugg in 1774)
    JULIAN baptised 8 June 1760 at West Down.
    ELIZABETH   baptised 14 July 1764 at West Down.
    (She may have married William Heddon in 1784)

--oo0Ooo—

JOHN COATES was baptised 31 July 1754 at West Down and married **ELIZABETH LAWRENCE** on 28 February 1775 at Ilfracombe.

Elizabeth Lawrence was baptised 16 December 1749 at Ilfracombe, daughter of Richard Lawrence and Elizabeth Chugg who married 16 Februarry 1747 at Ilfracombe.

More detail of Elizabeth Chugg's family on the page 57.

John and Elizabeth had seven children all baptised at West Down. (WD)

    * **PETER**   baptised   6 August 1776.
    RICHARD   baptised   28 May   1778.
    ELIZABETH   baptised   12 June   1780.
    MARY   baptised   25 October 1782.
    JOHN bapt 25 May 1784, died 28 September 1784, buried WD.
    GILLIAN bapt 19 January 1786, died 2 November 1789 buried WD
    JANE   baptised   7 June 1788.

ELIZABETH CHUGG was the eighth and final child of William and Joan Chugg of Ilfracombe. Their children were Mary baptised 27 February 1696, Jane 7 May 1698, John 29 July 170, Edward 17 August 1702, Pruscilla 3 September 1704, Joane 4 March 1706, Thomasine 1 May 1709 and Elizabeth baptised 8 May 1711.

At the time of the baptism registration of the first seven children, their mother's name was spelt Joane, however her name was spelt 'Joan' when daughter Elizabeth's baptism was recorded.

Father William died 8 April 1747. Buried at Ilfracombe Church-yard.

Mother Joan died 17 April 1758 and is buried with her husband.

--oo0Ooo--

PETER COATES was baptised 6 August 1776 at West Down. He described himself as 'Yeoman of Georgeham' when aged 36 he married **ELIZABETH CHAPPELL** aged 27, on 11 April 1812 at the Church of England in Fremington, Devon.

Elizabeth was the first daughter of George Chappell's second wife Susanna, and was baptised 11 November 1783 at Fremington.

A brief CHAPPELL TREE follows on page 59.

Peter and Elizabeth Coates had seven children…

HANNAH	bapt 25 April	1813 at Georgeham.	
ELIZA	bapt 23 October	1814 at Georgeham.	
PETER	bapt 16 June	1816 at " (he died 4 August 1853.)	
SUSANNA	bapt 25 May	1818 at West Down.	
JOHN	bapt 1 August	1819 at West Down.	
MARY	bapt 21 October	1821 at West Down.	
***JANE**	bapt 19 October	1823 at West Down.	

***Jane married JOHN THOMAS at Ilfracombe
on 16 March 1848 and later they came to New Zealand.***

In the 1841 Census, Peter Coates, 65, listed himself as 'Independent'.

His wife Elizabeth, son Peter (Agricultural Labourer) and their daughter Mary lived on Dean Farm. All the other children had left home.

The only Jane Coates of the correct age in this Census, was a servant and worked on a farm named 'Tarak', for Sarah Howard described as 'farmer' and Sarah's 4 year old daughter Mary.

Father Peter Coates died aged 69, at Dean Farm on
18 December 1845 and is buried at West Down.

--oo0Ooo--

New Zealand Company advertisement to entice people to New Zealand from England, Wales, Scotland & Ireland.

EMIGRATION
TO
NEW ZEALAND.

The Directors of the New Zealand Company, do hereby give notice that they are ready to receive Applications for a **FREE PASSAGE** to the

TOWN OF WELLINGTON,
AT LAMBTON HARBOUR,
PORT NICHOLSON, COOK'S STRAITS,

NEW ZEALAND,

From Agricultural Laborers, Shepherds, Miners, Gardeners, Brickmakers, Mechanics, Handicraftsmen, and Domestic Servants, **BEING MARRIED**, and not exceeding Forty years of age: also from **SINGLE FEMALES**, under the care of near relatives, and **SINGLE MEN**, accompanied by one or more **ADULT SISTERS**, not exceeding, in either case, the age of Thirty years. Strict inquiry will be made as to qualifications and character.

Apply on Mondays, Thursdays, and Saturdays, to Mr. **JOSEPH PHIPSON**, 11, Union Passage, Birmingham,

AGENT TO THE COMPANY.

TOWN and **COUNTRY SECTIONS** of **LAND** on sale, full particulars of which may be had on application as above.

The Fremington Church in Devon where ELIZABETH CHAPPELL married PETER COATES in 1812.

The <u>CHAPPELL's of FREMINGTON</u>, Devon.

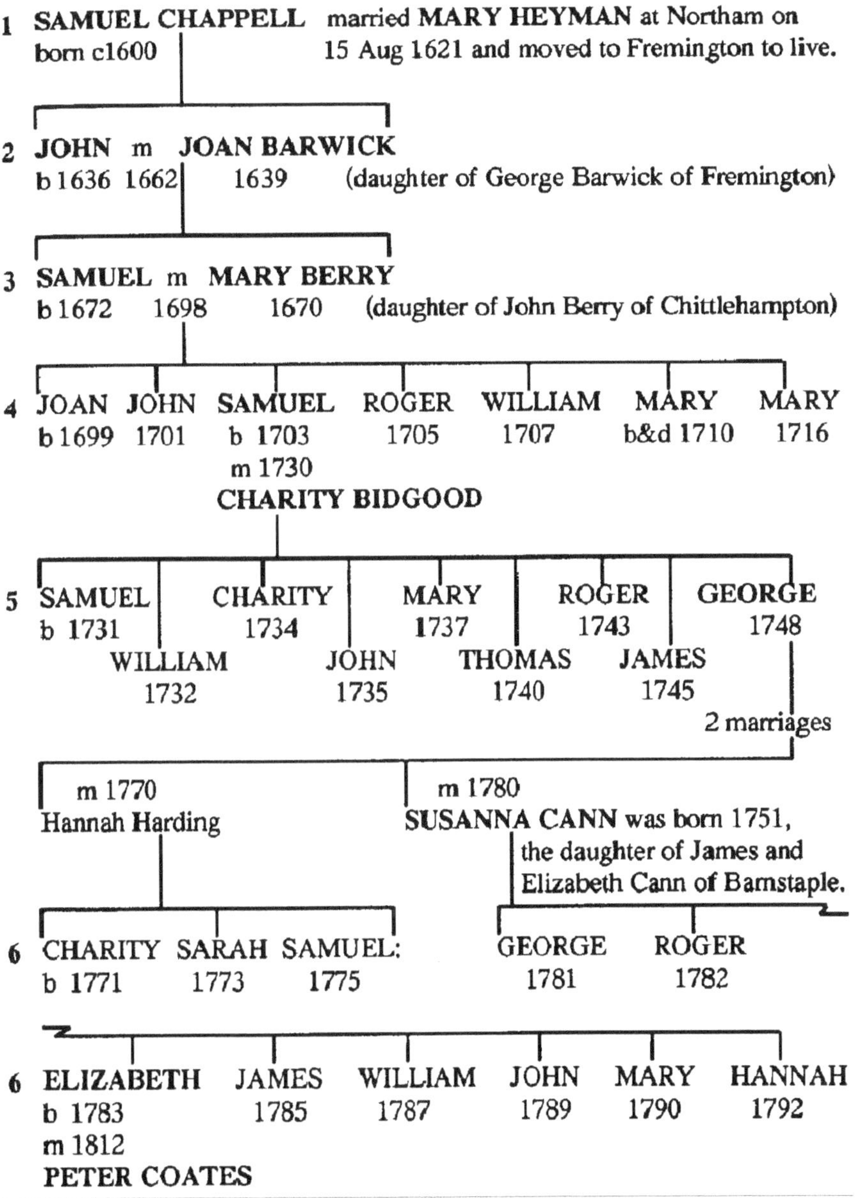

ELIZABETH THOMAS: (1859-1928)

1859... **ELIZABETH THOMAS** was born at Oakley's Creek, Whau in Auckland on 1 March 1859, the second daughter and fourth child of John and Jane Thomas.

1865... Elizabeth's father John died when she was only 6 years old.

1870... We wonder if Elizabeth when aged 8, 11 and 13, had any part in the wedding groups when her mother married Thomas Barraclough, or when her brother William married Eliza McKay, or when her brother John married Phebe Woods ?
  She must have completed her education at the Whau School.

1877... On 15 May 1877 Elizabeth was aged 18 and on this day she signed and dated an inscription inside a Bible she gave to her brother John and Phebe Thomas when they left Auckland for the South Island.

1878... Elizabeth aged 19 married **JAMES HILL** aged 23,
    on 28 May 1878 in Auckland. James was a 'Labourer'
    and was born in County Tyrone in Ireland.

1879... A son was born 6 March 1879 at Richmond in Auckland. They named him **William John Hill.**

1883... A second son was born 25 January at Paeroa, in the Kaipara District near Helensville. He was named **Robert Hill.** James aged 28 was still described as 'Labourer' (farm labourer). Elizabeth was 24 years old.
A letter in June 1989 from Mr D.R. Monk solves the location of Paeroa problem. *"My father lived in the area from 1860 to 1950. The area was called Paeroa by the Maori until about 1884 when the railway to Thames and Paeroa was built. To avoid confusion the name of this area was changed to Wharepapa, that being another local name. The only two farms occupied in this area were those of Monks and Phillips."* We think that this Hill family worked and lived on either of these two farms for a time.

Robert Hill served with the World War I Expeditionary Forces.

1903-1906... James Hill purchased a farm at Poi Poi and worked it with his son Robert for about thirty years.

Michael S Thomas (5th New Zealand generation, John Thomas' family) corresponded in 1972 with a Mr Duncan Inkpen of Ramarama and gained the following information which is still being investigated....

1.　　The family of four lived on a farm near Te Kuiti.
2.　　Son William, known as Bill, went to Peru, married and fathered two daughters called Dorothy and Gwen.
　　　　a... Dorothy had one daughter.
　　　　b... Gwen married a Scotsman named McLean.
　　　　He was an Ambassador in Peru for Great Britain.
　　　　They had two children Pat (Patricia?) and Donald.
3.　　Son Robert (known as Bob) married Edie (Edith) ..?..
and took over the farm. There was no issue.
It is thought that Robert died at Manurewa in November   ..?..
and Edie died in Auckland in December 1971.　　　　(End MST)

1928... New Zealand Herald 18 July:　　"Elizabeth Hill, in her 70th year,
　　　　died 16 July 1928 at her residence in Forbes Street, Onehunga.
　　　　She was buried at Hillsborough Cemetery on the 18th July.
At the Cemetery "Area 4, Row 27, Plot 2191" we found that she is buried with husband James Hill who died aged 79.

1933... James Hill died 6 September.
　　　　He was a retired farmer, then living at Forbes Street, Onehunga.
James' Will left his half of the Poi Poi farm to son Robert... who owned the other half. The farm was 1611 acres, section 11 and 12 in Block 6 of Maungamangaro District, about 50 miles south west of Te Kuiti.
　　　　When James signed his Will in 1923, Robert was described as of Haku in the County of Kwakino, NZ.　　(No mention of son Bill !)

We have not found any photos of Elizabeth or James Hill and to date have been unsuccessful in tracing any living descendants of Bill.

JOHN THOMAS (1851-1928)

1851... John Thomas was baptised 1 May 1851. When aged 4 he emigrated to New Zealand from Devon, England, with his parents John and Jane Thomas, and elder brother William.

> Full details of the life and descendants of this John Thomas, (the fifth in our family tree,) up to Easter 1993 is contained in the book ***"The THOMAS family of Devon and New Zealand"***,
> by the same author.   A brief summary follows.....

1865... John's father John Thomas died at Oakley Creek, Auckland and in 1867 his mother remarried to neighbour Thomas Barraclough.

1872... On 31 December JOHN aged 21 married PHEBE WOODS aged 17½ at the Primitive Methodist Church at Whau, Auckland. They moved into a new cottage erected on the three acre mill-land beside his mother's home.

> **PHEBE** was born the second of ten children to John Woods (a Mariner) and Mary Ann nee Lowe on 14 May 1855 in Auckland.
> Phebe's mother was aged 7 when she came to New Zealand with her parents Griffiths and Ann Lowe, on the *'Bolton'* landing at Wellington 21 April 1840, the sixth English immigrant ship to come to New Zealand. At that time it was a long five month journey.

Griffiths Lowe a farm labourer and Ann Griffiths were married at the Welsh town of Flint in 1830 and brought their daughter and four sons to New Zealand as assisted immigrants, leaving from the town of Threapwood where they had lived for about six years. Around 1850 Phebe's grandmother Ann decided Wellington was not a safe place to live due to the then frequent earthquakes) and travelled north by ship to make their home in Auckland. Mary Ann was then aged 17 and two years later she married John Woods at the Primitive Methodist Chapel in Auckland.

For more information on this family please contact this author.

1873... At the age of 21, eight days after he married, John was in charge of the families *"Star Flour Mill"* at Oakley Creek, when it caught fire and was totally destroyed. For full details of the fire see page 76 onwards.

CHILDREN: John and Phebe had fifteen children known as........
Mary, Arthur, *Albert, *Frederick, Jessie, John, *Percy, *George, *Syd, Elsie, *Jack, Charles, Bertha and *Roy.
The seven *sons, and daughter Elsie survived to old age. These seven sons married and have living descendants in year 2000. Son Charles was killed in France in 1916 during WWI. Daughter Elsie remained single.

1877... John and Phebe lived at Oakley Creek, Auckland, for the first five years of their married life, then on 25 May 1877 they moved to Christchurch to enjoy new opportunities of employment in Canterbury's rapidly expanding towns and farming districts. John spent some time at the Rangiora flour mills and was joined in Christchurch by brother William and family about 1880. A couple of years later when purchasing some land they described themselves as 'Corn Dealers' of Christchurch.

1882... ALLENTON:
At Allenton (now one of Ashburton town's northern suburbs) John and William purchased a nursery of 8 acres. This was sold in March 1893 and in signing the documents John described himself as 'Produce Dealer'.

1893... ASHBURTON SHOP:
J THOMAS GRAIN & PRODUCE STORE.
The Havelock Street shop was started in 1893 and saw income and employment for three John Thomas generations over the 60 years of its life. At the beginning John ran the shop and later on employed his sons when they left school.
When John retired sons Alfred, Percy, George and Jack formed a partnership and Thomas Brothers Ltd ran the business. Jack was soon bought out by the other three. In 1925 the author's grandfather Percy wanted to join his brother Jack in purchasing a nursery in Invercargill.
At the same time Alfred desired to have a grocery business and George became owner of the business. His children also became George's employees. Many Ashburton residential sections were owned by the family over the years for the shop and families stable, housing horses and gigs, shop delivery carts, etc, for their homes and for investment purposes.

1907... FAMILY PHOTO:

This photo was taken just prior to the death of daughter Jessie in September 1907. About this time John and Phebe were thinking of retirement.

JOHN and PHEBE THOMAS family photo 1907

L to R rear...   SYDNEY, PERCY, ELSIE, FREDERICK and GEORGE.
L to R front...   JACK, JESSIE, **JOHN** (V) and **PHEBE**, ALFRED,
                   CHARLES and young ROY.

1908... RETIREMENT:

For some reason John and Phebe did not settle down for retirement in Ashburton, Christchurch or Invercargill where their children were living at this time, but retired to the township of Coromandel.

In 1908 John aged 57 and Phebe 53, together with Elsie 22, Charles 20 and Roy aged 7 went to Coromandel. We found living in Coromandel Phebe's sister Agnes and husband Patrick Petley, which must have influenced them, along with the promise of a good climate. In Rings Road, Coromandel they purchased a large house which had been erected on one acre of land in 1876. Prior to John and Phebe moving in, it was owned by the British Government to house the Kapanga Mine Manager. When it finally left the Thomas family in 1937, the Coromandel Hospital Board purchased it for their Resident Doctor's housing. The hospital was situated diagonally across the road from the house.

JOHN did not go back to active employment but maintained an existing orchard on the property. He still had a share of the store in Ashburton and some land there, and he and Phebe made regular visits down to see their family. John also invested in the Petley's Fruiterer business in Coromandel and made some loans to new friends there. He financially supported, and was active in Sunday School and Church activities in Ashburton and became more involved in the Coromandel Methodist Church. He served terms as Circuit Steward, Trustee, often went off to church by himself, was a member of the Choir (as he loved to sing) and became a frequent Lay Preacher there.

PHEBE continued to keep busy meeting her children's needs. There are still many examples within the family of her knitting and crochet work and stories of how she was never idle, making many items and jerseys for her many grandchildren. Phebe enjoyed gardening and often decorated the church with flowers she had grown. When a good supply was available she would distribute some to the sick at the hospital.

1928… JOHN died 4 March 1928 after a heart attack at the age of 72.
The New Zealand Methodist Times records… *"A great gloom was cast over the township of Coromandel when it became known that John Thomas had passed away."* It was Harvest Festival at the Church and John had just completed a short practise of his part in the evening service, where he was to sing *"Sing unto the Lord a new song"*, when he walked into the vestry and collapsed.

1934… PHEBE died 23 June 1934 aged 79 after a short illness. She rests with John at the Coromandel Cemetery beside many of their Methodist friends. Their headstone carries the inscription under John's name…….....…
"I sing unto the Lord a new song".

--oo0Ooo—

WILLIAM THOMAS

ELIZA THOMAS

CHAPTER FOUR

6th Generation (2nd NZ)

WILLIAM THOMAS and ELIZA

(1848 - 1923)   (1851-1935)

1848... BIRTH IN ENGLAND:

William was born at Ilfracombe in Devonshire, England, on 26 December, the first child and eldest son of John Thomas (Miller) and wife Jane nee Coates. He was named after his paternal grandfather. Although we have found no record of his baptism at West Down or Ilfracombe his birth certificate shows that his parents were living in Ilfracombe at the time.

1855... EMIGRATION:

William when aged 6, left England with his mother, 4 year old brother John, and his father's younger brother George. They arrived in Wellington, New Zealand, on the *Sea Snake* on 25 May 1855. William's father had emigrated to New Zealand in 1853. (refer Chapter three.) We do not believe the family stayed in Wellington long but travelled quickly to Auckland, where father John had found a need for flour milling and a good site for a flour mill.

1859... SISTER ELIZABETH:

Nearly four years after settling here, William's sister Elizabeth was born at Oakley Creek, Whau, Auckland, on 1 March 1859.

1864... MILLER:

William must have completed his education at Whau and then, like his brother John, followed his father into the trade of 'Miller' at his father's Star Flour Mill on the Oakley Creek at Whau.

1864... MILITIA:

William aged 15, may have taken part in the Waikato Maori Wars but not with a gun. Many military records have not survived to the year 2000. We show detail in his father John's section, pages 48-50.

1865... FATHER DIED:

When William was 16 his father died.

1865... STAR FLOUR MILL:

In those days a young boy of 11 or 12 was considered old enough to do a man's job. Aged 16, William would have had as much as five year's experience as an assistant flour-miller to his father. However, at his father's death he would not have been legally allowed to carry on the management or ownership of the mill and it seems to have continued operating under his Uncle George's guidance.

1867... In August William's mother Jane married Thomas Barraclough.

1869... A half-brother to William was born and named Thomas Coates Barraclough. Unfortunately he died at the early age of 6 in 1875.

1870... MARRIAGE:
William aged 21 married **ELIZA McKAY** aged 18, on 28 May 1870, at the residence of the Rev. William John Dean in Beresford Street, Auckland.

The Weekly News 4 June 1870 page 12 advises readers...
"On May 28, at the parsonage, by the Rev Mr Dean, William Thomas of Star Mills, Whau, married Miss Eliza McKay of Point Chevalier."

William listed his occupation as 'Miller' and signed with an educated and firm hand. Eliza signed with an 'X'.
It is generally remembered that Eliza remained illiterate, however we have discovered she learnt to sign her name by 1875 when she registered son Jack's birth. There is no mention of *"her 'X' mark"* on this entry.

Eliza was the daughter of John McKay and Ann Carey. She was baptised... Euphemia Eliza Ramsey McKay... in Dundee, Scotland.
***   The McKay and Carey/Carrie stories commence on page 100.

14 CHILDREN:
William and Eliza had 14 children during the first 26 years of their marriage. They were known as Lizzie, Eliza, Jack, Harry, Annie, Arthur, Albert, Rose, Ethel, George, Edith, Alice, Jim and Ivy. All married except Jim, who died aged 22, and George, Alice and Ivy who died near to their births.

Interesting facts..... Daughters Lizzie and Eliza married brothers William and Herbert Sowry. Daughters Rose and Edith married brothers Harry and Arthur Dove. Lizzie's daughters Olive and Amy married brothers Bill and Fred Ansin, Veda and Alice married brothers Campbell and Alan Buchanan and sons Rupert and Walter married sisters Marjorie and Jessie Malcolm.

WILLIAM'S OCCUPATIONS:

This brief summary highlights the capabilities of William Thomas as a self-employed person, able to do what was required at the time.

May 1870 to mid 1871 Flour Miller in Auckland.

Mid 1871 to end 1874 Flour Miller in Waikato.

1875 to 1877 Miller / Carpenter / Wheelwright in Auckland.

1877 to 1880 Carpenter at Hastings.

1880 to 1882 Carpenter in Auckland.

1882 to 1887 Carpenter / Nurseryman in Ashburton.

1887 to 1898 Carpenter / Nurseryman, Ngawapurua, Woodville.

1898 to 1923 Farmer/Brickmaker/Orchardist/Retired. New Lynn, Auckland.

1870... MILL OWNER:

Shortly after his 21st birthday and his marriage to Eliza, joint ownership of The STAR MILL at Oakley Creek, was bestowed upon William.

Purchase... DEED 23D:486 #41575

This 1 June 1870 Deed of Conveyance was between David Nathan, (Gentleman, now on a visit to England), William Thomas and Thomas Barraclough of Oakley Creek, Storekeeper. Mr Nathan appears to have extended his Mortgage #28832 of £ 350 to five years instead of the original two because of father John's death. The deed reads in part, *"......and whereas default has been made in the payment of the principle £ 350 and the same still remains unpaid together with the sum of £ 9 interest thereon, David Nathan agrees to sell to WT & TB (all the land and buildings) for   £ 360, purchased as tenants in common........ with two thirds to WT at £ 240 and one third to TB at £ 120."*

Mortgage... DEED 14M:439 #41576

The new firm of Thomas & Barraclough, trading as The Star Mills, raised a mortgage of £ 450 at 10% pa, to run from 1 June 1870 to June 1872 with David Nathan, secured over lands and buildings plus machinery, tools of trade, goods, chattels and effects as contained in schedule (A).

(A)   1 water wheel with driving shaft, drums, cogs, wheels etc;   2 pair 4ft 6" mill stones; 1 dressing machine; 1 smutting machine; hoisting gear and chain; 2 pair of trucks; 1 mill-proof weighing machine with 11 weights for same; all belting required for driving above machinery all fixed in good working order; all other machinery which may during the continuance of the security be fixed on the land.

Transference... DEED 24D:195 #41755

On 15 July 1870, only one month after the above two deeds were signed...

> *"William Thomas (Oakley Creek, Miller) signed over to his brother John Thomas (Oakley Creek, Miller) one of his third shares in the mill company for the consideration of 10 shillings."*

This entitled John to one third ownership and one third of the £ 450 mortgage debt. Young John had only turned 19 on 1 May just past.

William and John signed in the presence of Eliza Thomas.

Mortgage... DEED 13M:825 # 46624.   15 July 1870.

The three man partnership raised further funds at this time from David Nathan now residing in London, of £ 100 to 18 Jan 1875 at 10% pa.

1870... ADVERTISEMENT:

The New Zealand Herald carried a Star Mill advertisement on page five of their 25 June issue which states...

> *"Thomas and Barraclough are now prepared to receive Wheat, Maize, Barley etc for Gristing, at either their Produce Store at Wellesley St East, (only a few doors from Queen St) or at the Star Mill, Oakley Creek... the only Grist Mill in Auckland."*

On sale at the store were...

> *"Flour, retail only; Sharpes; Bran; Maize, whole or crushed; Maize meal, always fresh; Barley, crushed for pig food, etc, etc,..."*

We have not found any photos, or the exact location of this Auckland produce store. Later in Ashburton, William's brother John opened a similar produce store that continued in the family for three generations.

1871... ELIZABETH:

William and Eliza's first child arrived 14 February 1871 at Oakley Creek.
She was Jane's first grandchild, named Elizabeth Jane Thomas and later became known to all as Lizzie.

1871... The WAIKATO:

For up to four years William and family lived in the Waikato. They seem to have moved south after the birth of Lizzie and they were back in the Oakley Creek area in January 1875 for son Jack's birth.

> In the middle of this period, on 8 January 1873, the Star Flour Mill was razed to the ground by fire. Details of the fire follow because

William still held a one third financial interest in the mill.
However, it was his brother John who was operating it at the time.

Daughter Eliza was born in 1872 at Ngaruawahia 30 days before the fire, and we assume that William and his family were still living in the Waikato when this event occurred. Also, the fact that William was never mentioned in any of the many newspaper reports on the fire, supports this theory.

Was William milling flour once again at the side of the Waikato River at Ngaruawahia, or was he employed now as a carpenter?
William didn't answer this question when he recorded his occupation on daughter Eliza's birth certificate... when asked he replied 'Settler'.
We believe he may have gone to the Waikato to mill flour, as carpentry did not appear on his children's birth certificates until Harry was born in 1877.

The book "Meeting of the Waters" by A M Latta records…
......a flour mill at Ngaruawahia on the north banks of the Waikato River, west of the rail bridge and just upstream from it's confluence with the Waipa River. The original mill was a wooden structure of two stories and there were 2 or 3 other buildings of wood alongside, apparently office accommodation and storage for it's products as well as grain. It unfortunately was destroyed by fire but was soon replaced by a three story concrete building. The mill was purchased by the Waikato Steam Navigation and Coal Mining Company in March 1863 from a Mr R Lamb."

23 December 1871:
This issue of the *'Nokomia Herald'* of northern Southland recorded....
"Absolute poverty seems to be rife in Auckland as during the first nine months of the year, no less than 1592 adults and 2642 children received assistance there."
If work conditions were as bad as this report implies, it is no wonder that William took his family south seeking greener pastures.
The same paper noted in it's 25 May 1872 issue these fascinating facts...........*"The entire population of NZ is 256,393 people, 811,028 Horses, 436,592 Cattle and 9,700,629 sheep."*

1872... ELIZA:
William and Eliza's family bible records the birth of their second daughter as 'Eliza, 8 December 1872, Waikato.'

Eliza the mother could not read or write, so we do not know when the entries in the bible were made or by whom, however in this case it was incorrect.

In the New Zealand Birth registers we could not find a registration of birth for an Eliza Thomas about this time. It appears that William went down to Hamilton on 12 December 1872 to register his new daughter's birth and gave her the name Elizabeth. We guess he was advised of his mistake when he returned home and found he now had two daughters named Elizabeth.

It is little wonder that one was soon known as Lizzie and the other as Eliza. Officially, Eliza was registered as born *24 November 1872 at Ngaruawahia.*

1872... William's brother John married Phebe Woods on 31 December at Whau, Auckland. (The Whau district in 2001 comprises suburbs, Waterview and Avondale.)

1873... FLOUR MILL FIRE:

The following record of the Mill fire and its re-building are a condensed version of newspaper items, as reported in 1873 in the copies of *the Auckland Star* 8 January, *New Zealand Herald* 8 and 9 January, *The Weekly News* 11 January and *The Daily Southern Cross* on June 20.

The City firebells rang out an alarm about one o'clock this morning (8 January 1873) as if the whole town were afire. A number of slumbering citizens were induced to forsake their virtuous couches and venture out into the drenching rain. The rival fire brigades under Superintendents Asher and Matthews also mustered at their engine sheds. It was soon discovered that the fire was some miles from the town and most returned to their respective domiciles. Mounted Police constable Bullen was dispatched to the spot.

The scene of the conflagration was The Star Flour Mills, situated at Whau. The property belonged to Mr Thomas Barraclough and his step son Mr John Thomas, and included besides the Mill, a small dwelling house, some out buildings and a new cottage in which Mr Thomas lived. The Mill, erected some 13 years ago, by Mr Thomas' father, stood by itself, and there was, therefore, no likelihood at any time that the fire would spread. Later that morning, pursuant to instructions received from Inspector Broham, Detective Tornahan proceeded to the scene of the fire. He found the Mill, which was a four storey building, had burnt to the ground, in less than one hour after the discovery had been made by the man in charge. The entire Mill, a portion of the waterwheel and all the machinery were destroyed.

It is very difficult to account for the probable origin of the conflagration, which had destroyed a valuable property and entailed a serious loss to the owners. It is possible that the machinery of the Mill, which had been working almost constantly night and day, had become heated by friction to such an extent as to cause ignition... or it may be that a spark dropped unperceived from a sperm candle placed on some sacks whilst some of the hands were at work on the evening of Tuesday.

A servant named John Lowndes states that he had been working to about 10.30pm, in the company of Mr Thomas who had been hoisting up maize to put through the hopper. In consequence of the recent dry weather, the water supply was getting short and Lowndes says he stopped the Mill and lay down on some sacks, intending to rest until the dam got a little fuller. Mr Thomas went to his home nearby. Mr and Mrs Barraclough also reside close to hand, and Mr Barraclough had been confined to his bed for some days past.

Lowndes states that he remained on the ground floor resting on the sacks, until about 12.30pm, when he perceived the smell of smoke and immediately jumped up and proceeded to search the Mill. He found the fourth floor on fire. It was filled with sacks of wheat and already the fire had made considerable progress. He immediately gave the alarm and called Mr Thomas who came promptly, and by their united exertions they endeavoured to extinguish the fire by throwing buckets of water on it. They soon perceived that their efforts were useless and they turned their attention to save some of the books and bags of flour and wheat. By this time the floor began to give way and they therefore deemed it inconsistent with their personal safety to remain any longer in the building.

The building which was valued at about £ 900 was insured at the Royal Insurance Company for £ 400 but the stock was uninsured. Three sacks of flour and one hundred sacks of wheat were all that could be saved. The loss consisted of the Mill, machinery, and the stock stored at the time... known to be 400 sacks of wheat, three tons of flour, eight sacks of bran, one ton and a half of meal, and fifteen bags of sharps, all estimated to be worth £ 600.

Heavy rain fell during the time of the conflagration, but had not the slightest effect upon the flames. (end of quote*)*

1873... MILL REBUILT:
The Daily Southern Cross newspaper on 20 June announced that...
"The Star Flour Mills at Whau were once again set in operation, after having been rebuilt on a more extended scale by Mr H Palmer, the contractor for the Hamilton Mill in the Waikato.
The building is substantially supported by a strong brick foundation. On the wheel side of the Mill a thick scoria and brick wall, surmounted by a solid beam of heart kauri, give the necessary strength for supporting the enormous weight here bought to bear. The sides elsewhere are weatherboard with heart kauri. The waterwheel is on the high-breast principle, and measures 20 feet (6.10m) in diameter by 5 feet (1.52m) on the face. It is composed of iron and kauri, with inverted segments. There are two pairs of stones of English manufacture. The mortice-wheels are furnished with wooden (Pohutukawa) teeth and work noiselessly. A creeper of ingenious formation contains the latest improvements and will convey the grist to the silk.
The work of grinding was commenced yesterday, in order to exhibit some maize-meal at the Show at Auckland. The trial working was in every respect satisfactory but a short time will necessarily elapse before everything is in perfect working order.
About 15 tons of flour can now be turned out each week." (end of quote)

Mr Walker recorded in his book, that the Star Mill's maize-meal entry at the New Zealand Market Exhibition, on 21 June 1873, was a winner.

1874... William's mother's second marriage fell apart about this time.

1874... MILL SALE:
>DEED 27D:684 #49858 dated 22 July 1874.

This 'Equity of Redemption' records the sale of William Thomas' one third share of everything to John Thomas and T Barraclough for £ 150.

The Star Mill story continues in the book *"The Thomas Family"* printed by this author in 1993. In brief, William's brother John and Tom Barraclough sold the Star Mill late in 1874 to William and John's Uncle George Thomas, and he sold it in March 1876. It became a Tannery and was demolished around about 1911.

We were advised that the Mill's grinding stones became fill for Auckland's North-Western motorway extensions beside Oakley Creek.

The new STAR FLOUR MILL of 1873.
…as shown in the New Zealand Graphic 10 September 1898.
"Auckland Public Library (NZ)" photo # A1683.

1871 - 1877: We have been unable to prove where William and family lived between the birth of Eliza in November 1872 at Ngaruawahia and the birth of Harry at Hastings in August 1877.
We feel that it was most likely that the family left Auckland mid 1871 for Ngaruawahia, and returned to live in Auckland around the time William signed the Mill sale papers (July 1874), and four or five months before the birth of son Jack on 6 January 1875.

Eliza recorded his birth five weeks later on February 13 and gave her address as 'Waterview', a housing district next to the Oakley Creek Mill site giving William's occupation as 'Miller'. This seems to imply, that after the sale of his share of the Mill, William continued working there for wages.

About now, William may have worked for a wheelwright making cart wheels. This business was opposite the original entrance to the old Mental Hospital (now Unitec) on the Great North Road near the Star Mill. (DT)

William and family possibly stayed here at Waterview until their big shift to Hastings, probably in the middle of 1877. William may have started his carpentry activities in the Waikato or soon after the birth of Jack.
William's brother John and family were living on the Mill land at Oakley Creek and they shifted to the South Island in the middle of 1877.

Soon after Hastings, William and John were in business together in Christchurch, before both moved their families to Ashburton.

1875... JACK: First son and third child John Coates Thomas (known as Jack) was born on 6 January 1875 at Waterview, near Oakley Creek.

1877... William's brother John and family moved to the South Island.

OCCUPATION CHANGE:

Due to the very seasonable nature of the flour milling industry, they needed other sources of income. It would appear that William took up carpentry for that is the occupation shown on son Harry's birth certificate in 1877. Apart from a brief spell as 'Nurseryman', his recorded occupation was 'Carpenter' for the next 20 years, up to the birth of his 14th child Ivy in 1896.

HASTINGS: 1877-80

1877... HARRY: He was born 13 August at Hastings and although known as Harry, he was christened William Henry Thomas. Eliza registered his birth and gave William's occupation as 'Carpenter' and their residence as Hastings! We have not found any other relations living in the area, so assume William won a carpentry contract there.

1878... In May, William's sister Elizabeth married James Hill in Auckland.

1880... AUCKLAND again:
ANNIE: Eliza and William's 5th child Mary Anne was born 13 August at Waterview and became known as Annie. William was a 'Carpenter'.
Eliza was back in Auckland again, and we think William and the other children were with her. It was a very long and arduous trip from Hastings to Auckland for a pregnant woman in those days by land and rail or sea and we can not imagine that she travelled by herself.

1880... PIGLET: Eliza told a grand-daughter that soon after her marriage, two of her sons bought her a piglet. She had it in the oven cooking, when a Maori came to the door and asked if she had seen a lost piglet. She denied any knowledge but was quite frightened. (DT) Her sons Jack and Harry, (now aged about five and three) may have been those concerned.

1880... Eliza's uncle Alexander Carrie died 1 October in Auckland.

1881... Mt ALBERT SCHOOL:
We found William Thomas enrolled his three eldest children... Lizzie, Eliza and Jack, at Mt Albert School on 20 April 1881. He stated all had previously attended the Whau School. But no Whau, Point Chevelier, Gladstone or Avondale records for these years have survived. The three of them sat exams on 29 March 1882, and we mention these in their individual chapters. The school record ends with them leaving 30 May 1882 to go to Christchurch.

1882... SOUTH ISLAND:
The children had left Mt Albert School by 30 May 1882 and William, Eliza and five children moved to the South Island. They signed for purchase of a Nursery near Ashburton in September 1882, and were living at Allenton when William enrolled son Jack at the Ashburton School in November 1882. William's brother John and wife Phebe who went to the South Island in 1877, were in 1881 living at Stix, near Christchurch, where he was initially employed as a 'flour miller'. We believe they must have got word to William of the work and good business opportunities in the area.

WHY: The question as to why William left Auckland and went to live and work in Hastings, and also why brother John left in 1877 and took his family to Christchurch, may never be factually answered.
We have found that Canterbury was a rapidly expanding area and obviously had not been hit as hard as other parts of New Zealand, by the world wide

depression of 1875 - 1895. Auckland suffered severely from falling prices, interest rates and profits. Because of this slump and the closure of their flour mill, we believe William and John may have had difficulty gaining carpentry or flour milling jobs. They may have been more farsighted, to notice greater opportunities in the South Island, with longer term work prospects and greater financial security for their families.

> In the 1870's another New Zealand immigration policy was put into effect. Between the 10 years 30 June 1870 to 1880 there were 100,000 assisted and nearly 40,000 unassisted immigrants arriving to all parts of New Zealand. 27,600 settled in Canterbury. (H.NZ)

With their twenty year experience of life in New Zealand and general business knowledge they could probably see these attributes as being more profitably put to use if they got into a secure position quickly, before the large number of immigrants did so. It would seem that they concluded the Christchurch area was the best place to be, to take up this opportunity.

D.N. Hawkins says in his book *'Rangiora'*, that there were 33 Grain Mills in Canterbury at that time and 10 of these within a dozen miles of Southbrook and Rangiora. At Southbrook there were 2 flour mills (Archers and Moirs). There was also a thriving Methodist community, a school and ample support businesses such as butchers, grocery stores, fellmongery, tannery, builder's yard and a large flax industry. There was a Post Office and the railway passed through, which made Christchurch only a short distant away.

'The History of Canterbury' advises… *"the slump that reached Canterbury in 1879 caused a great fall in prices. However, from 1896 relative ease and prosperity continued until 1914."*   Not easy times for our Thomas brothers.

1882… Son Jack, many years later, told George Wright, *"….his father once had a bakery in Christchurch."* It would appear to us that between June 1882 and October 1882 could be the period that this occurred.

No records of this business have been found to date.

1882… CORN DEALER:

From mid 1882 until September 1882, William and his brother may have been in partnership in a business they described, when signing land purchase papers, as 'Corn Dealers of Christchurch'. No documents have been found.

The author's grandfather Walter Percival Thomas was born in Christchurch in November 1881 and John described himself as… "Produce Dealer of Christchurch". Son Percy later said they lived at Stix when he was born.

SCHOOL: We thought William's children attending school in Christchurch might provide details of where they lived, but this search proved fruitless. Southbrook, Belfast and Papanui did not record Lizzie, Eliza and Jack as attending and the records of Addington and Rangiora were destroyed by fire.

1882... FREEHOLDERS:

The October 1882 edition of 'Freeholders of NZ' records William and John Thomas as joint owners of 8 acres of freehold land in the Ashburton district with a value of £ 1,000.

1882... ALLENTON NURSERY:

The Land Act was passed by the New Zealand Government in 1877 and land purchases began to be registered.

In September 1882, William and his brother John purchased a property of 8 acres at Allenton, which, at that time, was outside the boundary of the township of Ashburton. An article published in the *Ashburton Guardian* by Ray McCausland, states that on the property were old stables, barns, men's quarters and 3 cottages, before Mr W H Collins bought it in 1893.

We found this advertisement in the **10 July 1890** *Ashburton Guardian* for the sale of trees for J Thomas' Nursery. No mention of William. Was he only a financial partner? Did he occupy one of the nursery's houses and do his carpentry from there? We think so.

Auctioneer Mr T Bullock advises the nursery had 200 varieties of apple trees in this orchard. The advert makes interesting reading when compared with the wording used in today's advertisements.

We wish to call the attention of ol to the sale of trees by Mr T. Bullock Thomas' nursery, North belt, on next. The apple trees are proved g as Mr Thomas has over 200 varit orchard, but his experience has n confine his nursery stock to abc these, they being found most suitab district for bearing properties, qua value as a crop. Some of these are bli both roots and branches, and some keepers and suitable for export, vl Wolseley; Stone, Golden, Sturn Allonsbury pippins; Scarlet, N Majstin, and many others, both e late varieties for kitchen and desser

These 8 acres were in their joint names for 11 years until officially sold on 10 March 1893 to William Henry Collins. This gentleman (a local timber dealer) erected a very large and beautiful house on the property and called it

'Menorlue.' This building still existed in 1999 and was then occupied by the Ashburton College Community Division.

Allenton, in the year 2001, is a northern suburb of Ashburton.

William and John paid £ 1,000 for these 8 acres in September 1882 and arranged a mortgage with the previous owner. This was taken over by Dixon Investments in 1886. In March 1893 Dixon took control of the property for 10 shillings and 6 months later sold it for £ 620 to Mr Collins. This sale almost covered the mortgage debt of £ 700.

When John Thomas signed the sale documents on 10 March 1893 he described himself as 'Produce Dealer', implying his Ashburton shop was already in existence at that time. William Thomas signed describing himself as 'Nurseryman' living at Ngawapurua near Woodville in the North Island.

Comments:

1.   Whilst researching brother John's life, his grand-daughter Phoebe Ching recalled her mother telling her that during this period William and John had a great argument and they separated. She thought that William strongly believed younger brother John was being inconsiderate to his wife Phebe, by getting her pregnant so often. In January 1883 John and Phebe had been married 11 years, had 9 children and saw 4 of these die.

William and Eliza, who had been married longer at nearly 13 years, had only 6 children and all had survived. Maybe William did say something to John. In 1988 when talking to all of John and Phebe's grand-children, we found only Phoebe Ching had any knowledge of John having a brother. It was as if there really had been a difference of opinion and the 2 families had not communicated from that time on.

Alternatively, it could have been the obvious nursery business financial problems which caused the men to go their own separate ways. The nursery may have earned wages for John, but it does not seem to have made a profit for them at the time of the sale, and William as an investor would obviously not be too happy with having lost a lot of money.

2.   We wonder, as John and William's nursery was heavily into trees, if the special Gingko tree on the Menorlue site in 1999 was planted by them. No one knows the exact age of the tree except that it is very old, so it could have been planted during their 11 year ownership of the property. The Collins' house appears to have been designed to enjoy this lovely tree.

1882... ASHBURTON SCHOOL:
> Education to Standard 6 level was compulsory from 1875.

We found parent William Thomas of Allenton, registered his son John, (known as **Jack**) at the Ashburton Borough School on 13 November 1882.
> In 1882 **Lizzie** was 12 and **Eliza** 10 and they seem to have ceased schooling as neither of them attended this school. Both must have been useful about the nursery and in helping mother with 4 year old Harry and Annie aged 2, whilst she once again set up house and awaited the arrival of their 6th child, Arthur, in 8 to 10 weeks time.

William registered daughter **Annie** (aged 5) on 17 August 1885, she had not been to school before and their address was North East Belt, Ashburton. The records show Annie left school 19 August 1887 to go to the North Island.

William registered son **Harry** (aged 9) on 24 January 1887 stating prior to this he had attended Infant School in Christchurch but this has not been confirmed. Harry left the school 7 September 1887.

1882... ARTHUR:

On 29 December, Arthur Gordon Thomas was born at Ashburton and Eliza recorded William's occupation as 'Carpenter'.

This was only three months after the two brothers signed an agreement together to purchase the nursery. William was financially involved with the nursery for eleven years but seems to have taken little part in it.

1884... N.Z.P.O. Directory:

The 1885 issue (set in 1884) lists William as *'Nurseryman - Ashburton.'*
> We think William was still a carpenter as the births of his children consistently record this from 1877 to 1896. This entry in the Directory probably only recorded his major investment.... and not his occupation.

We have wondered if William felt there was more prestige attached to owning part of a business..... than to being a self-employed carpenter.

1885... ALBERT:

Albert Peter Thomas was born at Ashburton, the 7th Child of William and Eliza on the 23 March 1885. William's occupation was a 'Carpenter'.

1887.... ROSE:

Born at Ashburton on January 22 was William and Eliza's 8th child Eleanor Rose Beatrice Thomas, known as Rose. William was a 'Carpenter'.

1887... NGAWAPURUA:

It seems certain that the family shifted from Ashburton to Ngawapurua, near Woodville in the North Island, between the January 1887 birth of Rose and the October 1888 birth of Ethel. In fact we found 10 year old son Harry's last day of attendance at the Ashburton Borough School was 7 Sept 1887.

William was a **'Carpenter'** on the birth certificates of his next three children born in 1888, 1890, 1892 but in 1893 when signing the Ashburton Nursery sale documents and again in 1897 when registering for the Election Rolls he gave his occupation as **'Nurseryman'.** Another three children arrived in 1893, 1894, 1896 and William was a **'Carpenter'** each time. For the Electoral Rolls of 1890, 1893, 1894 and 1896 he is described as **'Settler''**!

We have not found a property registered in William's name in this area.
Did William buy land here or did he lease it from the Maoris? Where was the nursery situated? Did they live on the nursery land? Did he buy a pre-existing nursery or start one from scratch? Enquiries continue.

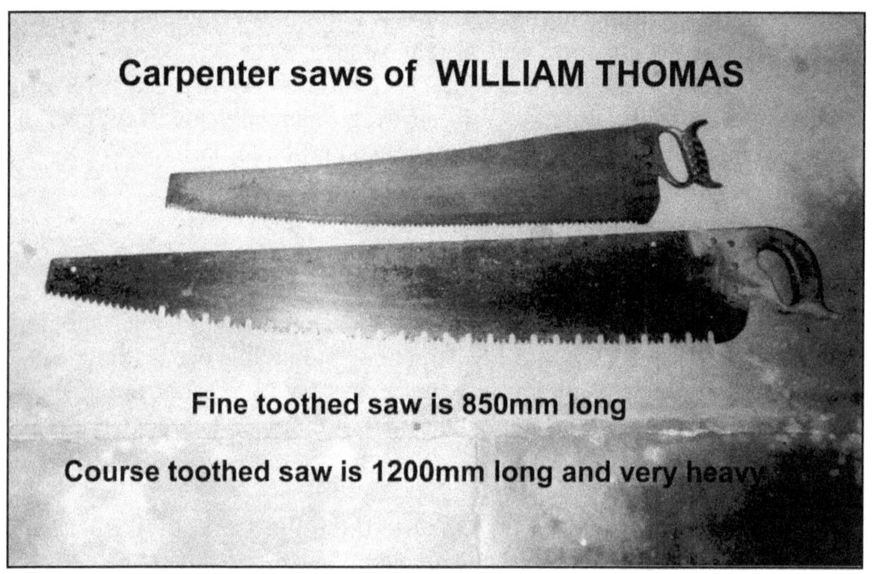

WILLIAM'S SAWS:

Delcie Twizell has these two saws used by her grandfather William Thomas who must have been quite strong to use the large one for any length of time.

NGAWAPURUA:

The farming community of Ngawapurua was 2 miles (3.2km) south from Woodville and 8 miles (12.8km) north of the township of Mangatainoka. By the time William and family arrived at Ngawapurua late in 1887, a good road to Woodville had been constructed in 1876. Woodville was a bustling town with all amenities including a school, library, newspaper, police and courthouse, banks, registry for birth, deaths and marriages, racing club and numerous churches. The bridge at Ngawapurua giving much easier access from Woodville to all points south had opened 14 July 1885. Before this a punt was available for all transportation across the Manawatu river.

The 10 June 1886 Tarawera eruption shook Woodville and some chimneys fell but this did not deter William and Eliza from moving there a year later. Mid 1887 saw Joseph Sowry elected as first Mayor of Woodville and a few years later two of his sons married William and Eliza's two eldest daughters. A contract to construct a railway station was let in August 1886. W.H. Nelson's Freezing Works commenced operation about 1891 and the Pinfold Road Creamery in 1892. There must have been lots of work for carpenters. In 1897 the railway reached Ngawapurua and the bridge served both trains and vehicle traffic, with gates at each end of the bridge. William and Eliza Thomas moved to Auckland in 1898 a few months after this event occurred.

SCHOOLS, 1888-1898:

Bert and Olwen Hammond supplied us with a lead into William and Eliza's children's education by finding 1897 records of three children's attendance at the Mangatainoka Public School, 12 kilometres south of Ngawapurua. Further investigations provided lots of information of school attendance at this and other schools and these details appear in each child's chapter. Through school attendance records we know Lizzie (17) and Eliza (15) were not enrolled at the Woodville School at the start of the 1888 school year. However Jack, Harry, Annie, Arthur, Albert, Rose and Ethel all attended Woodville School from 30 January 1888, as and when each was old enough, with Ethel enrolled on 29 November 1893, soon after her 5th birthday. Some of the children went on to attend the Mangatainoka school.

1888... ETHEL:

William was aged 40 and Eliza 37 when Ethel Isabel Thomas was born on 1 October at Ngawapurua, their 9th child. William was a 'Carpenter'. We believe she received the name Isabel after Eliza's Aunt Isabel Carrie.

1890 & 1891... GEORGE:

William and Eliza's 10th child George Alexander Thomas was born at Ngawapurua on 31 December 1890. William's occupation, 'Carpenter'.
George died when he was 6 weeks old on 18 February 1891 and was buried at the Old Woodville Cemetery.

1892... EDITH:

Edith May Thomas was born 25 February at Ngawapurua, the 11th child of William and Eliza Thomas. William's occupation, 'Carpenter'.

1892... Daughter Eliza married Herbert Sowry on 15 June at the Methodist Chapel, Mangatainoka, ten kilometres south of Ngawapurua.

1893... The Ashburton Nursery sale documents were signed in March.

1893... WOMEN VOTE:

The first time women were allowed to vote in a New Zealand Parliamentary Election was in 1893. In the Waipawa Electoral Roll we found...
#3314   William Thomas   Ngawapurua.   Settler.
#3315   Eliza Thomas   Ngawapurua.   Household Duties.
#3316   Elizabeth Jane Thomas   Woodville.   Household Duties.

1893... GRANDMOTHER:

While pregnant with daughter Alice, Eliza Thomas became a grandmother.
> Alfred George Sowry was born 18 April 1893 at Woodville to daughter Eliza and Herbert Sowry and 6 days later Alice was born.

By the time Eliza Thomas' 14th child Ivy was born, she had 3 grandchildren, daughter Eliza's Alfred and Leonard, and Lizzie's son Hector.
Their grandchildren knew William and Eliza as...   Granddad and Grandma.

1893... ALICE:

Alice Agatha Thomas was born 24 April 1893 at Ngawapurua, the 12th child of William and Eliza Thomas. Sadly she died almost 10 months old. She was buried beside her brother George at the Old Woodville Cemetery, on the hill over-looking the Palmerston North / Gisborne main road and railway line.

1893... William's mother Jane Thomas died in Auckland on 25 July 1893 aged 72. William was 44 at this time.

1893... Eldest daughter Elizabeth Jane (Lizzie) married William Sowry at Woodville on Xmas day 1893. The two sisters, Eliza and Lizzie Thomas married two brothers Herbert and William Sowry.

1894... Daughter Alice died on 21 February.

1894... JIM:

Walter James Thomas was born 8 November 1894 at Ngawapurua and was known as Jim. William and Eliza's 13th child. William was a 'Carpenter'. Jim died tragically at the age of 22 in 1917. (Details in Chapter 15)

1895... FRUIT TREES:

We found two advertisements in the *Woodville Examiner* on 21 June and 17 July 1895 advising that William Thomas at his **"TERRACE NURSERY"** (between Woodville and Pahiatua), had hundreds of blight free apple trees for sale and many other tree types too.
These provide some proof that William had at least two sources of income.... his nursery and his carpentry work.

1896... IVY:

On January 24 at Ngawapurua, Ivy Gladys Thomas was born, their 14th and final child. William was nearly aged 49 and Eliza was aged 44.

Ivy died March 26 when only 2 months old and is buried at Old Woodville Cemetery beside her brother George and sister Alice in Plot 28 Block 11.

FIRST ANNUAL CLEARING SALE OF FRUIT TREES, &c., &c., Now going on at the Nursery.

BLIGHT-PROOF Apple Trees a speciality. I have early season sorts, midseason sorts, late season sorts, and keeping sorts. Blight-proof Roots and Branches. Hundreds of them.

—ALSO—

Plums, Peaches, Quince, Cherry, Pear, Small Fruit, Shelter Trees, Shrubs, Bushes, &c.

Catalogue on application.

All trees not sold by the end of the season will be sold by auction without the slightest reserve.

WM. THOMAS,
TERRACE NURSERY,
Between Woodville and Pahiatua.
POSTAL ADDRESS—Woodville.
84186

Dr. H. T. Dawson recorded she died after suffering five days from acute bronchitis and syncope. The Rev. James Wrigley, a Methodist minister took the burial service. Ivy's death certificate notes her eldest unmarried sister Annie, then aged 16, registered her death and recorded *"she was present at Ivy's death"* and that her father William was still occupied as a 'Carpenter'.

1897... Electoral Roll:
We found in the Pahiatua Electoral Rolls for 1897...

William Thomas	Nurseryman.	Ngawapurua.
Eliza Thomas	Married Woman.	Ngawapurua.

We have not found the location of this Nursery at Ngawapurua..... yet!

1898... HOT LAKES or AUCKLAND !
The *Woodville Examiner* newspaper recorded on 6 June 1898......
"Mr William Thomas, nurseryman at Ngawapurua, and his son-in-law Mr William Sowry, started today on a trip by road for the Hot Lakes via Napier, and they will return via Hunterville. They intend camping on the journey, which is expected to occupy about six weeks."

My wife and I searched all pages to end January 1899 and there was no item about their safe return or their adventures around the hot lakes. We believe this entry was made by William Thomas, as details of his residence and occupation are noted but not those of his travelling partner William Sowry.

The June 1898 item may be a 'red herring' (*"Anything that diverts attention from a topic or line of enquiry"*... Collins) We have come to believe that William found out (probably from his solicitor) about the Riverview Farm being for sale, for a cheap amount, as it was a mortgagee sale and so organised a trip. He then placed the above mentioned comment in the paper so as not to advise others of his interest in the farm and not to alarm his nursery and carpentry customers and debtors. If he did not buy the land then no harm was done to his businesses at Ngawapurua. Who better to take with you to investigate and advise on the purchase of a large farm, than one's son-in-law William Sowry... a farmer.

Maybe they did 'rough it' and camp out on their way to and from Auckland via the hot-lakes, however it was mid-winter with low temperatures and probably some snow about. Not ideal holiday and sightseeing weather.

We have learnt from school records that William and Eliza moved from Ngawapurua to Auckland, late in 1898 and before February 1899. Their daughter Ethel attended Mangatainoka School in 1898 and attended the New Lynn Public School in Auckland for about seven months in 1899 before that years 22 September school exams. The three youngest children, Ethel, Edie and Jim were the only ones attending school in Auckland from 1899.

William 50, Eliza 47, and five of their children (Arthur 15, Albert 13, Ethel 9, Edith 6 and Jim 3) moved north to live at New Lynn in Auckland.

Their eldest two girls Lizzie and Eliza were by this time married, their eldest two sons Jack and Harry were living near Levin and soon married there. Daughter Rose was living with her sister Lizzie and attended Nikau School in 1900 aged 13. Daughter Annie was aged 18, working in the area and three children who had passed away, were sadly left at the Woodville Cemetery.

--oo0Ooo--

1898... 88 ACRES: RIVERVIEW FARM :

We thank Mr Eric Smith for his valuable assistance in locating and determining the details of William Thomas' 88 acre property.   (T)

PURCHASE... DEED #144537…   dated 5 September 1898.
(13A-page 94, and book R53-page 933)

William purchased 88 acres at New Lynn, Auckland, known officially as *Allotment 139 in the Parish of Waikomiti, Auckland.* (now spelt Waikumete) Documents registered 11 October 1898 show it was purchased from Walter Alison McCaul, a Gentleman, by William Thomas of Avondale, a Farmer.

The farm land was known as **'RIVERVIEW'** and it was a mortgagee sale.

It seems it was owned by Dorothy and Walter McCaul who sold it to George Thomas Hogg. Mr Hogg gained a mortgage of £ 450 plus interest from the McCauls which was made out in Mrs McCaul's name.   Dorothy Susan McCaul died 13 July 1897 and the mortgage transferred to her husband Walter on 19 November 1897. Mr Hogg defaulted on mortgage payments and Mr McCaul exercised his right of 'Power of Sale' and sold the land to William Thomas for £ 400 ($800) on 5 September 1898.

William appears to have paid the £ 400 in cash, as it was 14 months later when he raised his first mortgage on the property.

A story, originating from son Jack, tells of *"Eliza inheriting money"* (maybe from Grandma Isabel or her father in Scotland) *"with William and their solicitor using this without her knowledge."* (V+GW)

If she was at Ngawapurua, and William was in Auckland and very keen to buy Riverview Farm, we can imagine him using some of her money which their solicitor was probably investing on her behalf. Later William did take out three mortgages over the farm land, either for farm improvements, or to build the brickworks, or maybe to pay Eliza back.

THE HOME OF WILLIAM AND ELIZA THOMAS
Rata St, New Lynn, 1898 when they moved in.

**THE RATA ST HOME after William had restored it
and added a conservatory to the right.**

1899... MORTGAGE... DEED #149667.   (R64-190)
On 1 December, William Thomas (Avondale Farmer) raised a mortgage of £ 300 with the Superintendent of 'The Government Advances to Settlers Office'.   Repaid 19 July 1905. Receipt #174532.

1902... MORTGAGE... DEED #159019.   (R80-29)
On 29 April, William Thomas (Farmer of 'Riverview', Avondale) raised another mortgage of £ 100 with the same organisation mentioned above.
Repaid 4 July 1905. Receipt #174535.

1905... MORTGAGE... DEED #174534.   (R116-21)
On 26 June William Thomas raised a mortgage of £ 650 with Joseph Glenny, Schoolmaster, plus interest at 7% per annum, payable quarterly.
Repaid 6 July 1910. Receipt #204378.

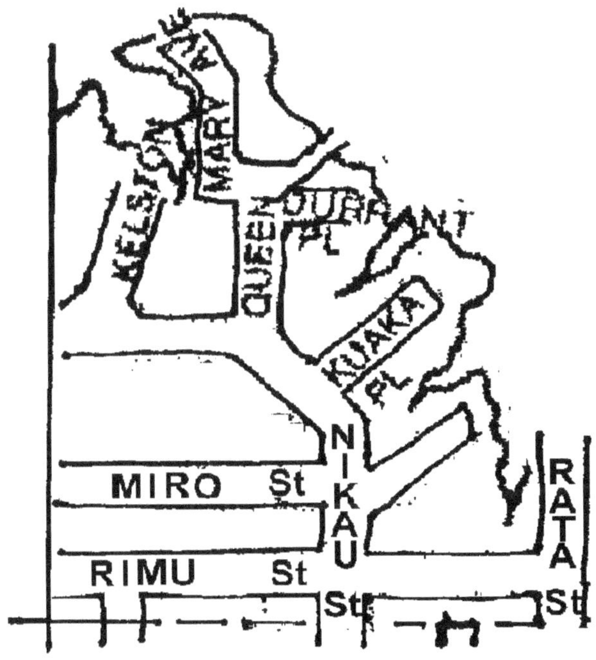

The 88 acres in year 2000

What did William Thomas do on his 88 acres at New Lynn ?
We have found he was a Farmer, Orchardist, Brick-maker and Developer.

FARMER:

Grain: From descendants, we found he farmed the land, growing oats and was one of the first in the New Lynn district, to own a 'reaper and binder' (a machine for cutting grain and tying it up into bundles or sheaves.) (DT) Initially William would have used horses about the farm and we found the location of his stable on Plan #7823.

Orchards: The Department of Land Information has a copy of Plan #7823 which shows two large areas fenced off and marked 'Orchard'. William Thomas was an "Orchardist" on a 1910 mortgage application.

In October 2000 we found at the Henderson Library, Auckland, an unnamed author had at some time toured the New Lynn district's businesses and at Rata Street he had noted... *"Thomas family. Delicious apples".* Grandson Athol recalled William supplied Turners and Growers with fruit. (GC)

Trees: This same Plan #7823 also shows William had a small plantation of, and two long fences of pine trees.

Fowls-Eggs. On Plan #43488 a large building was drawn and described as 'Fowl-house', situated between his home and the brick works site.

> We have put together a composite sketch plan showing all these items on William's reduced 36 acre 1912 farm. See page 96.

BRICKWORKS:

We have not found any record or photos of the Brickworks, its erection or money specifically gained to pay for the building and machinery.

But it did exist. William did erect a brick works on his property, at the bend in today's Queen Mary Avenue, just above today's footbridge over the creek and where the creek channel runs closest to the land. Deed R296-4 describes the original straight piece of Queen Mary Avenue that goes north at Nikau St as *'Wharf Road'* and confirms the location of the brick works, with the wharf at the end used to load and unload bricks and supplies. The New Lynn Council changed the name when they formed a proper roadway there.

William employed 3 of his sons, Harry, Jack and Albert. All three became brickmakers, and with their families lived on the farm in separate houses.

William built a scow and son Albert sailed it. With this *'flat bottomed unpowered barge with sail'* they delivered their bricks wherever needed. Some of them were used on the Chelsea Sugar Works and the Parnell Post Office. (DT) The return trips often carried supplies, timber, firewood or coal. (OTW2) Some of their bricks were despatched by J. J. Craig the carriers, for their own builders and for others further afield. (AWT)

John T Diamond wrote in his second edition of *'Once –The Wilderness'*…..
       (Possible correction. We think it should be 1898 or 1903 as
       William Thomas did not leave Ngawapurua until late 1898)
"In 1893 William Thomas started making bricks at the foot of Queen Mary Avenue, Kelston. He built a bridge across a narrow arm of one of the inlets of the Rewa Rewa Creek over which he brought clay to his works while he used his own scow to transport the bricks to Auckland and the shore settlements until 1908 when he closed down. This was the last brick-works to be built on the banks of the Whau Creek."

In another section of the same book Mr Diamond writes…..
"The old saying 'time and tide wait for no one' was true on the Whau. One old seaman who sailed on the scow 'Glenae' with coal from Whangarei for Thomas' brickyard, said that if they arrived off the Whau at night as the tide was running in they went in with it, unloaded the cargo of coal, took on a cargo of bricks and sailed out again on the tide. Under the light of kerosene lanterns the unloading was done with the aid of wheelbarrows which when loaded with coal had to be pushed up a plank onto the breastwork and thence to the dump. Although at this stage the crew were sober, there were several instances when the wheelbarrow and pusher fell into the dark murky waters. If the tide was full in, it was much easier to extricate both, but they were filthy muddy messes if they had to be rescued from mud covered with a few inches of water." (OTW2)

We learnt from Dick Scott in his book *"Fire on the Clay"*…
that in 1905 competition for supply of bricks and pipes became fiercer in Auckland with the arrival of Albert Crum, an ambitious, hard driving, builder and brickmaker from Ashburton in the South Island.
Crum's business expanded at such a rate that it promptly challenged the established larger companies of Clark, Gardner, and Craig's hold on the market. Bricks sold at 45 shillings per thousand ($4.50 per 1000) when Mr Crum arrived at New Lynn. His success in capturing a large slice of the market within three years was a signal for savage price-cutting that lowered the rate to 30 shillings ($3 per 1000) in 1908.

       In 1908, at near enough to 60 years of age, we can imagine William Thomas deciding to close his brickworks, because the big boys were going on a price war and thereby making his business unprofitable.

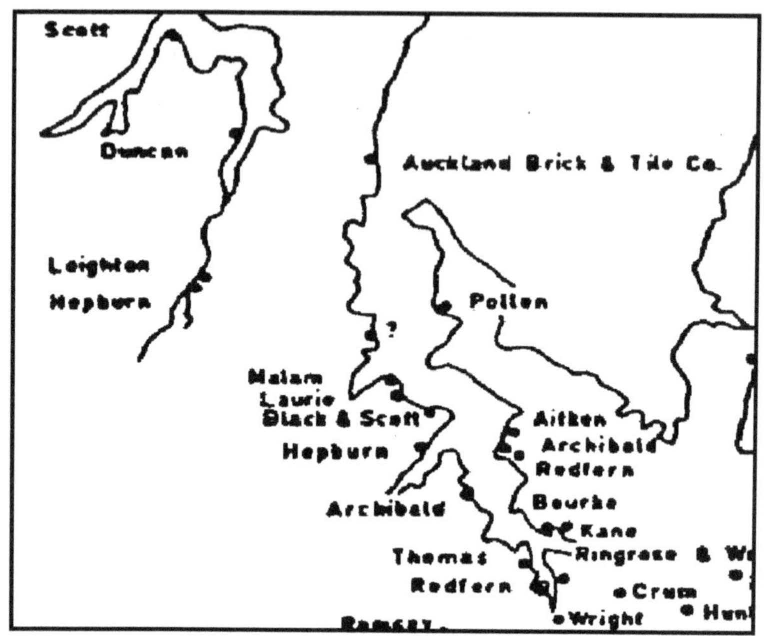

THE INNER WAITEMATA HARBOUR:

This MAP shows the lower part of the Waitemata and the concentration of brick and pipe works around the Whau estuary. William Thomas' brickworks is shown lower middle, and to the upper right is depicted the Oakley Creek site of his father John's Star Flour Mill and brickyard.

Memorial: In 1984 the New Lynn Rotary Club erected beside the Great North Road in New Lynn a 'memorial plaque' to the pioneer brick, pipe and pottery industry in the Western Districts of Auckland. This lists all the works and a map shows their locations including William Thomas' brickworks.

--oo0Ooo--

1899... Eldest son Jack married Alice James on 25 December at Levin. Mother Eliza (49) and William (51) was described as 'Nurseryman' (why?) on Jack's wedding certificate.

1900... The Nikau School Roll, dated 7 March, lists Rose Thomas (aged 13) as a pupil in Standard 7. We believe she didn't move north with her parents but was allowed to stay with her eldest married sister Lizzie.

1904... SALE… DEEDS… #171352 & #171353   (R107-58)
On 17 October William Thomas agreed to sell 46 acres (The Homestead block in Rata Street plus 6 acres towards the Whau waters) for £1,000, to   J. C. Colbeck to be settled in one month. The deal was never finalised.

--ooOOoo--

1904... Daughter Annie married Len Gardner on 27 July at Nikau.
1905... Son Harry married Mary Close on 26 July at Levin.

--ooOOoo--

1909... NEW LYNN 88 ACRES SUBDIVIDED:

SALE… DEED #204377... dated 30 October 1909. (23A-362, R176-237)
William Thomas, settler of New Lynn, sold 52 acres (part of his 88 acre farm of Allotment 139 in Waikumete parish) to his three sons, Jack, Harry and Albert for £ 900. All three were listed as 'Brickmakers'.
This sale was finally registered 21 July 1910.

> (The 36 acre balance was retained by William Thomas, now aged 60, and in 1912 he subdivided these 36 acres.)

This Deed mentions that William agreed *"about July 1903 to sell to his three sons that portion of said Allotment 139 for £ 900 and subject to the payment of Annual Right and Rent charges."*
The document advises these three sons *"took possession of the land about 1903 and paid William £ 250."* Since that date the three sons *"have effected on this land, conveyed out of their own proper moneys, all the improvements on the said land."*
The three sons agreed in October 1909 to *"the conveyance of the said land to them for the balance payment of £ 650 plus interest."*

The three sons became *'Tenants in common in equal shares of the 52 acres'.*
They agreed to pay……(1) the £ 650 mortgage off, (J. Glenny 174534) and (2) to provide William Thomas and wife Eliza Thomas (or the survivor) during their lifetimes *"a continuing clear annual sum or yearly rent charge of £ 52, without any deductions what-so-ever, paid on the 6th day of February, May, August and November, with the first payment due 6th day February next (1910)."* A paragraph was included that *"should any such sum or rent fall in to arrears (21 days after due date) then William or Eliza could exercise Right of Sale over the property to recover all moneys due and all expenses incurred by the action."* and (3) to provide *"a free and uninterrupted Right of Way as well as a horse way and a footway and either with or without horses, cattle or other animals, carts, carriages and other vehicles, laden or unladen, at all times, at his or their will and pleasure, in, through, over or along the Right of*

Way." The document was signed by all four persons. (There is no description on the document of type, number or location of the buildings on the property. T)

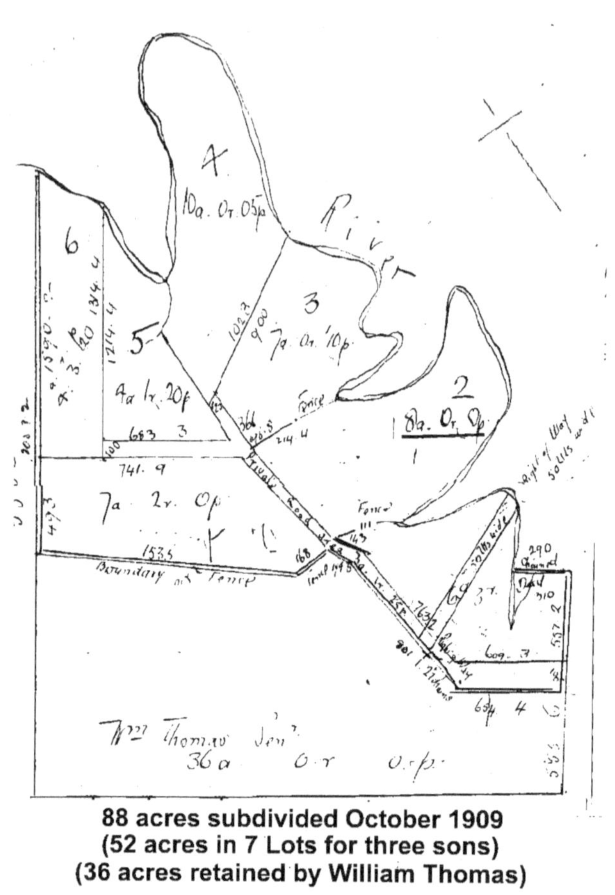

88 acres subdivided October 1909
(52 acres in 7 Lots for three sons)
(36 acres retained by William Thomas)

1910... MORTGAGE... DEED #204378   (R176-242)
This document, signed by Joseph Glenny, records that on 6 July 1910 he received all the monies to pay off William Thomas' Mortgage # 174534.

1910... RIGHT & RENT CHARGE... DEED #204379 (R176-242)
**   and DEED #204381 (R179.322)**
Very wordy documents detailing William's and then the three sons' obligations and agreement regarding Right & Rent Charges, as above.

1910... MORTGAGE... DEED #204380   (R180.27)
On 7 July the three brothers raised a mortgage of £ 450 with New Zealand State Guaranteed Advances Office, secured over the 52 acres.

52 ACRES: We do not know what the three brothers did to this land between 1909 and 1912 but imagine much discussion, due to the fact that in 1913 and 1914 there were many sales made of pieces of the 52 acres. Some of the original seven lots (ranging from 4 to 10 acre pieces) were sold as one block, many were reduced by council roads, public reserve and state housing needs and others were subdivided into many smaller lots for houses.

> There are many many records of land transfers, mortgages etc available at Land Information, Auckland, but too many to record in detail here. However, here are some notable items we found.

Lot 2, suitable in 1914 for residential housing, seems to have been swapped for a larger parcel of farm land at Brigham's Creek, at Massey.

Jack was the only brother to live on the 52 acre land, with a house on the south side of the corner of Nikau Street and Queen Mary Avenue. Harry and Arthur had houses close to their parents in Rimu Street, on the 36 acre block.

Harry Thomas' father-in-law William Close of Levin made mortgage money available in March 1913 to 1918 and again from June 1918 to 1921.

About 1909 before completing the subdivision, roads were needed and son Harry cleaned up the brickyard-site by removing all unsold and broken bricks and set these out as a foundation for part of the road now named Queen Mary Avenue. Harry always felt that due to his hard work and enterprise, the northern leg at least should have been named *Thomas Street.* (DT)

--oo0Ooo--

1910... Son Arthur married Elsie Wilmshurst on 29 September at Stratford.

1911... Eliza's aunt Elizabeth Carrie died 14 February aged 84 in Auckland.

1912... Son Albert married Ethel Ladbrook on 9 October at New Lynn.

1913... Daughter Rose married Harry Dove on 22 January at New Lynn.

1910... MORTGAGE... DEED #204382   (R179.325)
On July 7, William Thomas, Orchardist, gained a £ 300 mortgage from New Zealand State Guaranteed Advances over the 36 acre balance of his land.

1912... SECOND LAND SUBDIVISION:
In June 1912 Plan #7823 was submitted to 'Land Information'. This was the first of the subdivisions of William Thomas' 36 acre New Lynn property.

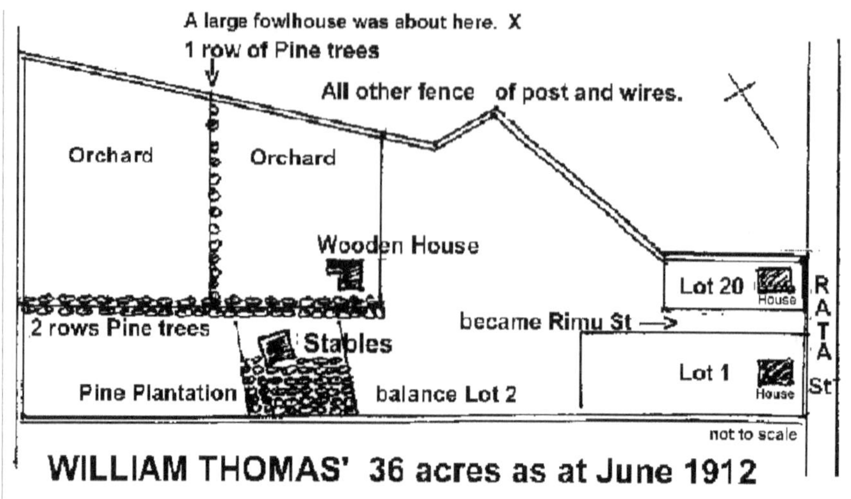

WILLIAM THOMAS' 36 acres as at June 1912

1912... Plan #7823 shows three divisions of these 36 acres of land…
Lot 1 of 2 acres. South corner Rata and Rimu. Includes William's residence.
Lot 20 of 1 acre. North corner Rata and Rimu. Included son Arthur's home.
Lot 2 of 28a,2r,29.8p is balance of 36 acres with orchards, stables, etc.
This plan was registered 24 June 1912.

In May 1917, after William died, Lot 1 above was further subdivided into 5
lots on Plan #11688. New Lots 1,2,3 faced Rata Street and new Lot 4 & 5
faced Rimu Street. Lot 5 was where Harry's home was. Eliza's home was
now located on Lot 3 on the corner Rimu and Rata Streets.

1912... MORE LAND… DEED #223512   (25A/176, R216/228)
On 10 September, William Thomas purchased Lot 9 of 1 rood 32.44 perches
for £ 70. This land, situated over Rata St from his 88 acres, ran down to the
Whau Creek. It was still in his ownership when he died. However, on 19 May
1916 William had made an agreement to sell this land to Mr James Hunter,
manufacturer of Auckland for £ 125 and had received a £ 10 deposit. DEED
#323215 (R407/332) details William's Will and passes ownership to
William's executors. DEED #334890 (R430/498) dated 27 June 1924
transfers this land to Mr Hunter after he paid the £ 115 balance.

1912... THIRD SUBDIVISION:
Plan #8034 dated August 1912 shows William's 36 acres, with new streets
named Rimu, Miro and Nikau adjoining Rata Street. All New Zealand native
trees. The land is also divided into Lots 1 to 53 and Lots 63 to76.

The largest sale William made involved Lots 42,43,44,45,46,47, + 51,52,53, +74,75,76 registered on 1 August 1913 via Vol 206/276 totalling 5 acres, 2r, 17.8p. Part of the deal was for William to hold a mortgage (#55108) over Lots 42,43,44,+45 as recorded on Vol 211/111.

The purchaser Mr James Caddell paid off the debt 5 September 1929.

We also found another family member involved. Harry Dove owned Lot 24 facing Miro St for approximately six months during 1921.

JANUARY 1915 Birthdays: Jack 40, Marjorie 1, Rose 28, Irene 14.
(left to right) Jack, Harry, Jim, Harry Dove and   ?
Roland, Edie, Marjorie, Violet, Eliza, Mary, Ethel, Gladys, Rose and Irene.
Athol, Ivy, Edna, Flossie, Eileen and Gwen.

1914... In a three-brother's land sale document of 7 December, William and Eliza Thomas are described as... *'The Annuants'*.

Around 1914 William Thomas made concrete slabs with metal chips, like terrazzo, as a hobby for who ever wanted them. (DT)

1915... NZPO Directory listed at New Lynn... William Thomas...'Settler', also sons Albert Thomas...'Mariner', and Arthur Thomas...'Builder'.

1916... Daughter Edith married Arthur Dove on 18 April at New Lynn.
William travelled to his Solicitors on 22 May and signed his Will.
1917... Son Jim was killed in work related accident. (details Chapter 15)
1921... Daughter Ethel married Laurie Hawken on 6 August at Taihape.

1922... Electoral Roll for Eden records...........

      William Thomas   Rata Street, New Lynn. Retired.
      Euphemia Eliza Thomas   Rata Street, New Lynn. Married.

1923... WILLIAM THOMAS DIED:

      On 25 February 1923, William Thomas died at his residence in Rata Street, New Lynn, Auckland aged 74.

His funeral procession left his home at 11am Tuesday 27 and he was buried at Waikumete Cemetery in Presbyterian Block D, Section 6, Plot 39.

      William is remembered by his granddaughter Mary England as a man of medium stature standing near the fireplace at Rata Street, and that he had a long beard. She was nearly seven when he died.

      Grandson Athol recalled entering his grandfather's room at Rata Street. Athol could hardly see for smoke from the dark Havelock Tobacco. On the shelf above William's desk were many empty tins.

The WILL of WILLIAM THOMAS was signed on 22 May 1916.

William's Will was probated 13 April 1923 and he left an estate of nearly £ 4,500. The 'Motion to Probate' shows he made his wife Euphemia Eliza Thomas his Executrix and Albert Peter Thomas ('Carpenter' of New Lynn) and Arthur Gordon Thomas ('Farmer' of Okura, Taranaki) to be Executors. All three signed that they *"had seen his dead body after death."*

      Special bequests detailed in the three pages of the Will were.....

      Albert Peter Thomas... the cancellation of a mortgage of £ 338, held by William and secured by Lot 34 Allot 16 of Parish of Waikumete.

      Arthur Gordon Thomas... the cancellation of a mortgage of £ 200 held by William. No details given of security.

His trustees were to hold the balance of the estate in trust, for the use of his wife *'during the term of her natural life'*.

Had she remarried she would have received one third of the estate, the balance being divided equally amongst his children.

Eliza did not remarry and so after she died William's estate was equally divided amongst all his children. Had one of his then living children died before Eliza, that child's children would have received equal portions. There was no mention of that child's spouse receiving anything.

William Thomas' Will was signed by himself, by J. M. Melville, Solicitor and Raymond Farmer, Law Clerk. No obituary has been found for William.

**WILLIAM'S SIGNATURE
ON HIS WILL................**

--ooOOoo--

1923... ELIZA:

Immediately after William's death, daughter Edith, husband Arthur and their children moved into the Rata Street house and for twelve years took care of Eliza there. About 1934 the Dove family moved back to their Mt Albert home and here Eliza spent her final year.

1935... ELIZA DIED:

Eliza Thomas (nee McKay) died on 6 March 1935, aged 83, at 53 Mt Albert Road, the home of Edith and Arthur Dove.

Her funeral procession left the Dove home at 11am Friday 8 and she joined husband William at Waikumete Cemetery. If Eliza made a Will, it does not appear to have survived for us to read.

ELIZA THOMAS nee McKAY

William and Eliza's headstone reads.........
          IN LOVING MEMORY OF WILLIAM THOMAS
            DIED 25 FEBRUARY 1923 AGED 75 YEARS
              ALSO HIS BELOVED WIFE ELIZA
              DIED 6 MARCH 1935 AGED 84 YEARS
              AND THEIR SON WALTER JAMES
              DIED 27 JUNE 1917 AGED 22 YEARS.
                    --ooOOoo--

ELIZA THOMAS nee McKAY

(1851 - 1935)

1851... SCOTLAND:

Eliza McKay was the second child of John McKay and Ann nee Carey and was registered as Euphemia Eliza Ramsey McKay.

She was born on 1 November 1851 at Dundee in Scotland and baptised in the Church of Scotland (Anglican) on 22 November 1851.

We are advised that two weeks after her birth her mother died.

We do not know for sure who brought baby Eliza up in Scotland until she was aged five, but feel that her mother's Carey / Carrie family were involved.

We are very grateful of the help provided by Eliza's New Zealand grand-daughter Delcie Twizell, who, some years ago did a lot of this research and gained various certificates of births and marriages mentioned in this chapter. The family tree which follows, lists Eliza's predecessors we have found.

1858... NEW ZEALAND: Aged 6, Eliza McKay came to New Zealand.

Auckland's Southern Cross and the Comber Index advise us....

"The 600 ton barque "Tamar" with Mr J. Ross as Captain, left Gravesend, London on 11 October 1857, on the 16th passed the Lizard, November 7 Spk 6N 24W, November 10 (30th day) crossed the Equator 27'21" west, December 15 Cape of Good Hope in heavy weather, sighted Van Dieman's Land 11 January, unsettled weather to The Three Kings where she was detained 5 days (wind ESE / ENE) under double reefed topsails and making no headway the whole time. After 109 days she berthed at Auckland, New Zealand on 28 January 1858."

Eliza celebrated her 6th birthday on the ship.

The ship's papers no longer exist, so details of the passengers (ages, occupations etc) and of the voyage are unknown, except for the few comments recorded in Auckland's papers.

The Southern Cross newspaper states...

"The Tamar brought a very superior class of passengers, a large portion of whom are farmers and farm labourers. There were a dozen female servants and a few ladies described themselves as Governess."

There were 98 passengers, including Isaac Carrie, Isabel Carrie and Eliza McKay. The paper gave them the name 'Currie' and their accent probably accounted for this error. Eliza travelled under the Carrie name, probably for simplicities sake. In New Zealand she appears to have been brought up by her grandmother Isabel and her uncle Isaac Carrie.

We believe that Eliza's grandfather Joseph Carrie died in his mid-fifties before his family left Scotland in 1857, and that her father John McKay stayed in Scotland, raised her brother John and maybe re-married.
The name Carrie seems to be spelt either Carrie or Carey, depending on whoever did the recording. Earlier Scottish Church records have it as Carrie, but when Ann married John McKay the Minister used the Carey version. When Ann's children were baptised the Carey spelling was again used and this was the way it was recorded in New Zealand by Eliza's family.

Eliza would have had no schooling before leaving Scotland and appears to have had very little in New Zealand. She could not write her name when she married in 1870, but she did sign the registration forms for all her children's births following daughter Annie's in 1880, when she was aged 29, and signed as Executrix of her husband William's Will in 1923.

AUCKLAND:
1858... First night in New Zealand. Eliza told her grand-daughter Flossie, about the first night she and her relations spent in Auckland. They had to cut four posts from trees to make a thatched room in which to sleep. They placed wire around and over the posts and interwove Manuka branches throughout. It rained that night and it leaked. Each person sat in a rug with the corners drawn up and sat under umbrellas. (FT)

QUEEN STREET:
There appears to be two occasions when Eliza's family could have lived in Queen St, Auckland, either early in 1858/9 immediately after their arrival, or about 1867/8. There were very few shops there then and only a few houses, and Eliza told Delcie that *"they lived at the bottom of Queen St in an old shop on the left hand side looking seawards"*. Years later Delcie's father pointed out the "Guardian" building with its columns opposite Shortland St, as the area where Eliza had lived awhile. This reminded Flossie that Eliza said that if the family went to bed, or went out for the day and left the door unlocked, the police would soon be along to tell them to be more careful.

1859... MOTUIHE ISLAND:

Isaac Carrie, a farmer in Scotland, found employment on Motuihe Island (as it is known today) as a farmer, and we believe that his mother Isabel and niece Eliza aged seven in 1859, went with him.

Many of her grandchildren have said that Eliza mentioned she had lived for a while on Motutapu Island. There was no record of Isaac on Motutapu, however in the March 1861 and the 1865 Electoral Rolls for the district of Franklin, we found Isaac Robert Carrie listed, so it would seem correct that they lived on the not-so-well-known Motoihe Island, next to Motutapu.

Tracing Isabel Carrie was difficult, because women at that time were not mentioned on Electoral Rolls, property registrations or in town directories.

When Delcie was seeking knowledge of Eliza, she received a letter from Flossie's mother Elsie Thomas. In part it reads.. *"When she (Eliza) was a girl, she used to go in a boat from one island to another by herself. One day as she was getting into the boat she looked into the water, saw the danger and got a fright. That was the last time she went in the boat."*

'Chapman's New Zealand Almanac' of 1862 described Moto-Ihi Island as... *"A fertile island lying between Waiheke Island and the Tamaki River entrance, about 10 miles from Auckland."* The booklet 'Motuihi' advises this 441 acre island (also known as Tayler's Island) was mostly used for farming. It was sold by the Maori into Pakeha ownership in 1839 to W. H. Fairburn. He sold in 1840 to Henry Tayler, who sold in 1843 to William Brown & John Logan Campbell, who in February 1858 sold to John Graham. Finally, in 1872 the island became the property of Her Majesty Queen Victoria and was used as the Quarantine Station for New Zealand.

During the John Graham ownership, we found Isaac occupying a dwelling on Motuihe Island. The writer believes that Isaac moved there in 1859 or 1860. He was listed first in March 1861, then in each of the following Electoral Rolls, until he bought land in 1869 at Point Chevalier in Auckland.

Eliza told granddaughter Delcie that *"they felt very safe on that island especially while the Maori Wars were taking place,"* over the years 1860-1864.

Elsie's letter also advised Delcie... *"When they were living on the island, some Maori came over to where they were living but never touched them."*

According to Elsie's letter *"Eliza lived with Isabel until she married."*

ISABEL CARRIE'S HEADSTONE.

By 1865, Isabel would have been aged in the mid 60's, may have been of deteriorating health and thinking of the then 14 year old Eliza's future.
Did she suggest that Isaac should find a wife so that he could continue being 'father' and provider for Eliza?

At age 40 in 1865, (NZ ref 59) and while living on Motuihe, Isaac married Martha Gordon. They had three sons and two daughters.

ISABEL DIED.
She died on 16 September 1866 of 'Decay of Nature' and was interred at Auckland's Grafton Cemetery, plot 156, Presbyterian section.

The informant on Isabel's death certificate was 'John Goldie'.
Was he one of Isaac's or Alexander's daughter's husbands or a close family friend?

Buried with her are her son Alexander and his wife Selina, and Isabel's daughter Elizabeth and possibly a grandson named John Carrie. Alexander and Elizabeth must have followed Isabel and Isaac out to New Zealand.

Isabel's headstone reads............
SACRED to the memory of ISOBEL CARRIE (nee GORDON)
relict of JOSEPH CARRIE,
farmer of Knockhills Forfarshire, Scotland,
who died September 16th 1866, and of
ALEXANDER CARRIE their son settler at Matakana
who died October 1st 1880 and his wife
SELINA who died November 8th 1917. Also
ELIZABETH CARRIE Died 15th February 1911 aged 84.

The Wills of Isabel, Isaac, Martha and Elizabeth Carrie have not survived.

1868-1870… About 1868, Eliza aged 17 or 18, moved to live in Point Chevalier, probably with her Uncle Isaac and Martha. While there she met, and agreed to marry, William Thomas of nearby Oakley's Creek, in 1870. As her life became part of William Thomas' when they married, other facts we have found about Eliza are included in that earlier story.

--oo0Ooo--

FAMILY IN SCOTLAND.

This photograph from Scotland came to New Zealand with Eliza. Her mother Ann died when Eliza was two weeks old.

It could depict her mother's Carrie family or the McKay family.

We believe it to show Eliza's mother Ann McKay nee Carrie, with her grandmother Helen Carrie nee Allan and an unknown young male and family dog.

The camera was invented in 1826, and suitable photograph papers were available from 1839 when Ann Carrie was aged 11. This young lady could be ANN aged between 10 and 13 years. (DT&T)

ISAAC ROBERT CARRIE:

We detail Isaac's life now, as he acted as Eliza's 'Dad' here in New Zealand.

1869... The *'Newton Highway's District Roads Board'* set rates of 9 pence per acre for the calendar year 1869. Assessed for these rates was Isaac Carrie who paid £ 1-2 shillings, 6 pence on 30 acres of part Lot 20 and 21 at Oakley's Creek. The balance of Lots 20 and 21 were owned by... Joseph Cunningham 10.75 acres, James Coupland a half acre, John Collins 2 acres, Mr Crago 5 acres, Mr Sutton 10 acres, Richard Walker 50 acres, John White 30 acres, Robert McDonald 31 acres and Mr Greenway 18 acres.

1873... *'The Auckland Directory'* lists nine families living in the Point Chevalier district of Auckland. Three of these are of interest to us.
The nine families were named.... <u>Isaac Carrie</u>, Patrick Dignam, William Motion, Capt. Seymour, Richard and Thomas Henry Walker, <u>Barraclough and Thomas of Star Mill, Oakley Creek,</u> and W. Edgecombe.
    (Mrs Barraclough was William's mother Jane, and
    Mr Thomas was William's brother John.)

1866 - 1882... Isaac and Martha had 5 children, Joseph b1866, Robert Gordon b1868, Martha b1871, John b1872 & Elizabeth b1875. They all attended Mt Albert School from 1 January 1878 to October 1882 and during these years lived in Kingsland Road, now known as 'Sandringham Road'.

1889... Isaac Robert Carrie's last known address was Kingsland Road, Mt Albert where he died 19 January 1889 aged 64. The Rev. R. S. West interred Isaac at Waikumete Cemetery's Presbyterian section, Row 4.
The headstone detail is quite long and reads..............
"Sacred to the memory of Isaac Robert Carrie beloved husband
of Martha nee Gordon, born Knockhills, Forfarshire, Scotland.
22 March 1825, died Mt Albert, Auckland 19 January 1889.
Also grandson Isaac Robert Andrew Carrie,
died 20 August 1898 aged 5 days,
also Martha, relict of the above who passed peacefully away
on 29 August 1932 in her 93rd year."

We also found an Isaac Gordon Carrie, farmer, died 9 Dec 1930 in Auckland aged 71 and buried at Purewa (ref #3181). He seems to fit into this family - perhaps he was one of Isaac or Alexander's sons?

Was there a blood relationship between Isaac's mother Isabel nee Gordon, and his wife Martha nee Gordon?   Martha was 14 years younger than Isaac.

1893... Martha, aged 54, was on the Womens Suffrage Electoral Roll...
#605 Eden... Martha Carrie of Kingsland Road... Tailoress.
****

The CARRIE FAMILY TREE:

1780?.. ISAAC CARRIE   (spelt Carey on the wedding record)
married 30 December 1800 at Saint Vigeans, Angus, Scotland.
to **HELEN (ELEANOR) ALLEN.** We found evidence of 4 children....
> **Joseph Carrie** bapt (twin) 21 Oct 1801 Camyllie, Scotland
> Robert Carrie bapt (twin) 21 Oct 1801 Camyllie, Scotland
> > Recorded at Camyllie as Carrie.......
> Ann Carrie   bapt 21 March 1804, Inverkeilor, Angus, Scotland.
> John Carrie   bapt 4 October 1807, Inverkeilor, Angus, Scotland.
> > Recorded at Saint Vigeans and Inverkeilor as Carey.

SCOTLAND: Saint Vigeans is in the northern part of Arbroath town.
Camyllie 6 miles west of Arbroath.   **Inverkeilor** 7 miles NE of Arbroath.
Kirkden (in Forfarshire, now Angus County) is 6 miles NE of Arbroath.
Kirkden Parish in 1887 had 5406 acres and 1205 people. (Gazetteer)
--oo0Ooo--
1801... JOSEPH CARRIE (farmer, died Forfarshire, Scotland.)
married 5 December 1818 at Kirkden, Angus, Scotland.
to **ISABEL GORDON** (spelt Gorden at wedding and Gordon at baptisms)
We have found 5 children.....
> John Carrie   baptised 8 March   1819.
> Alexander Carrie   "   19 December 1821.
> Elizabeth Carrie   "   2 June   1823.
> Isaac Robert Carrie   born 25 March 1825, baptised 17 April 1825.
> **Ann Carrie**   baptised 28 April   1828.
> All children were baptised at the Kirkden Parish Church.

We have found that Alexander came to New Zealand and married, Elizabeth came to NZ and remained single, and Isaac Robert Carrie came to NZ with mother Isabel and sister Ann's child Eliza McKay.
Alexander and Elizabeth were not with Isabel on the ship *'Tamar'*.

1828... ANN CARRIE / CAREY
married 17 Dec 1849 at the Parish Church in Dundee, Scotland.
to **JOHN McKAY** (a bachelor and 'Merchant' of Dundee)
John C. Baxter was the Minister.
They had two children. Ann died two weeks after Eliza was born.
John Gordon Maxwell McKay born 24 October 1850
and baptised 10 November 1850 at Dundee.
Euphemia <u>Eliza</u> Ramsey McKay born 1 November 1851
and baptised 22 November 1851 at Dundee.

****

The **1851 Census in Dundee** shows 6 families living at 3 Crescent Street, Dundee. One of these families was recorded as…
John McKAY   head   married   26   Wine and Spirit Merchant.
Ann McKAY   wife   married   22
Elizabeth CARRIE   servant unmarried 26
(son John (aged 5 months) was not recorded as being at home.)
(Elizabeth Carrie was wife Ann's sister.)

****

1851... Eliza (6) came to New Zealand and later married William Thomas.

****

The McKAY FAMILY TREE

1800... ALEXANDER McKAY
married **BETTY (ELIZABETH) MAXWELL** on
24 December 1820 at Dundee, Angus, Scotland.
We have found two children.....
Christian McKay born 18 November 1821 at Dundee.
John McKay   born 29 October   1824 at Dundee.

John McKay married Ann Carey in 1849 at Dundee.

****

CHAPTER FIVE

7th Generation (3rd NZ)

ELIZABETH JANE THOMAS

(1871-1951)

1871... BIRTH - AUCKLAND:

On 14 February 1871 at their Oakley Creek home in Auckland, the first child of William and Eliza Thomas was born.

They named her Elizabeth Jane Thomas but she was known as 'Lizzie'.

1876... SCHOOL: Auckland.

Mt. Albert School enrolment registers state Lizzie first attended the Whau School (Avondale) but no records prior to 1883 have survived to date.

She may have attended school at Hastings where the family lived for a time.

The Mt. Albert School registers show Lizzie (10) was enrolled here by her father, along with sister Eliza and brother Jack on 20 April 1881.

On 29 March 1882, Lizzie aged 11 sat Standard 2 exams. She passed reading, spelling, dictation and arithmetic but failed writing and geography. There were 21 in the class and 8 failed something. Her attendance for the year was low at 296 out of 430 half days which may have contributed to the results. Lizzie left this school on 26 May 1882 *"to go to Christchurch"*.

1882... ASHBURTON: Lizzie aged 11, moved south with her parents and

may have attended school in Christchurch. No record has been found. When the family moved onto the Allenton Nursery at Ashburton, Lizzie would have enjoyed the company of her first cousins, (Uncle John's children) Lizzie, nearly 12 years old, was not enrolled at the Ashburton Borough School along with her younger siblings. We think her education was considered to be completed. She probably was most helpful to her mother with the younger children, also becoming very useful with household chores.

1887... NGAWAPURUA:

In her 17th year, the family moved to Ngawapurua in the North Island near Woodville. She, and seven siblings travelled with her parents and Lizzie must have provided valuable assistance, during this long trip.

1893... ELECTORAL ROLL: The Waipawa Electorate.

Elizabeth Jane Thomas...   resident of Woodville...   Household duties.
William Sowry...   resident of Woodville...   Butcher.

E. J. (Lizzie) SOWRY

1893... MARRIAGE:

On Christmas Day 25 December 1893, Lizzie (22) was married by the Rev. C. Penny at the Methodist Church in Woodville, to WILLIAM SOWRY (30). They lived all their married life on William's Nikau farm property.

Lizzie and sister Eliza married two brothers... William and Herbert Sowry.

William Sowry was the second son of JOSEPH SOWRY and wife HANNAH nee STROTHER. He was born at Waitaki in Canterbury on 13 May 1863. Later during the 1880's William, together with brothers Arthur and Albert operated a bakery in the Woodville township. (AS)

Further Joseph Sowry family detail follows on page 158.

NIKAU FARM:

Parts of the Nikau, Makomako and Mangahao districts formed the Woodville Mangahao Special Settlement Block. About 1887 William purchased a piece of this, Section 7 of 93 acres at Nikau, a bush settlement property a few miles south

LIZZIE and WILLIAM SOWRY (JR)

west of Pahiatua. Over many years they finished clearing the bush and progressively established a dairy farm. William supplied the Creamery at Makomako with his milk, and this entailed sledging and then carting it over four miles of very rough country. (AS)

William and Lizzie's home on Marina Road, Nikau. (ND) The house was set back from the road on top of a small hill overlooking the rest of the farm. In the paddock next to the house was a good sized orchard and granddaughter Anita recalls the many berries and fruit she ate whenever her family visited the farm. Anita also remembers as a wee girl, being fascinated by a small tin toy hen that Lizzie would wind up and she watched as it moved and ate bread crumbs. (AH)

Later on Lizzie had a row of lawsonias planted on the boundary, where she would be shielded from the view of her neighbours, while unloading her shopping from her car boot. (NS)

William died in 1932 after farming this property for 45 years. The farm was then worked by his family for another 35 years, when it finally left Sowry hands.

William, Lizzie and Malcolm and dog Rover in 1908 (NB+MMacD)

William's obituary in the *'Pahiatua Herald'* advises us *" .... he was one of the first settlers in the Nikau district, an enterprising and progressive farmer, being a firm believer in top-dressing and ensilage making."*

CHILDREN:

Lizzie and William Sowry had 11 children they named... Hector, Olive, Amy, Veda, Vivian, Mavis, Rupert, Walter, Malcolm, Thelma and Norman. Their children all attended the Nikau School in Omata Road until it closed. Then the younger ones completed their education at the Marima School.

The Nikau School started in a slab whare in January 1895 and when Lizzie's eldest child started school in 1900 the roll had reached 35 children. The teacher at the time was Miss Wilson. In 1901 a new and larger school was built on the same site.(M) The schoolteacher boarded at Lizzie's home.(NB)

It is a credit to Lizzie and William that all of their eleven children survived to adulthood. Their descendants are detailed at the end of this chapter.

LIZZIE and WILLIAM SOWRY'S children. in 1810/11

at back HECTOR, OLIVE.

in centre AMY, THELMA, VIVIAN, MALCOLM, MAVIS.

in front RUPERT, VEDA, WALTER.
(OH)

1897... ELECTIONS: In the Pahiatua Electorate we found Lizzie *'Married Women'* and William *'Farmer'* living at Nikau.

1898... Lizzie's parents, William and Eliza Thomas, and some of her younger siblings moved to live in New Lynn, Auckland.

1910... POST MISTRESS:
Lizzie became Post-Mistress for the Nikau district on 29 October 1910. She received mail three times a week until November 1920 when the horse and trap started making daily deliveries. In June 1925 Lizzie lost the mail activity when a rural service started to cover the area from Pahiatua.
A telephone link had been obtained by a line that crossed the Mangahao River from Mangamaire to the room in their farm-house set aside for Post Office use. From June 1925 Lizzie continued to operate the telephone being paid a fee for each call. The telephone office was closed down on 31 December 1930. (M)

1926... ELECTIONS: William Sowry............ Nikau Dairy Farmer.
(Waipukurau Electorate)   Elizabeth Jane Sowry.. Post Mistress.

1914-18 WAR: The First World War saw eldest son Hector Sowry travel to France and an item appeared in *The Pahiatua Herald* 4 June 1918. From a letter to his mother he described conditions in the trenches as *'...very hard, with mud and water up to his knees... standing in this for up to 14 days... he had a sheet of iron over his head to shelter from the rain... etc.'* (AS)

1920... Grandchildren. First grandchild was Noeline Olive Ansin, born 19 August to daughter Olive. Lizzie became known as 'Grandma Lizzie'. (NB)

MEMORIES: Those early years for pioneer settlers were times of great hardship and a great many difficulties to overcome, to survive and to succeed. Lizzie and William had the necessary qualities to survive and were successful. Grandma Lizzie was an industrious person and made and sewed the family's clothes. From a large orchard she preserved fruit and made jam and they also had a large vegetable garden too. (OH)

It is remembered that Lizzie would demand to know where any missing child was, when they sat down for a meal. She would also take this time to issue orders for things to be done by each member of the family. (OH)

Another memory of Lizzie's daughters, was coming home from school to find their mother getting to the end of the big family wash and the girls would have to wash a large pile of socks. Many of the never ending chores, such as the churning of cream to make butter, was done in the evenings.

After some years, Lizzie would 'take-a-break' and go to Auckland to stay with relations for several months at a time and the older children would take care of the house and the younger children. (OH)

E. J. (Lizzie) SOWRY (FT)

1927... RADIO: About 1927 William and Lizzie had the first radio in the Nikau area. It was battery operated. (O+BH)

1932... 3 SONS:
In January of 1932, three of Lizzie's sons, Rupert, Walter and Malcolm left the Woodville area and travelled to Northland and bought land to farm.
Here they married and each raised a family.

Daughter-in-law Jessie advises that Lizzie enjoyed holidaying with them when ever she made the long journey from Palmerston North. (JS)

1932... WILLIAM DIED:

In 1932 William Sowry was visiting his sons in the Whangarei district. On March 16 he was on a Waiotu farm and after helping erect new fences, he felt exhausted and sat under a Totara tree for a smoke and a rest. Here he died. (LA+AH) William was buried at the Hukerenui Cemetery, Whangarei.

Grand daughter Ngara has his memorial card which carries the verse.........
> *"The call was short, the shock severe*
> *To part with one we loved so dear,*
> *Our hopes in heaven that we may meet*
> *and then our joy will be complete. "* (NB)

William Sowry's Will, which he signed 26 January 1929 at Pahiatua, left all his estate valued at £1739.17.00, to his wife Lizzie. (Nat Arch)
After his death, son Vivian took over the management of the farm.

RETIREMENT: During the late 1930's Lizzie retired to 299 Featherstone Street, Palmerston North. Granddaughter Avyce recalls Lizzie's life evolved around her children and grandchildren. She was always sewing for them.(AS) She always had someone living with her. She boarded her grandsons, while they attended the nearby Boys High School. (AH)

Anita did not see a lot of her grandma but she recalls Lizzie seeming to have a preference for two piece woollen suits and woollen stockings. They did not live far from her in Palmerston North and they visited her... she seldom visited them. On one visit Lizzie sent Anita to the butchers for some meat for her tea... it had to be a "lean-mid-loin-chop". Lizzie enjoyed her garden. She was always available to meet her family's needs. (AH)
Grandma Lizzie was endlessly involved in Church and Institute affairs. (NB)

1951... LIZZIE DIED:

At Awapuni on 22 August 1951 at the age of 80, Lizzie Sowry died and was buried at Palmerston North's Kelvin Grove Cemetery, Block 2, Plot 23.
> Her headstone is very simple and reads...
In loving memory of Elizabeth Jane Sowry.   1871 - 1951 "At Rest"

Lizzie's Will left her estate, valued at £ 4,145, to be divided equally among her children, except for son Vivian, who was excluded because she felt he had been otherwise sufficiently provided for. (Nat Arch)

HEIRLOOMS:

Two pieces of Lizzie's china have survived to date and are now treasured by granddaughter Olwen Hammond.
A 12½ inch (32cm) tall 'Victorian' vase and a Royal Albert cup with two saucers.

Lizzie's granddaughter Avyce Simpson is looking after Joseph Sowry's 1867 *"Book of Sermons"* by Henry Ward Beechers.

--oo0Ooo--

It is such a rare occasion to find five generations of one family living at the same time, we have added this photo of Lizzie's daughter Thelma's family.

From left to right are ....
Rachel and Judith, Merle standing, and in front are Samantha and Thelma.

1990..... 5 GENERATIONS:

E. J. (LIZZIE) THOMAS FAMILY TREE:

3rd Generation

ELIZABETH JANE THOMAS............married.............................**WILLIAM SOWRY**

b 14 February 1871 (Lizzie)	25 December 1893	b 13 May 1863
at Oakley Creek, Auckland.	at Woodville.	at Waitaki, Canterbury.
d 22 August 1951 (80)		d 16 March 1932 (68)
Bur Palmerston North.		Bur Hukerenui, Whangarei.

William was the son of   JOSEPH SOWRY and HANNAH nee STROTHER

Lizzie and William had eleven children known as Hector, Olive, Amy, Veda, Vivian, Mavis, Rupert, Walter, Malcolm, Thelma and Norman.

4th Generation	5th Generation	6th Generation	7th Generation
HECTOR LYLE SOWRY	**IAN LYLE SOWRY**	**BRENT LYLE SOWRY**	**JAY BRENT SOWRY**
b 7 January 1895	b 7 December 1927	b 1 August 1953	b 26 December 1986
at Woodville.	at Wellington.	at Lower Hutt.	at Wellington City.
d 29 July 1984 (89)	d 18 Feb 1966 (38)	m 8 Sept 1984 ======	
Bur Featherston.	Bur Masterton.	at Wellington.	
m 5 August 1925=====	m 26 April 1952 =====	**LISA ALICE NEEDHAM**	**GEMMA HELEN SOWRY**
at Petone.	at Petone, Wellington.	b 9 December 1959	b 27 October 1988
MARY ETHEL RULE	**MERLE BROWN**	at Wellington City.	at Wellington City.
b 15 April 1901	b 24 October 1929		
at Oamaru.	at Wellington.		
d 28 Dec 1974 (73)	(daughter of John		
Bur Featherston.	Edward Brown and	**PAUL JOHN SOWRY**	**ANDREW LIAM SOWRY**
(daughter of William	Annie Elizabeth nee	b 18 August 1956	b 30 April 1990
Henry Rule and	Bailey)	at Lower Hutt.	at Auckland City.
Mary nee Kennedy)		m 20 April 1985 =====	
They had one child.		at Auckland City.	
		LEE ANDRA SUTHERLAND	**JONATHAN PAUL SOWRY**
		b 28 May 1957	b 20 July 1992
		at New Plymouth.	at Auckland City.
			EMMA ELIZABETH SOWRY
			b 28 March 1997
			at Auckland City.

LIZZIE continued

4th Generation	5th Generation	6th Generation	7th Generation
Hector & Ethel continue	Ian & Merle continue	**MARK IAN SOWRY** b 28 March 1960 at Masterton. m 29 Dec 1992 ====== at Masterton. **BRIGITTE ANNE CORLETT** b 9 November 1970 at Masterton.	**JACK IAN SOWRY** b 21 April 1994 at Masterton.
		NEIL ALLAN SOWRY b 7 July 1965 at Masterton.	
OLIVE ANNIE SOWRY b 8 August 1896 at Pahiatua. d 30 August 1965 (68) Bur Palmerston North. m 8 Oct 1919======= at Makomako. **WILFRED ANSIN** (Bill) b 16 August 1898 at Portland Island, NZ. d 8 May 1962 (63) Bur Palmerston North. (son of John Victor Emile Ansin and Janet nee Waugh.) They had 3 children.	**NOELINE OLIVE ANSIN** b 19 August 1920 at Palmerston North. m 20 Nov 1945 ====== at Palmerston North. **PATRICK CLAUDE ALLENBY COLLINS** b 7 October 1918 at Palmerston North. d 14 Aug 1990 (71) Bur Palmerston North. (son of Edward Collins & Susan nee McGlone)	**WENDY NOELINE COLLINS** b 9 August 1946 at Palmerston North. m 13 March 1971 ==== at Palmerston North. **PETER GERALD GILLESPIE** b 8 April 1945 at Christchurch.	**KATE ELIZABETH GILLESPIE** b 16 January 1974 at Palmerston North. **MEG GERALDINE GILLESPIE** b 26 June 1975 at Palmerston North. **TIMOTHY PETER GILLESPIE** b 17 February 1979 at Palmerston North.
		PETER WILFRED COLLINS b 16 March 1949 at Palmerston North. partner SUSAN (Sue)== **ENID STEWART** b 14 September 1955 at Masterton.	**KATE LAURA SHERLOCK** b 29 January 1978 at Christchurch.

4th Generation	5th Generation	6th Generation	7th Generation
Olive & Bill continue	**LEON WILFRED ANSIN** b 8 May 1923 at Palmerston North. 1st m 19 June 1948 === at Feilding. **GLADYS <u>AVERILLE</u> WILCOCK** b 11 November 1926 at Palmerston North. d 21 Dec 1964 (38) Bur Palmerston North. (daughter of John Wilcock and Gladys nee Looker) : 2nd m 3 Dec 1966 at Palmerston North. **ELIZABETH** (Betty) **DAWN WATSON** b 19 January 1931 at Wellington. (nee McKay)	**RAYMOND LEON ANSIN** b 5 July 1949 at Palmerston North. m 31 March 1986 ==== at Dunedin. **JOCELYN AMARANTHA ELAINE BROUGHTON** b 26 September 1954 at Dunedin.	**FREYA ELIZABETH AVERILLE ANSIN** b 31 May 1988 at Hamilton. **CHRISTOPHER ANSIN** b 5 November 1991 at Hamilton.
	AVYCE MARGARET ANSIN b 3 November 1930 at Palmerston North. m 27 Feb 1954====== at Palmerston North. **LAURENCE BRIAN SIMPSON** (Laurie) b 14 November 1929 at Palmerston North. (Laurie was son of Thomas Simpson and Gladys May nee Dickel)	**GRANT LAURENCE SIMPSON** b 26 September 1956 at Palmerston North. m 2 April 1983 ====== at Maitland, Sydney, A. **LYNNE MARY O'HARA** b 9 November 1957 at Singleton, N.S.W, Australia.	**BRENT GARETH SIMPSON** b 10 February 1986 at Adelaide, Australia. **LAURA DAWN SIMPSON** b 3 September 1988 at Adelaide, Australia. **TAYLA MARY SIMPSON** b 31 December 1991 at Adelaide, Australia.
		ROSEMARY next page	EMMA next page

LIZZIE continued

4th Generation	5th Generation	6th Generation	7th Generation
Olive & Bill continue	Avyce & Laurie continue	**ROSEMARY ANN SIMPSON** b 12 November 1960 at Palmerston North. m 9 Dec 1989======= at Mt Ruapehu, NZ. **TONY RICHARD JAMES** b 12 December 1964 at Auckland.	**EMMA KATE JAMES** b 5 January 1999 at Palmerston North. **REBECCA ROSE JAMES** b 31 July 2000 at Palmerston North.
AMY ISOBEL SOWRY b 24 June 1898 at Pahiatua. d 4 Jan 1977 (78) Cremated Hastings. m 28 June 1922 ===== at Makomako. **FREDERICK WILLIAM ANSIN** b 4 August 1896 at Riverton, Southland. d 14 July 1975 (78) Cre Hastings. (son of John Victor Ansin and Janet nee Waugh.) They had 4 children. Fred was brother of Bill Ansin who married Amy's sister Olive.	**TREVOR FREDERICK ANSIN** b 11 May 1924 at Palmerston North. d 4 November 1967 Cremated Napier. m 31 Jan 1948 ====== at Napier. **KATHLEEN <u>MAY</u> SHAW** b 24 May 1924 at Napier. (daughter of Henry Ernest Shaw & Victoria Georgina nee Tucker) : : : : : : : : : : : : : :	**MARGARET GRACE ANSIN** b 21 May 1950 at Napier. m 25 Oct 1969 ====== at Napier. **WILLIAM ARTHUR CAIRNS** b 8 October 1945 at Gisborne. (son of Roger Patrick Cairns and Mavis Constance nee Wright)	**MARK ANDREW CAIRNS** b 28 March 1970 at Carterton. partner **STELLA DIANA NEAL** b 9 September 1960 at Oxford, England. *Mark and Stella have 8th Generation children…..* *ELSIE MAY CAIRNS b 17 October 1999 at Wellington.* and *CAIRNS b 2001 at Oxfordshire, England.* **LINDA NAOMI CAIRNS** b 24 October 1971 at Masterton. m 17 February 1996 at Cambridge. MICHAEL next page

4th Generation	5th Generation	6th Generation	7th Generation
Amy & Frederick cont..	Trevor & May continue	Margaret and William continue	Linda married **MICHAEL GRAHAM BOOTH** b 15 December 1965 at Avondale, Auckland. *Linda & Michael have 8th Generation children* ***SHANNON MICHAEL BOOTH*** *b 4 June 1997 at Waitakere City.* and ***RENEE NICOLE BOOTH*** *b 11 January 1999 at Waitakere City.* and ***MITCHELL WILLIAM BOOTH*** *b 12 September 2000 at Waitakere City.*
	:	**ROGER JOHN ANSIN** b 1 May 1952 at Napier. 1st m 26 May 1973 === at Napier. **RAEWYN GAIL KAVANAGH** b 29 June 1951 at Hamilton. : 2nd m 12 Dec 1992 at Auckland. **PATRICIA** (Pat) **LIDDELL** nee Taylor b 1 March 1949 at Middlesbrough, Yorkshire, England.	**CHRISTOPHER JOHN ERNEST ANSIN** b 10 February 1978 at Napier. **JAMES TREVOR ANSIN** b 28 December 1982 at Rotorua. d 29 January 1983 Bur Napier.
	:	BARBARA next page	DANIEL next page

LIZZIE continued

4th Generation	5th Generation	6th Generation	7th Generation
Amy & Frederick cont..	Trevor & May continue :	**BARBARA JEAN ANSIN** b 21 November 1956 at Napier. m 1974 =========== at Napier.	**DANIEL JAMES SMART** b 26 December 1981 at Hamilton.
	:	**MICHEIL GEORGE SMART** b 1950 at Hamilton.	**MEGAN JEAN SMART** b 12 November 1983 at Hamilton.
	:	**CHRISTINE ROBYN ANSIN** b 15 October 1958 at Napier. m 12 Nov 1983====== at Napier. **JOHN PETER WILLIAM TREAGUS** b 14 April 1958 at Woodville.	**HAYDEN JOHN TREAGUS** b 25 October 1985 at Napier.
	:		**SIMON DAVID TREAGUS** b 30 June 1988 at Napier.
	:		**BENJAMIN PETER TREAGUS** b 26 August 1990 at Napier.
	:	**BERYL MAY ANSIN** b 18 May 1960 at Napier m 10 Oct 1981 ====== at Napier	**SONYA NICOLE FENN** b 17 August 1986 at Hastings.
	May remarried on 11 August 1979 at Napier. **LESLIE JOHNSON** b 28 April 1924 at Taumaranui.	**ALEXANDER FENN** b 5 April 1959 at Napier.	**JOSHUA KYLE FENN** b 4 April 1991 at Napier.
	REX next page	LYNNETTE next page	MICHAEL next page

4th Generation	5th Generation	6th Generation	7th Generation
Amy & Frederick cont..	**REX INNIS ANSIN** b 15 April 1926 at Napier. d 23 May 1999 (73) Bur m 28 Oct 1950====== at Napier. **ELIZABETH JEAN MYERS** (Betty) b 21 March 1928 at Waipukurau. d 14 Jan 1999 (70) Bur (daughter of Bingley Myers and Margaret nee Sands)	**LYNNETTE MARGARET ANSIN** b 5 August 1951 at Napier. m 16 Feb 1974 ====== at Hastings. **ALEXANDER LESLIE ZACHAN** b 24 June 1949 at Napier.	**MICHAEL JAMES ZACHAN** b 6 June 1976 at Hastings. m 22 January 2000 at **JEANETTE FLORENCE BRAININGG** b 28 November 1970 at : *Michael & Jeanette have 8th Generation* **HARRISON MICHAEL ZACHAN** *b 22 May 2000 at Auckland.*
			NATASHA MEGAN ZACHAN b 17 October 1977 at Hastings.
		RAEWYN JOY ANSIN b 6 November 1956 at Napier. m 14 Feb 1976====== at Hastings. **DAVID GRAHAM ANDERTON** b 10 October 1954 at Hastings. : : Raewyn remarried on 11 April 1998 at Wellington. **RICHARD PERRY HARRISON** b 20 December 1943 at Napier.	**JASON DAVID ANDERTON** b 25 December 1976 at Hastings.
			MARK ANDREW ANDERTON b 4 August 1979 at Hastings.

4th Generation	5th Generation	6th Generation	7th Generation
Amy & Frederick cont..	**YVONNE GRACE ANSIN** b 3 April 1929 at Napier. m 12 Aug 1950 ===== at Napier. **JOSEPH JOHN KING** (Joe) b 18 December 1926 at Napier. (son of Thomas King and Alice nee Brown)	**DENNIS JOHN KING** b 27 June 1952 at Napier. m 16 May 1980====== at Christchurch. **YVONNE QUINT** b 4 September 1955 at Christchurch.	**CLAUDIA NICOLE KING** b 14 April 1983 at New Plymouth. **FRASER ALEXANDER KING** b 12 October 1985 at New Plymouth.
		JANET MIRIAM KING b 21 February 1954 at Napier. m 14 April 1973 ===== at Eskdale, Napier. **DAVID LESLIE ROTHWELL** b 1 December 1948 at Blenheim.	**KELLY ANNE ROTHWELL** b 12 March 1975 at Napier. **TESSA MAIRE ROTHWELL** b 2 December 1976 at Napier. **GREG DAVID ROTHWELL** b 19 October 1978 at Napier.
		RHONDA GRACE KING b 7 September 1957 at Napier. m 7 Feb 1981 at ===== Te Pohue, Hawkes Bay **WARWICK (Rick) JONES** b 17 March 1956 at Tauranga.	**SARAH GRACE JONES** b 10 February 1988 at Adelaide, Australia. **TIMOTHY PRYCE JONES** b 14 July 1989 at Adelaide, Australia.
		HEATHER next page	EMMA next page

LIZZIE continued

4th Generation	5th Generation	6th Generation	7th Generation
Amy & Frederick cont..	Yvonne & Joe continue	**HEATHER MARGARET KING** b 9 July 1959 at Napier. m 26 March 1990==== at Napier.	**EMMA GRACE WRIGGLESWORTH** b 20 December 1992 at Auckland.
		ADRIAN CHARLES WRIGGLESWORTH b 26 September 1958 at York, England.	**JESSIE LAURA WRIGGLESWORTH** b 6 November 1995 at Auckland.
		PERRY JOSEPH KING b 18 April 1965 at Napier. m 25 March 1989 ==== at Auckland.	**ANNIE GRACE KING** b 10 December 1991 at Napier.
		KATHERINE MARY SANDELIN b 14 January 1964 at Auckland.	**FREDERICK JOSEPH KING** b 7 September 1994 at Napier.
	JUNE MARGARET ANSIN b 22 June 1940 at Napier. m 27 Jan 1962======= at Napier. **ROBERT GLYN ROY** (Rob) b 20 December 1938 at Wairoa. (son of Edwin Keith Roy and Nancy nee Burgis)	**ANTHONY COLIN ROY** b 29 Aug 1963 (Tony) at Napier. d 10 October 1966 Bur Napier.	
		VERNON ROBERT ROY b 12 April 1966 at Napier m 3 October 1998 ==== at Rotorua.	**KEITH ANTHONY ROY** b 23 June 1995 at Rotorua.
		JENNIFER HELEN GASCOYNE b 9 August 1961 at Aldershot, England.	**HELEN EMILY ROY** b 6 December 2000 at Rotorua.
		BEVAN next page	

LIZZIE continued

4th Generation	5th Generation	6th Generation	7th Generation
Amy & Frederick cont..	June & Rob continue	**BEVAN WAYNE ROY** b 5 August 1968 at Napier. partner **ANDREW RICHARD RUMBLES** b 13 Feb 1966 at Te Awamutu.	
		LYNDA JUNE ROY b 18 Oct 1971 (a) at Napier. m 12 March 1994 ==== at Rotorua. **ALBY PADDY TIPIWAI** b 24 May 1962 at Murapara.	**ASHTON ROBERT WILLIAM TIPIWAI** b 1 September 1999 at Rotorua.
		NICOLA MARGARET ROY (a) b 23 December 1974 at Napier. m 20 August 1999 at Sydney, Australia. **DANIEL DONATO BOVE** ========== b 21 March 1978 at Sydney, Australia.	**PATRICK ROY-DEAN** b 12 April 1994 at Rotorua. **BAILEY ROY BOVE** b 17 April 2000 at Sydney, Australia.
VEDA MAY SOWRY b 21 October 1900 at Pahiatua. d 21 June 1978 (77) Bur Palmerston North. m 3 June 1925 ====== at Pahiatua. **ARCHIBALD CAMPBELL BUCHANAN** b 1 December 1898 at Kakaremea, Taranaki.	**ARCHIBALD <u>IAN</u> BUCHANAN** b 7 November 1928 at Palmerston North. m 8 Dec 1951======= at Dannevirke. **JEANETTE HELEN GRAHAM** b 22 January 1931 at Wellington. (daughter of James Graham and Vera Louise nee Sparwath)	**GRAHAM CAMPBELL BUCHANAN** b 20 July 1953 at Palmerston North. m 18 Dec 1976 ====== at Palmerston North. **JOYCE PATRICIA MOORMAN (Joy)** b 20 October 1955 at Patea. IAN next page	**LISA JOY BUCHANAN** b 4 January 1983 at Palmerston North. **KARL GRAHAM BUCHANAN** b 13 July 1985 at Palmerston North. EMMA next page

4th Generation	5th Generation	6th Generation	7th Generation
Campbell continued d 11 January 1974 (77) Bur Palmerston North. (son of David Buchanan & Rosa nee Campbell.) They had 3 children.	Ian & Jeanette continue	**IAN JAMES** **BUCHANAN** b 1 January 1955 at Palmerston North. m 23 Aug 1975 ===== at Pahiatua. **SHERYL** **MARGARET DOAK** b 22 October 1954 at Manaia, Taranaki.	**EMMA MARGARET** **BUCHANAN** b 20 October 1979 at Palmerston North. **DAVID IAN** **BUCHANAN** b 11 September 1981 at Palmerston North.
		ANDREA LOUISE **BUCHANAN** b 5 August 1956 at Palmerston North. m 25 October 1975 at Palmerston North. **ROBIN ASHLEY** **DAVIES** b 22 January 1955 at Dannevirke.	
		BRIAN CRAIG **BUCHANAN** b 22 April 1958 at Palmerston North. m 9 Nov 1985 ====== at Melbourne, Australia. **KAREN** **ELIZABETH** **RENDALL** b 6 October 1961 at Rochford, Essex, UK.	**ELIZABETH KATE** **BUCHANAN** b 3 July 1988 at Palmerston North. **ROSS WILLIAM** **BUCHANAN** b 4 December 1990 at Palmerston North. **PENNY ROSE** **BUCHANAN** b 13 April 1994 at Palmerston Noth.
		DIANA next page	MARK next page

LIZZIE continued

4th Generation	5th Generation	6th Generation	7th Generation
Veda & Campbell cont..	Ian & Jeanette continue	**DIANA MARY BUCHANAN** b 18 March 1960 at Palmerston North. 1st m 18 March 1978 == at **GRAHAM DANN** b at (son of and nee : : : : : : : : : : : :	**MARK GRAHAM HARRY DANN** b 11 October 1978 at Palmerston North.
			MICHELLE LINDA DANN b 23 April 1980 at Palmerston North. m 4 Sept 1999 at Toowoomba, Q. Aust. **MARK JAMES LEAMAN** b at : *Have 8th Generation* ***BETHANY SKYE LEAMAN*** *b 16 Nov 1999 at Toowoomba, Q. Aust.*
		2nd m June 1986== at **PETER HOLMES** b at (son of and	**MATTHEW PETER HOLMES** b 17 January 1987 at Taupo.
			PAUL ANDREW HOLMES b 25 June 1988 at Taupo.
			MARY-LOUISE JEANETTE HOLMES b 8 February 1997 at

4th Generation	5th Generation	6th Generation	7th Generation
Veda & Campbell cont..	**OLWEN VEDA BUCHANAN** b 31 January 1929 at Palmerston North. m 14 July 1951 ====== at Palmerston North. **HERBERT HEBER HAMMOND** (Bert) b 14 July 1928 at Woodville. (son of Herbert William Hammond and Isobel nee Pallant)	**JENNIFER ELIZABETH HAMMOND** b 17 January 1953 at Woodville. m 10 Nov 1973====== at New Plymouth. **BRUCE LESLIE McCARTHY** b 6 November 1945 at Melbourne, Australia. : partner ========== **JAMES MURRIE** b 30 April 1949 at Adelaide, Australia.	**STACY ANN McCARTHY** b 28 October 1982 at South Port, Gold Coast Australia. **TERESA ELIZABETH MURRIE** b 2 August 1992 at South Port, Gold Coast Australia.
		BARRY CAMPBELL HAMMOND b 31 August 1954 at Woodville. m 7 May 1977 ====== at Hamilton. **SALLY LAWTON** b 2 December 1957 at Hamilton.	**CLARE MELANIE HAMMOND** b 2 January 1980 at Hamilton. **CAMPBELL ROSS HAMMOND** b 1 December 1981 at Hamilton. **ANGELA KAY HAMMOND** b 9 May 1984 at Hamilton. **NICOLE FRANCIS HAMMOND** b 13 February 1986 at Hamilton.
		PETER next page	

4th Generation	5th Generation	6th Generation	7th Generation
Veda & Campbell cont..	Olwen & Bert continue	**PETER JOHN HAMMOND** b 7 June 1957 at Woodville. m 20 June 1987 at Palmerston North. **SYLVIA HART** **nee HARRIS** b 9 May 19 at Praze-an-Beeble, Cornwall, England. d 18 November 2000 Bur Palmerston North.	
	ELIZABETH ROSA BUCHANAN b 22 March 1939 at Palmerston North. d 14 March 1961 (21) Bur Palmerston North. m 23 January 1960 at Palmerston North **ROBIN BOND WARE**		
VIVIAN WILLIAM SOWRY b 2 December 1901 at Pahiatua. d 6 April 1954 (52) Bur Ballance. m 11 June 1941 ===== at Dannevirke. **CORA LOUISA HARDING** b 16 February 1913 at Dannevirke. d 23 Nov 1985 (72) Bur Ballance. (dau of Leolin Harding & Louisa nee Ebbett)	**EARL VIVIAN SOWRY** b 3 September 1945 at Pahiatua. d 13 April 1966 (20) Bur Ballance. (died in car accident)		

LIZZIE continued

4th Generation	5th Generation	6th Generation	7th Generation
MAVIS MYRTLE SOWRY b 8 January 1903 at Pahiatua. d 26 October 1989 (86) Bur Palmerston North. 1st m 16 April 1924=== at Pahiatua.	**COLLIN ARDEN WILLIS** b February 1925 at Pahiatua. d 5 March 1925 Bur Mangatainoka. (aged 6 weeks)		
STANLEY WILLIS b 1898 at Pahiatua. d 5 March 1925 (27) Bur Mangatainoka. :			
2nd m 25 March 1926 = at Woodville. **HUIA ARAPUKE HOULBROOKE** b 25 November 1896 at Waterfalls, Wairarapa. d 3 Sept 1974 (77) Bur Palmerston North. (son of Leonard Houlbrooke & Alice Mabel nee Davies) They had 3 children.	**NGARA BETTY HOULBROOKE** b 25 October 1926 at Woodville. m 30 March 1948 ==== at Palmerston North. **ROBERT FRANCIS BATTERSBY** b 19 June 1926 at Feilding. (son of William Francis Battersby (Frank) and Thelma Ellen nee Short (known as Trix)	**KEITH RICHARD BATTERSBY** b 5 January 1949 at Palmerston North. m 31 March 1975 ==== at Tawa Flat. **MONICA MARY BODERICK** b 28 October 1952 at Carterton.	**CLAIRE MARY BATTERSBY** b 5 December 1977 at Palmerston North. **JAMES RICHARD BATTERSBY** b 23 September 1979 at Palmerston North.
		BRUCE ROBERT BATTERSBY b 2 December 1950 at Feilding. 1st m 18 July 1970==== at Wanganui. **ANNETTE KAY MAIN** b 24 March 1951 at Wanganui. : : : : : : :	**DEAN MATHEW BATTERSBY** b 29 December 1970 at Palmerston North. **MELANIE CHRISTINA BATTERSBY** b 2 December 1973 at New Plymouth. m 7 January 2000 at Owhanga, Taumarunui. **BRETT OWEN MARTIN** b 7 January 1960 at Taumarunui.

LIZZIE continued

4th Generation	5th Generation	6th Generation	7th Generation
Mavis & Huia continue	Ngara & Robert continue	BRUCE remarried on 12 March 1983==== at Palmerston North. **PATRICIA (Trish) MARGARET WILLS** b 3 December 1956 at Wanganui.	**REBECCA TINA BATTERSBY** b 12 June 1985 at Palmerston North.
			ANNA MAREE BATTERSBY b 18 June 1987 at Palmerston North.
		ANNE MARGARET BATTERSBY b 11 December 1952 at Feilding. married **COLIN GEORGE SIM** born	
		JOHN EDWARD BATTERSBY b 2 December 1954 at Feilding. m 1972 =========== at Palmerston North. **DIANE EDITH MAY FENTON** b 1 October 1955 at Feilding. : : : : 2nd m 23 Aug 1997 at Healdsburg, California, USA.	**CAROLINE DIANE BATTERSBY** b 25 May 1973 at Palmerston North.
			JOANNE MARIE BATTERSBY b 2 February 1977 at Palmerston North.
			DOUGLAS JOHN BATTERSBY b 2 February 1981 at Hamilton.
		DARCIE KAY ELLYNE ======== b at	**RACHEL LOUISE BATTERSBY** b 5 July 1999 at San Francisco, USA.

4th Generation	5th Generation	6th Generation	7th Generation
Mavis & Huia continue	Ngara & Robert continue	**KATHRYN PAMELA BATTERSBY (Kate)** b 30 August 1957 at Feilding. Father of David====== **GERARD NEIL CAREY** b 19 October 1945 at Palmerston North.	**DAVID MICHAEL BATTERSBY** b 17 September 1986 at Palmeston North.
	ANITA MARJORIE HOULBROOKE b 20 October 1931 at Woodville. m 4 May 1952 ====== at Palmerston North. **BRIAN HAROLD SHIRLEY** b 27 February 1925 at Palmerston North. (son of Hercules Shirley & Lillian nee Larcombe. Lillian born at Patea in Taranaki, NZ and her father was Mayor)	**PAMELA ANNE SHIRLEY** b 30 December 1953 at Wanganui. single parent ========	**KERRY BRIAN SHIRLEY** b 4 October 1972 at Auckland City. **TODD ANTONY JOSHUA SHIRLEY** b 21 October 1988 at Howick, Auckland. **ANNA-LEA SHIRLEY** b 25 January 1991 at Howick, Auckland.
		CHRISTINE DAWNE SHIRLEY *(twin)* b 28 April 1955 at Wanganui. partner =========== **GIAMPAOLO MONTESANTO** b 26 September 1963 at Palermo, Sicily, Italy.	**ANITA LARA MONTESANTO SHIRLEY** b 23 February 1992 at Lisbon, Portugal.

KATHRYN next page   NICHOLAS next page

4th Generation	5th Generation	6th Generation	7th Generation
Mavis & Huia continued	Anita & Brian continue	**KATHRYN MARGARET SHIRLEY** *(twin)* b 28 April 1955 at Wanganui. partner =========== **MICHAEL DUNCAN HIKUROA** b 18 March 1954 at Auckland City. :	**NICHOLAS MICHAEL HIKUROA** b 5 October 1978 at Howick, Auckland.
		partner =========== **RICHARD OLIVER POWELL** b June 1942 at Somerset, England. :	**KAHN SILLAURE POWELL** b 9 September 1980 at Brisbane, Australia.
		partner =========== **DUNCAN NEWINGTON** b at	**ALICE MAE SHIRLEY** b 4 May 1990 at Howick, Auckland.
		JUDITH ROBYN SHIRLEY b 22 September 1958 at Howick, Auckland. m 27 July 1990 ====== at Haines, Alaska. **DANIEL GREGORY CURRY** b 31 December 1946 at Seattle, Washington, U.S.A.	**CONRAD HOULBROOKE CURRY** b 14 August 1993 at Juneau, Alaska. **KILLIAN HUIA CURRY** b 1 August 1995 at Elfin Cove, Alaska.
		MICHAEL JOHN SHIRLEY b 11 May 1961 at Howick, Auckland. m 19 April 1997 ===== at Taupo.	**JOPHIEL HERCULES SHIRLEY** b 19 December 1997 at Thames.

4th Generation	5th Generation	6th Generation	7th Generation
Mavis & Huia continued	Anita & Brian continue	Michael married **SHONA MARIE WALTERS** b 3 January 1960 at Ohakune.	
	PAMELA MAVIS HOULBROOKE b 16 August 1936 at Woodville. m 27 April 1963 ===== at Woodville. **GAVIN FREDERICK WILSON** b 18 June 1937 at Christchurch. (son of Gavin Trengrove Wilson and Esther Mary nee Purvis)	**MARK GAVIN WILSON** b 6 October 1965 at Palmerston North. m 17 April 1999 at Christchurch. **USHA GANDA** b 2 February 1966 at Christchurch. **NICOLA LOUISE WILSON** b 8 January 1968 at Palmerston North.	
RUPERT CLARENCE SOWRY b 23 October 1904 at Hawkes Bay. d 28 Dec 1975 (71) Bur Maunu, Whangarei. m 24 May 1938 ===== at Hawkes Bay. **MARJORIE FLORA MALCOLM** (Margie) b 18 October 1911 at Hawkes Bay. d 22 April 1984 (72) Bur Maunu, Whangarei. (Margie was the daughter of Alexander Lumsden Malcolm & Annie nee Andrew) They had 5 children.	**LESTER ALEXANDER SOWRY** b 2 December 1939 at Whangarei. m 2 Sept 1961 ====== at Whangarei. **MAVIS MERLE REED** b 25 October 1939 at Whangarei. (daughter of Frederick James Reed and Lorna Constance nee Thorburn)	**GREGORY ROSS SOWRY** b 30 September 1963 at Whangarei. m 28 Jan 1989 ====== at Whangarei. **JANINE MARIE LONG** b 19 August 1969 at Dargaville. **PETER ALAN SOWRY** b 23 June 1965 at Whangarei. m 15 Oct 1988 at Whangarei. LISA next page	**TAYLAH LEE SOWRY** b 31 December 1997 at Whangarei. **LUKE DANIEL SOWRY** b 4 October 1999 at Whangarei.

4th Generation	5th Generation	6th Generation	7th Generation
(Margie was a sister of Jessie who married Rupert's brother Walter Claude Sowry)	Lester & Mavis continue	Peter married **LISA ELLEN PHILLIPS** b 2 July 1967 at Warkworth.	
		LEANNE MERLE SOWRY b 26 August 1966 at Whangarei. m 16 July 1988 at Whangarei. **WARREN JOHN HERBERT** b 25 June 1962 at Hastings.	
	ANNE ELIZABETH SOWRY b 25 October 1942 at Whangarei. m 16 June 1962 ===== at Whangarei. **WILLIAM ALEC MEADES** b 8 March 1937 at Nonington, Kent England. (son of William George Meades and Alice nee Keene)	**PAUL WILLIAM MEADES** b 2 October 1965 at Whangarei. m 27 March 1999 at Whangarei. **DIANNE MAREE HENWOOD** b 23 May 1972 at Whangarei.	
		DAVID JOHN MEADES b 10 April 1968 at Whangarei.	
		SANDRA BETH MEADES b 29 December 1970 at Whangarei. d 29 December 1970 Bur Whangarei.	

4th Generation	5th Generation	6th Generation	7th Generation
Rupert & Margie cont..	Anne & Alec continue	**MICHAEL JAMES MEADES** b 22 February 1973 at Whangarei. d 22 February 1973 Bur Whangarei.	
		JULIE ANNE MEADES b 20 November 1973 at Henderson. partner =========== **ERIC MALCOLM SHORTLAND** b 23 January 1971 at Whangarei.	**BROOKE ANNE SHORTLAND** b 6 November 1996 at Whangarei. **CYRIL BOYD SHORTLAND** b 12 February 1999 at Whangarei.
	LYNNETTE JEAN SOWRY (Lynne) b 9 June 1945 at Whangarei. m 16 Oct 1965 ====== at Whangarei. **COLIN HAROLD ALEXANDER** b 12 August 1940 at Whangarei. (son of Mona and Eric Harold Alexander)	**ROBERT COLIN ALEXANDER** b 14 August 1970 at Whangarei. **JANINE LYNNE ALEXANDER** b 15 March 1973 at Whangarei.	
	BRUCE WILLIAM SOWRY b 19 December 1946 at Whangarei. m 21 April 1973 ===== at Whangarei. **MARILYN EDMUNDS** continued next page	**MAREE ANN SOWRY** b 7 April 1977 at Whangarei. **SUZANNE LEE SOWRY** b 21 May 1978 at Whangarei.	

LIZZIE continued

4th Generation	5th Generation	6th Generation	7th Generation
Rupert & Margie cont..	Marilyn was born on 24 October 1952 at Carleon, Wales. (daughter of John Edmunds and Sylvia May nee Carne)	**CHRISTINE GAYE SOWRY** b 8 July 1980 at Whangarei.	
		JOANNE CARA SOWRY b 6 January 1984 at Whangarei.	
	JANICE MARGIE SOWRY b 8 August 1948 at Whangarei. m 11 Dec 1970====== at Whangarei. **ALAN HUGH GOING** b 5 January 1949 at Whangarei. (son of Hugh Charles Going and Frances Rona nee Cotterill)	**KYLIE MAREE GOING** b 20 April 1973 at Cairns, Australia.	
		DUANE SCOTT GOING b 7 July 1974 at Cairns, Australia.	
WALTER CLAUDE SOWRY (Wally) b 29 September 1905 at Pahiatua. d 7 October 1969 (64) Bur Maunu, Whangarei. m 14 July 1932 at ==== Waipawa, Hawkes Bay. **JESSIE ANNIE MALCOLM** b 10 October 1909 at Ormondville, NZ. (daughter of Alexander Lumsden Malcolm and Annie nee Andrew) They had 3 children.	**NALDA ANN SOWRY** b 12 August 1933 at Whangarei. m 3 Sept 1966 ====== at Whangarei. **LESLIE WILLIAM DOBSON** b 4 February 1931 at Maidstone, England. (son of William Frank Dobson and Elsie nee Norton) VALERIE next page	**KATHRYN JILL DOBSON** b 4 August 1968 at Maidstone, England. m 26 September 1992 at Rotorua. **PETER GEORGE MAHER** b 16 April 1964 at Sydney, Australia. DENISE next page	SHANE next page

4th Generation	5th Generation	6th Generation	7th Generation
Jessie was a sister of Margie who married Wally's brother Rupert Clarence Sowry)	**VALERIE MAY SOWRY** b 28 June 1938 at Whnagarei. m 1 Nov 1958======= at Whangarei. **ROYCE LESLIE JOBE** b 26 April 1937 at Whanagrei. (son of Augustus Edward Jobe and Dulcie Elizabeth nee Thorburn)	**DENISE VALERIE JOBE** b 21 July 1960 at Whangarei. m 3 April 19892 ===== at Waiotu, Northland. **STUART ROSLYN SWAN** b 21 July 1956 at Palmerston North.	**SHANE ANTHONY SWAN** b 1 July 1983 at Kawakawa. **LANCE ROY SWAN** b 18 December 1985 at Kawakawa.
		DAVID LESLIE JOBE b 2 January 1963 at Whangarei. m 10 May 1986====== at Hikurangi, Northland. **BARBARA THREASA MARY LENSSEN** b 7 November 1964 at Morrinsville.	**CHAREE FRANCES JOBE** b 19 January 1999 at Whangarei.
	DAWN CAROLINE SOWRY b 21 October 1942 at Whangarei. m 20 Oct 1962 ====== at Whangarei. **RICHARD IVAN THORBURN** b 9 April 1940 at Whangarei. (son of Ivan Terence Thorburn and Alma Joy nee Orams)	**CAROL ANN THORBURN** b 17 August 1964 at Whangarei. m 8 Feb 1986 ======= at Whangarei. **KERRY CHARLES MARTIN** b 14 August 1963 at Whangarei.	**AARON CHARLES MARTIN** b 8 March 1995 at Whangarei. **ELLA DAWN MARTIN** b 27 November 1999 at Whangarei.
		ROSS IVAN THORBURN b 8 March 1967 at Whangarei. m 14 Oct 2000 ====== at Whangarei. MILA next page	**CULLUM RICHARD THORBURN** b 27 February 1997 at Whangarei.

LIZZIE continued

4th Generation	5th Generation	6th Generation	7th Generation
Wally & Jessie continue	Dawn & Richard cont..	**MILA MARY ALLEN** b 2 July 1971 at Holland.	
		LISA DAWN THORBURN b 1 February 1971 at Whangarei. m 18 March 1995 at Whangarei. **DAVID VINCENT PARKES** b 13 July 1968 at Whangarei.	
MALCOLM SOWRY b 6 April 1907 at Pahiatua. d 11 January 1974 (66) Bur Maunu, Whanagrei. m 23 June 1936====== at Hastings. **AGNES KITCHING** b 8 February 1910 at Blackburn, England. d 5 June 1992 (82) Bur Maunu, Whangarei. (daughter of John Kitching and Mary Agnes nee Fenton) They had 4 children.	**MARGARET ELIZABETH SOWRY** b 28 April 1937 at Whangarei. m 17 May 1958====== at Whangarei. **RONALD CHARLES MacDONALD** b 15 March 1934 at Whangarei. d 23 January 1999 (65) Bur Maunu, Whangarei. (son of Percy William MacDonald and Edna Laura Kathryn nee Clarke)	**KATHRYN PATRICIA MacDONALD** b 16 May 1959 at Whangarei. m 20 Sept 1980====== at Whangarei. **RONALD JAMES BOWMAR** b 26 January 1955 at Whangarei.	**DANIEL JOSEPH BOWMAR** b 22 February 1980 at Whangarei. **JESSICA MARY BOWMAR** b 8 May 1981 at Whangarei. **SARAH ELIZABETH BOWMAR** b 20 October 1982 at Whangarei. **MAC CHARLES BOWMAR** b 19 March 1985 at Dargaville.
		JUDITH next page.	

4th Generation	5th Generation	6th Generation	7th Generation
Malcolm & Agnes cont..	Margaret & Ron cont...	**JUDITH ANNE MacDONALD** b 23 October 1960 at Whangarei.	
		MICHELLE ELIZABETH MacDONALD b 17 October 1962 at Thames.	
		PAUL CHARLES MacDONALD b 20 September 1963 at Thames. m 17 Nov 1990====== at Whangarei.	**ANDREA KATHERINE MacDONALD** b 5 April 1992 at Auckland.
		THELMA KATHLEEN REYNOLDS b 7 February 1962 at Warkworth.	**CLAIRE LAURA MacDONALD** b 25 March 1995 at Whangarei.
		DIANE MARGARET MacDONALD b 24 July 1965 at Thames. m 11 May 1991 ===== at Whangarei.	**JARROD THOMAS DOWLING** b 6 April 1996 at Whangarei.
		PETER THOMAS DOWLING b 30 August 1961 at Waitara.	**KATELYN ROSE DOWLING** b 27 September 2000 at Auckland.
	JOHN DAVID SOWRY b 1 November 1938 at Whangarei. WYNNE next page	**AVERIL GAI SOWRY** b 21 September 1966 at Whangarei. SIMON next page	

4th Generation	5th Generation	6th Generation	7th Generation
Malcolm & Agnes cont..	John married on 8 June 1963 ====== at Tamworth, NSW, Australia. **WYNNE LILLIAN DAVIDSON** b 5 July 1941 at Uralla, Australia. (daughter of David Leslie Davidson and Belva Jean nee Cooper)	Averil married on 23 January 1993 at Whangarei. **SIMON GARY LEWIS-ROBERTS** b 13 December 1962 at Northwitch, UK.	
		ROSS DAVID SOWRY b 12 September 1968 at Whangarei. m 22 April 1993 ===== at Whangarei. **JENNIFER SHARON PATRICIA SNOOKS** b 11 July 1962 at Whangarei.	**JOEL DAVIE SOWRY** b 8 October 1995 at Whangarei. d 3 September 1999 at Whangarei.
		MARK ALLEN SOWRY b 14 June 1971 at Whangarei.	
		FLEUR MICHELLE SOWRY b 28 September 1972 at Whangarei.	
	BARBARA ANNE SOWRY b 21 September 1942 at Whangarei. m 31 Jan 1961 ====== at Whangarei. **COLIN BEN THORBURN** b 2 October 1941 at Whangarei. continued next page	**KERRY MAREE THORBURN** b 28 July 1961 at Whangarei. m 20 March 1982 ==== at Whangarei. **STUART CRAIG McMILLAN** b 7 May 1959 at Whangarei. (3 children)	**TARA MAREE McMILLAN** b 26 December 1985 at Whangarei. **ADELE JANE McMILLAN** b 31 December 1987 at Whangarei.

4th Generation	5th Generation	6th Generation	7th Generation
Malcolm & Agnes cont..	(Colin was son of Ivan Terence Thorburn and Alma Joy nee Orams.) : : : : : : : : 2nd m 18 July 1975 at Whangarei. **RICHARD GILMOUR GELLERT** b 21 April 1940 at Tolaga Bay. NZ.	Kerry & Craig continue	**HAYDEN CRAIG McMILLAN** b 29 August 1991 at Hamilton.
		TERENCE COLIN THORBURN b 23 October 1962 at Te Kopuru, Norrthland. m 14 March 1987 ==== at Manurewa, Auckland. **ROSEMARY ELIZABETH WILLIAMS** b 2 December 1965 at Morrinsville.	**EMMA ROSE THORBURN** b 28 April 1990 at Papakura, Auckland. **MATTHEW BEN THORBURN** b 4 April 1994 at Papakura.
	CATHERINE MARY SOWRY b 30 November 1948 at Whangarei. m 15 July 1968 ====== at Whangarei. **WILLIAM JOHN REED** b 19 November 1946 at Whangarei. (son of William Mervyn Reed and Flora nee Hay)	**DEBBIE ANN REED** b 12 December 1970 at Whangarei. **JENNY MAREE REED** b 5 May 1972 at Whangarei. m 17 Dec 1994 ====== at Whangarei. **RAY CHEE** b 5 January 1962 at Kuala Lumpa, Malaysia.	**JOSHUA WILLIAM CHEE** b 21 June 1998 at Auckland.
		WILLIAM MURRAY REED b 11 November 1974 at Whangarei.	

LIZZIE continued

4th Generation	5th Generation	6th Generation	7th Generation
ALICE ETHEL <u>THELMA</u> SOWRY b 22 March 1910 at Pahiatua. d 19 July 1993 (83) Bur Palmerston North. m 6 July 1932======= at Pahiatua. **ALAN DAVID BUCHANAN** b 26 May 1904 at Kakaremea, NZ. d 29 April 1962 (57) Bur Palmerston North. (son of David Buchanan and Rosa nee Campbell. They had 4 children. (Alan was brother of Campbell Buchanan who married Thelma's sister Veda)	**<u>MERLE</u> THELMA BUCHANAN** b 16 January 1935 at Palmerston North. m 19 June 1954====== at Palmerston North. **IAN FREDERICK NAGEL** b 18 November 1929 at Palmerston North. (son of Frederick Nagel and Violet Myrtle nee Gundersen)	**JUDITH MERLE NAGEL** b 9 April 1955 at Palmerston North. m 11 Sept 1971====== at Opiki, near P-Nth. **BRUCE ELLIOT PROCTER** b 26 April 1954 at Foxton. : : : : 2nd m 1983 at Ohau, near Levin. **STUART JOHN MACDONALD** b 14 September 1960 at Levin.	**SAMANTHA JUDITH PROCTER** b 21 February 1972 at Palmerston North. partner ====== **KERRY JOHN WALKER** b 19 February 1971 at Hastings. *They have two 8th Generation children....* ***RACHEL JUDITH PROCTER-WALKER*** *b 28 August 1990 at Palmerston North. and* ***SEAN KERRY PROCTER-WALKER*** *b 15 November 1992 at Levin.*
		ALAN IAN NAGEL b 11 July 1956 at Palmerston North. m 1975 == at **ROBYN LINLEY STRICKET** b at : : : : : : : : : : :	**MAREE ROBYN NAGEL** b 4 December 1975 at Levin. *Maree has three 8th Generation children.* ***ADRIANNA*** *b* ***TYRONE*** *b* ***TIMOTHY*** *b* **MARC KENNETH NAGEL** b 25 May 1978 at *Marc has one 8th Generation child*

4th Generation	5th Generation	6th Generation	7th Generation
Thelma & Alan continue	Merle & Ian continue	Alan remarried 2nd m === at **VIRGINIA JUNE HORNE** b at	**HAYDEN IAN NAGEL** b 20 March 1981 at Palmerston North.
			KERRIE ALANA NAGEL b 13 December 1987 at Levin.
		DARYL JOHN NAGEL b 23 October 1958 at Palmerston North. m 16 May 1980====== at Levin. **LARISA ANN OCTAVIA CORNELL** b 19 October 1961 at Levin.	**CASEY LARISA NAGEL** b 2 September 1980 at Palmerston North.
			JADE DARYL NAGEL b 18 April 1982 at Levin.
		GRAEME ANTHONY NAGEL b 11 August 1960 at Palmerston North. m 10 Jan 1986 ====== at Hawera. **NGAITIA <u>NGAIGA</u> JOSEPHINE GATE** b 8 May 1961 at Hamilton.	**KELLY ANN NAGEL** b 17 February 1982 at Palmerston North.
			MATTHEW GRAEME NAGEL b 3 July 1985 at Levin.
			LUKE ANTHONY NAGEL b 13 June 1989 at Palmerston North.
		FIONA next page	SARAH next page

4th Generation	5th Generation	6th Generation	7th Generation
Thelma & Alan continue	Merle & Ian continue	**FIONA KIM NAGEL** b 15 November 1962 at Palmerston North. m 23 Feb 1991 ====== at Lesmurdie, Perth, Australia.	**SARAH JAYNE FRANCES HAWKES** b 19 September 1991 at Kalamunda, Perth.
		JOHN JOSEPH HAWKES b 6 December 1959 at Hammersmith, London.	**TIMOTHY JOSEF HAWKES** b 29 July 1993 at Kalamunda, Perth.
		CAROLYN LEE NAGEL b 8 September 1969 at Palmerston North. m 14 April 1990 ===== at Tauranga.	**TRACY LEE POTTS** b 20 December 1992 at Tauranga.
		PHILLIP JOHN POTTS b 23 July 1968 at Lower Hutt.	**JESSICA ANN POTTS** b 6 January 1999 at Tauranga.
	DAVID WILLIAM BUCHANAN b 1937 at Palmerston North. m 18 Jan 1958 ====== at Palmerston North. **DIAN MURRAY** b 27 August 1938 at Wanganui. (daughter of Henry David Murray & Delma Iris nee Moosman)	**DENISE DIAN BUCHANAN** b 11 July1958 at Palmerston North. m 15 June 1984 at Palmerston North. **CHRISTOPHER GRAHAM BRYANT** b 21 February 1958 at Palmerston North.	
		DEBRA LYNNE BUCHANAN b 13 October 1960 at Palmerston North. m 6 Sept 1980 ====== GORDON next page	**CAMERON GORDON MORRISON** b 2 July 1989 at Palmerston North.

LIZZIE continued

4th Generation	5th Generation	6th Generation	7th Generation
Thelma & Alan continue	David & Dian continue	Debra married at Palmerston North. **GORDON RAYMOND MORRISON** b 31 March 1957 at Wellington.	
		KATHRYN LEE BUCHANAN b 10 July 1962 at Palmerston North. m 23 Oct 1981 ====== at Palmerston North. **RICHARD HENRY WHALE** b 15 May 1963 at Farnborough, England. ⋮ ⋮ partner =========== **ROBERT DONALD NEWBY** (Bobby) b 13 July 1968 at Geneva, Switzerland.	**MADISON DAVID WHALE (Buchanan)** b 31 May 1987 at Palmerston North. **KEENAN MICHAEL WHALE (Buchanan)** b 19 October 1988 at Palmerston North. **CHARLEE DIAN BUCHANAN-NEWBY** b 9 September 2001 at Palmerston North.
		CHRISTINE LISA BUCHANAN b 27 September 1966 at Palmerston North. partner **ANDREW JAMES WARD** b 8 April 1964 at Dunedin.	
	ISLA DEIDRE BUCHANAN b 6 June 1939 at Palmerston North. 1st m 9 June 1962====	**JOHN BRUCE KENNERLEY** b 12 September 1963 at Pahiatua.	

4th Generation	5th Generation	6th Generation	7th Generation
Thelma & Alan continue	Isla married at Palmerston North. **BRUCE ARNOLD KENNERLEY** b 31 August 1938 at Dannevirke. (Bruce was son of Arnold Kennerley and Hazel nee Ingram) : : : : : : :	**DAVID MICHAEL KENNERLEY** b 3 February 1965 at Pahiatua. m 9 July 1994 at Ngaio, Wellington. **JACINTA MARY BROCKIE** b 8 March 1973 at Wellington.	
		LISA JANE KENNERLEY b 25 August 1969 at Pahiatua. m 5 January 2001 at Palmerston North. **TODD ANDREW MESSENT CHARTERIS** b 23 March 1971 at Tapanui, Southland. (son of John Charteris and Pamela Ruth nee Minson)	
	2nd m 2 June 1990 at Palmerston North. **IAN NORMAN LEWIS** b 17 March 1938 at Palmerston North. (son of Gordan Lewis and Myra nee Benton)		
	COLIN ALAN BUCHANAN b 8 December 1942 at Palmerston North. m 15 Feb 1964 ====== at Palmerston North. **MARIE VERA BUSCH** b 4 July 1944 at Martinborough. (daughter of Charles Henry Busch and Vera Gwendoline nee Thomas	**ALAN COLIN BUCHANAN** b 24 February 1965 at Palmerston North. m 7 March 1992 ===== at Havelock North. **ANDREA RAEWYN TONG** b 3 September 1965 at Palmerston North.	**CAMPBELL SCOTT BUCHANAN** b 13 May 1995 at Palmerston North.
			GEORGIA LOUISE BUCHANAN b 11 January 1997 at Palmerston North.
		ANDREW RICHARD BUCHANAN b 4 December 1968 at Palmerston North. m Jan 1992 =====	**ELLIOTT ANDREW BUCHANAN** (Drew) b 13 August 1995 at Palmerston North.

LIZZIE continued

4th Generation	5th Generation	6th Generation	7th Generation
Thelma & Alan continue	Colin & Marie continue	Andrew married at Wellington. **JOANNE MARIE CHEYNE** b 16 June 1968 at Wellington.	**ANGUS DEAN BUCANNAN** b 13 July 1997 at Palmerston North.
		JAMES DAVID BUCHANAN b 28 March 1978 at Palmerston North.	
NORMAN TREVOR SOWRY b 6 April 1912 at Nikau.Pahiatua. d 17 July 1969 (57) Bur Upper Hutt. m 31 July 1935 ====== at Wellington. **MAJORY FRANCES TRELIVING DRILLER** b 4 June 1909 at Wellington. d 14 Jan 1948 (38) Bur Upper Hutt. (daughter of Francis Summerhayes Driller and Lilian Edith (Edie) nee Duck) : : : : : : : : : :	**ROBERT TREVOR SOWRY** (Rob) b 7 June 1938 at Wellington. 1st m 24 Feb 1962==== at Wellington. **ANNE--MARIE SMITH** b 12 August 1942 at Lower Hutt. (daughter of Cameron Smith and Angela Anne nee Mitten) : : : : : : : Robert remarried 2nd m 8 July 1994 at Plimmerton, Wgtn. **DULCIE GREGORY EVELYN THOMAS nee WELLER** (Greg) b 14 December 1940 at Wanganui.	**GLEN ROBERT SOWRY** b 21 July 1962 at Lower Hutt. m 27 Aug 1994====== at Auckland City. **SANDRA MARY GRANT** (Sandy) b 21 December 1957 at Toronto, Canada. **VICKI-MARIE SOWRY** b 10 December 1963 at Lower Hutt. **TRACY LEIGH SOWRY** b 25 October 1967 at Lower Hutt. m 4 November 1995 at Fendalton, ChCh. **JONATHAN RODNEY CHELL WILSON** b 15 December 1969 at Christchurch.	**KANE GRANT SOWRY** (a) b 14 September 1997 at Auckland.

LIZZIE continued

4th Generation	5th Generation	6th Generation	7th Generation
Norman & Majory cont. : : : : :	**EDITH ELIZABETH SOWRY** b 2 January 1941 at Wellington. 1st m 30 April 1960=== at Upper Hutt.	**KIM MARGARET NIXON** b 24 October 1960 at Kawerau. m 22 Sept 1990 ===== at Auckland City.	**MADISON FRANCES BARNETT** b 8 November 1994 at Auckland City.
: : : : : :	**RAYMOND CHARLES NIXON** b 21 February 1938 at Sydney, NSW, Aust... (son of Charles Nixon & Kathleen nee Loughlan)	**MICHAEL FRANCIS BARNETT** b 18 June 1949 at Hamilton. (son of George Barnett & Raphael nee Cronin)	**FINLAY FRANCIS BARNETT** b 4 July 2000 at Auckland City.
: : : : : :	: : : : : :	**WAYNE RAYMOND NIXON** b 17 December 1962 at Kawerau. d 21 December 1962 Bur Kawerau.	
: : : : : : : : :	: : : : : : : : :	**LANCE ANDREW NIXON** b 18 November 1966 at Upper Hutt. m 15 Feb 1991 ====== at Auckland City. **TREENA LEANNE MILLER** b 10 June 1966 at Howick, Auckland.	**COURTNEY SAMANTHA NIXON** b 8 August 1991 at Auckland City. **GEORGIA MONIQUE HARRIET NIXON** b 21 January 1995 at Takapuna, NSC.
: : : : : :	2nd m 6 Feb 1975 at Auckland. **BARON ANTHONY CARTER** ======== b 2 June 1949 at Auckland. (son of Arthur Carter & Alma nee Gascoigne) :	**GARETH OLIVER CARLYLE CARTER** b 6 May 1975 at Auckland.	**CLAUDIA HOLLY NIXON** b 1 October 1996 at Takapuna, NSC.

LIZZIE continued

4th Generation	5th Generation	6th Generation	7th Generation
Norman & Majory cont.	**EDITH ELIZABETH MARILYN FRANCES SOWRY** b 8 September 1942 at Upper Hutt.	**GAVIN BRUCE CAMPBELL** b 14 November 1964 at Upper Hutt. 2/m 23 April 1993 ==== at Huapai, Auckland.	**MADELEINE SIAN CAMPBELL** b 10 June 1994 at Auckland City.
:	1st m 28 Sept 1963 === at Upper Hutt. **ALISTAIR BRUCE CAMPBELL** b 7 March 1942 at Lower Hutt. (son of Geo. Alexander Campbell and Alma Margaret nee McLeod)	**JULIE ANITA THOMPSON** b 24 December 1962 at Papakura, Auckland.	**JORDAN ALEXANDER CAMPBELL** b 11 July 1998 at Auckland City.
:	:	**HEATHER MARGARET CAMPBELL** b 21 March 1966 at Upper Hutt. m 30 Nov 1991====== at **ANDREW KEITH GARRATT** b 20 November 1964 at Hokitika.	**JACKSON ALISTAIR GARRATT** b 30 May 1994 at Lower Hutt.
:	2nd m 5 Nov 1977 at Upper Hutt. **CLIFFORD William George GOODWIN** b 15 December 1933 at Shauldham, Thorpe, East Anglia, England.	:	**TRUDY ANNA GARRATT** b 9 October 1996 at Whangarei. d 9 October 1996 Crem Whangarei.
Norman remarried 2nd m 28 April 1950 at Upper Hutt.		**BARBARA ANN CAMPBELL**======= b 20 August 1967 at Upper Hutt.	**VIRGINIA FRANCES CAMPBELL** b 20 August 1993 at Auckland City.
MARGARET ====== **McKIDDIE FERGUSSON-- HARTLEY** nee GRAY b 6 June 1917 at Lower Hutt. d 28 June 1995 (78) Bur Upper Hutt. (daughter of David Gray and Margaret McKiddie nee Lundie [Meg])	**DAVID WILLIAM SOWRY** b 22 March 1953 at Lower Hutt. m 16 Feb 1989 ====== at Nelson. **JENNIFER LOUISE ALLAN** (Jenny) b 17 August 1958 at Dunedin. (dau of Barry Clarke Allan and Ruth Olive nee Perry)	**MERIDA LUCY SOWRY** b 30 December 1997 at Dunedin.	

CHAPTER SIX

7th Generation (3rd NZ)

'ELIZA' THOMAS

(1872-1949)

1872... BIRTH - NGARUAWHAHIA:

On 24 November 1872 at Ngaruawahia in the Waikato, Eliza Thomas was born, the second child of William and Eliza Thomas.

She was registered as Elizabeth (see page 71) but known always as "Eliza".

1877... SCHOOL: Auckland.

It is probable that Eliza first attended school at Hastings, as she reached the age of 5 only three months after her brother Harry was born there. She may then have attended the Whau School, but no records exist today.

The Mt Albert School registers show Eliza (8½ years) was enrolled by her father, along with sister Lizzie and brother Jack, on 20 April 1881.

Eliza, on 29 March 1882 (9 yr 4 m) sat Standard 1 exams and passed all four subjects of reading, spelling / dictation, writing and arithmetic. She was marked 'present' for 341 half days.

Eliza left this school on 26 May 1882 *to go to Christchurch'*.

1882... ASHBURTON:

Eliza aged 9½ years, moved south with her parents and may have spent a month or so at school in Christchurch, but to date, no records found.

Soon afterwards the family moved into one of the houses on their Allenton nursery land at Ashburton to join Eliza's uncle John, Phebe and family. Eliza was not enrolled at the Ashburton Borough School and at nearly aged 10, her parents may have considered her education complete.

1887... NGAWAPURUA:

When about age 15 Eliza travelled with her parents, brothers and sisters from Ashburton to Ngawapurua, near Woodville in the North Island. She would have helped her mother and older sister Lizzie in minding the six younger children during this trip. It would have taken many days by horse and cart (or coach), boat and in some parts by rail.

Grandson Trevor Sowry advises that soon after the family settled at Ngawapurua, Eliza gained work at a bakery in the township of Woodville a short distance away.

1892... PAHIATUA:
During March of 1892 Eliza travelled to Pahiatua where she had found a new job. We believe the family attended the Methodist Church near there and this may have helped her gain new employment.

1892... MARRIAGE:
On 9 June, Eliza Thomas and Herbert Sowry filled in an 'Application to Marry' form which shows she was 19 and he was 25. Eliza gave her 'location of dwelling' as Pahiatua and as being employed there for 'three months on Household Duties.' Herbert had only been in the town for three days and his occupation was given as 'Carrier.'

At the Free Methodist Chapel in the small town of Mangatainoka, near Pahiatua, the Rev. Charles Penney from Woodville, married ELIZA THOMAS and HERBERT SOWRY on 15 June 1892.

The 16 June edition of the *'Examiner'* (Woodville) shows that.....
"Mangatainoka was gay yesterday on the occasion of the marriage of Mr Herbert Sowry, son of Mr Joseph Sowry of Woodville, to Miss Eliza Thomas, daughter of Mr William Thomas of Ngawapurua." It also mentions there was *"a goodly attendance"* and that *Misses Thomas* (two sisters ?) *and Emily Walker were Bridesmaids and Mr Arthur Sowry was Best Man."* Eliza who *"looked charming, was given away by her father."*
The wedding breakfast was held at the brides parents' residence and *"games and amusements kept up till late in the evening when the bride and groom left for their future home in Woodville amid the congratulations of their friends."*

Herbert was the fourth son of Joseph Sowry and Hannah nee Strother, and brother of William Sowry who wed Eliza's elder sister Lizzie.
Herbert was born in Christchurch on 20 January 1867.
SOWRY family details are at the end of this chapter.

CHILDREN: There were seven children born to Eliza and Herbert......
Alfred 1893, Leonard 1895, Horace 1897, Doris 1903,
Roy 1905, Leo 1907 and Ethel 1913.
In 1917, son Leonard was killed in France during World War 1.
All the other children married and raised families.

More detail of these children, and their descendants' details,
follow in <u>Eliza's Family Tree</u> at the end of this chapter.

CARRIER:
Grandson Trevor Sowry reports that Herbert started out with a horse and cart and carted anything, and anywhere in the district.

The book *"Woodville 1875-1975"* mentions Herbert on page 37 as..... *'Mr Monteith's man'.*
It would seem that in the very early days Herbert was employed by Mr Monteith....... the local General Storekeeper, as his carrier. It also contains an interesting account by historian Richard T. Roberts of *"Herb Sowry carting stores and swags up the Manawatu River for Alex and Charlie McDonald, for George, Jack and Bert Mills and for Mr Roberts, heading for Kumeroa."*

The *'Pahiatua Herald'* on page 5, 13 March 1931, in Herbert's obituary, mentions that prior to 1900 and *"Previous to purchasing land at Makomako, Herbert was a familiar and welcome figure to many of the old pioneer settlers as he used to pack stores to the various camps and outlying farms before the days of roads and bridges. He was somewhat renowned for his strength in those days although a man of no great stature."*

1892-1900:

Eliza and Herbert Sowry lived the first years of their lives together in the township of Woodville.

> Eliza's sister Rose started school at the Woodville School aged 7 on 28 March 1894 and her address was given as *"staying with Mrs Sowry until 22 June 1894."*

Eliza and Herbert's first three children were born at Woodville and the final four were born at the Makomako farm.

ELECTIONS:

The Waipawa Electoral Rolls of 1893 and 1894 show Herbert still employed as 'Carrier'. In 1897 Eliza (married woman) joins Herbert (carrier) on the roll, both living in Woodville.

In the 1902 rolls Herbert is described as 'Farmer of Makomako'.

HERBERT and ELIZA SOWRY FAMILY (November 1916)
at back L to R, **Leonard, Horace, Alfred.**
at front, **Doris, Herbert, Ethel, Roy, Eliza and Leo.** (TS)

1895... ROSEFARM:

In 1895-6 Herbert Sowry purchased Section #19 of 146 acres, in the district of Makomako a few kilometres south of Woodville, when the Woodville Special Settlement Block was opened up for sale. In the early days Herbert travelled to the farm from Woodville. They had to clear the section of bush to create farm land. Mostly the farm produced income as a dairy farm, but they also ran a few sheep for their own use. Herbert farmed until his death.

1898... Eliza's parents and some of her younger siblings moved to New Lynn, Auckland, late in 1898 when Eliza was aged 26.

1900... FARM HOUSE: About 1900, Herbert and Eliza built a house at Makomako and a special feature was the concrete floor and exposed beams in the kitchen. Now, 100 years later, their grandson Trevor Sowry is living in that house. Eliza and Herbert named that property **"ROSEFARM",** by which it is still known today. In the year 1900, Eliza's sister Rose aged 13, was living there and attending the Nikau School at the same time as her nephews Alfred (aged 7, son of Eliza) and Hector (aged 5, son of Lizzie).

The *Pahiatua Herald* of 13 March 1931 advises us... *Although Herbert Sowry did not enter actively into local politics, he was for a number of years a member of the school committee and for several of these was chairman. He was also a director of the Co-operative Creamery Company.*

1915. CHURCH LAND

Methodism was the prominent religion of the settlers who came to settle Woodville in the 1870's. These settlers' sons took up the new sections in the Nikau district in the late 1890's and Methodism spread to this area.

Residents recall initially services were held in Mrs Andrew Gardner's home in Gardners Road, Nikau and church picnics were held in one of their paddocks. Then in 1915, Herbert Sowry generously donated some of his land at nearby Makomako and in 1916 a Methodist Church was erected.

The Nikau Methodists attended the fortnightly services. Also, the Anglican and Presbyterian people used this Church at regular intervals, and often locals attended a service regardless of their particular faith. (M+MC)

1931... HERBERT DIED on 11 March 1931 aged 64.

The *Pahiatua Herald's* obituary describes Herbert as......

"widely esteemed for his integrity... was most deservedly popular, one who had a kindly word for all and was ever ready to give a helping hand or advice to a neighbour."

Herbert's death seems to have occurred as follows...... *"He had taken some sheep to a paddock near the Makomako Road. Then rode to the junction of the Nikau-Makomako Roads and waited for the mailman as was his custom. Mr Currie, driver of the cream lorry, discovered Herbert in a semi-kneeling position, one elbow being on the wire fence near the road and the other hand still clasping the bridle of his horse. The animal was standing quite still. Apparently Herbert had been seized by a heart attack. Mr Barnes the mailman subsequently arrived and assisted Mr Currie in attending to the body."* They mention Herbert had been suffering from heart trouble for some time and was under medical care at the time of his death. (PH)

Herbert was buried at the Ballance Cemetery.

WILL: Herbert signed his Will on 25 May 1929 and appointed the Public Trustee as Executor, with John Harding of Woodville and Leolin Harding of Hopelands as Advisor-trustees. His estate of £ 3,700 was divided as follows:

a.   *Wife Eliza to receive his motor cars, plate, linen, china, glass, books, pictures, prints, furniture and other items of household or ornamentation, and all the livestock.*

b.   *Horace to receive all his vehicles, tools, agricultural and farming implements, machinery and plant, (including milking machines, cans etc).*

c.   *The balance to be put in Trust for use by Eliza, and when she died to go to Alfred, Horace, Hannah, Roy, Ethel and Leo in equal shares.*

1949... **ELIZA DIED** on 22 June 1949 aged 76.

After Herbert died Eliza lived a further 18 years. She spent 12 of these at Rosefarm with son Leo doing the heavy farm work, and then moved to Pahiatua to spend her final years sharing a house there with Leo.

Eliza and Herbert are buried together at Mangahao Cemetery at Ballance, not far from their farm.

Eliza signed her Will on 27 January 1943 and appointed daughter Hannah and son Leo as her Trustees. Her Will is very detailed and the Trustees must have had no problems dividing her £ 1016 estate. A few items mentioned were two pictures of English hunting scenes to son Leo, her piano to daughter Ethel and her three piece chesterfield suite to daughter Hannah.

Another view of 'ROSEFARM'

The SOWRY family.

Joseph Sowry was born in Leeds, England, the youngest of five children to John and Hannah Sowry. Joseph, aged 21, married Hannah Strother in the Parish Church at Leeds in 1858. They had two children but the first, Annie, died when aged two. Soon after, they emigrated to New Zealand with son Arthur, arriving Lyttleton, 24 May 1862 on the "Zealandier". (B+AS)

Joseph was not only a builder and architect, but also very involved in local organisations, taking a prominent role in the Woodville area development. In 1876 he formed the Woodville Small Farm Association and became its secretary and manager. In 1884 he took on the job of chairman of the Woodville Town Board. Two and a half years later in 1887 Woodville was proclaimed a borough, and Joseph Sowry was elected unopposed as Mayor of Woodville. He served for three terms then, in 1889 after losing the mayoralty, he was appointed Borough Overseer & Inspector of Works, a position he held until his death in 1904.

Joseph Sowry also took a prominent role in the Woodville Methodist Church, holding early meetings in his home and later designed their first church building. He was an active champion of the Temperance movement (against consuming alcohol) and established the Rechabite Tent in Woodville.

The above are extracts from Pahiatua's *"The Bush Telegraph"* of
19 May 1987 pages 6, 7 and 8, which contain much more detail.

Joseph's first wife Hannah died aged 42, leaving twelve children. His second wife Martha died aged about 38, leaving another four children.
Joseph married again to Rhoda, but there were no more children.

Eliza Sowry's grandson Athol Sowry is prepared to provide further details.

SOWRY FAMILY TREE

Generation 1	**BENJAMIN SOWRY** married 1784 **SARAH CLIFF** W.Yorkshire, England. b1762 d1816 at Leeds. b 1764 d1826 both buried Wortley. 7 children
Generation 2	Samuel, Elizabeth, William, Hannah, Sarah, Thomas, **JOHN.** b 29 May 1804 Wortley d 9 May 1878 Leeds. m 6 Nov 1825, Leeds. **HANNAH HOWGATE** b 24 April 1806 Wortley d 28 March 1872, Leeds. 5 children
Generation 3	Alfred, Benjamin, William Howgate, Robert Howgate, **JOSEPH** b 18 Oct 1837 Leeds. d 12 March 1904 Woodville. m 13 Dec 1858 Leeds. **HANNAH STROTHER** b 1 April 1837 Leeds d 16 April 1879 Woodville. 12 children
Generation 4	Annie, Arthur, **WILLIAM**, Albert, **HERBERT**, Mary, Hannah H, Ernest, Marmaduke, George, Walter, and Wilfred.

Joseph remarried 21 Nov 1879
MARTHA MATILDA WILLING
b c1852
d 26 Oct 1890 Palmerston North.
4 children

Evangeline, Lavina, Mabel, Ivy.

Joseph remarried 17 Nov 1891
RHODA MITCHELL
b 14 July 1851 Brighton, England.
no children

Herbert married 15 June 1892 **ELIZA THOMAS**
b 24 November 1872 and d 22 June 1949
7 children

Generation 5   Alfred, Leonard, Horace, Doris, Roy, Leo, Ethel.

William married 25 December 1893 **LIZZIE THOMAS**
b 14 February 1871 and d 22 August 1951
11 children

Generation 5   Hector, Olive, Amy, Veda, Vivian, Mavis, Rupert, Walter, Malcom, Thelma, Norman.

For more Sowry detail contact... Betty and Athol Sowry, 336 Valley Road, RD2, Woodville 5473. NZ.

E. (ELIZA) THOMAS FAMILY TREE:

3rd Generation

ELIZABETH THOMAS...................married.....................................**HERBERT SOWRY**

b 24 November 1872 (Eliza)	15 June 1892	b 20 January 1867
at Ngaruawahia, Waikato.	at Mangatainoka,	at Christchurch.
d 22 June 1949 (76)	near Pahiatua.	d 11 March 1931 (64)
Bur Mangahao Cemetery, Ballance.		Bur Mangahao, Ballance.

Herbert was a son of JOSEPH SOWRY and HANNAH nee STROTHER

Eliza and Herbert had seven children... Alfred, Leonard, Horace, Doris, Roy, Leo and Ethel.

4th Generation	5th Generation	6th Generation	7th Generation
ALFRED GEORGE SOWRY b 18 April 1893 at Woodville. d 27 Sept 1932 (39) Bur at Ballance. m 29 August 1928 ==== at Levin. **MARJORIE McLEAVEY** b 17 January 1904 at Ohau, Levin. d 17 July 1993 (89) Bur at Ballance. (daughter of Alfred McLeavey & Emma Amelia nee Petersen) They had one child. : Marjorie remarried to HAROLD TERRY who died 17 July 1993 Bur Palmerston North.	**MARGARET ROSE SOWRY** b 25 May 1931 at Auckland City. m 21 Sept 1957====== at Palmerston North. **ARTHUR GLYNN GRIGG** b 14 October 1930 at Morrinsville. (son of Arthur Henry Grigg and Delia Mary nee Glynn)	**EMMA PATRICIA GRIGG** b 19 December 1964 at Auckland City. m 5 Feb 1993 ======= at Auckland City. **ANDREW STEWART McINTYRE** b 20 February 1963 at Wanganui.	**LUKE ARTHUR JACKSON McINTYRE** b 16 February 1995 at Wellington City. **REBECCA ALICE ROSE McINTYRE** b 13 October 1997 at Wellington City. **THOMAS STEWART GLYNN McINTYRE** b 1 November 2000 at Wellington City.
		OWEN GLYNN GRIGG b 14 Feb 1968 at Auckland City. m 2 April 1994 ====== at Melbourne, Australia. **JOANNE MARY REID** b 17 September 1967 at Melbourne, Australia.	**MAX OWEN GRIGG** b 30 August 1998 at Auckland City. **SAMANTHA MARY GRIGG** b 1 June 2001 at Auckland City.

LEONARD next page

ELIZA continued

4th Generation	5th Generation	6th Generation	7th Generation
LEONARD HERBERT SOWRY b 5 June 1895 at Woodville. killed 11 Aug 1917 WWI in France. Burried at Tancrez Farm Cemetery, Ploegsteert, Belgium.			
HORACE JOSEPH SOWRY b 2 December 1897 at Woodville. d 12 August 1967 (69) Bur at Ballance. 25 June 1936 ======= at Pahiatua. **ANNIE <u>RETA</u> HARDING** b 22 March 1907 at Dannevirke. d 9 March 1990 (83) Bur Ballance. (daughter of Loelin Harding and Louisa nee Ebbett) They had four children	**NEVILLE HARDING SOWRY** b 27 June 1937 at Pahiatua. m 13 May 1961 ===== at Bunnythorpe, near Palmerston North. **GLENNIS LORRAINE BOOTH** b 11 April 1942 at Palmerston North. (daughter of Lyall Earnest Booth and Edna Annie nee Pinfold) : : : : : : : : : : : : : : : : :	**CRAIG NEVILLE SOWRY** b 2 July 1962 at Pahiatua. m 6 Feb 1995 ====== at Makomako, near Pahiatua. **AROHA** (Lausa) **TANGIWAI** b 4 September 1968 at Murapara, Rotorua. (Div May 1997)	**ADRIAN HAMUERA JAMES SOWRY** b 6 February 1986 at Palmerston North. **TE AOMIHI ANNE SOWRY** b 3 June 1987 at Palmerston North. **KIMBERLEY GLENNIS SOWRY** b 13 October 1988 at Palmerston North. **DARRYLL TIEKE CRAIG SOWRY** b 15 August 1992 at Pahiatua.
		HEATHER <u>ANNIE</u> SOWRY b 30 July 1964 Pahiatua. m 10 Oct 1992====== at King Lake West, Melbourne, Australia. **TREVOR JOHN McERLAIN** b 20 May 1958 at Melbourne, Australia.	**KELSIE ANNE McERLAIN** b 21 November 1995 at Melbourne, Australia. **TIFFANY MAY McERLAIN** b 20 February 1997 at Melbourne, Australia.

ELIZA continued

4th Generation	5th Generation	6th Generation	7th Generation
Horace & Reta continue	Neville & Glennis cont.	**STUART GORDAN SOWRY** b 6 July 1967 at Pahiatua. m 30 March 1991 ==== at Dannevirke.	**STEVEN WALTER SOWRY** b 29 October 1993 at Palmerston North.
	:	**CYNTHIA ANNE TYACKE** (Cindy) b 26 March 1969 at Palmerston North. (dau of Walter Glanville Tyacke and Valma Amelia nee Moorecock)	**SCOTT JAMES SOWRY** b 29 March 1996 at Palmerston North.
	:	**BRYCE LANGLEY SOWRY** b 24 September 1968 at Pahiatua. m 6 Jan 1996 ======= at Pahiatua.	**AARON BRYCE SOWRY** b 7 October 1997 at Palmerston North.
	:	**DIANE MARIE LASKEY** b 25 September 1968 at Pahiatua. (daughter of Kenneth Maxwell Laskey and Carol Aileen nee Nielsen)	Diane brought three children with her. Tara Jane Sowry b 14 September 1985 Emma Marie Sowry b 12 January 1989 Katie Aileen Sowry b 31 January 1991
	(Neville and Glennis divorced and Neville married 26 June 1993 at Pahiatua. **TERESA CARMELLA BEDFORD (nee SPERANZA)** b 26 January 1944 at Palmerston North.	**DELWYN MARIE SOWRY** b 13 September 1969 at Pahiatua. m 23 Jan 1999 ====== at Dannevirke. **JAMES BRIAN WALKER** b 27 June 1968 at Dannevirke. (son of William Alexander Walker and Susan Louise nee Armstrong)	**DARCY JAMES WALKER** b 8 May 1998 at Townsville, Queensland, Australia.

ELIZA continued

4th Generation	5th Generation	6th Generation	7th Generation
Horace & Reta continue	**TREVOR ALFRED SOWRY** b 30 December 1939 at Pahiatua.		
	RUSSELL HORACE SOWRY b 6 February 1942 at Pahiatua. m 3 March 1962 ===== at Pahiatua. **MARILYN JOY KING** b 5 February 1943 at Te Awamutu. (daughter of Brian Newton King and Naida nee Keats)	**LEE-ANNE JOY SOWRY** b 25 September 1962 at Pahiatua. 1st m 15 September 1984 at Putaruru. **STEPHEN ROBERT McGREGOR** b 11 September 1963 at Putaruru. : Lee-Anne remarried 2nd m 5 Dec 1993 === at Rotorua. **MICHAEL GEORGE DUFF** (Mike) b 15 April 1961 at Tokoroa. (son of Graham John Duff & Eileen Florence nee)	**ETHAN JARED DUFF** b 21 March 1991 at Rotorua. **AARON JOHN DUFF** b 15 December 1994 at Rotorua.
		SHANE RUSSELL SOWRY b 3 August 1964 at Pahiatua. m 18 May 1988 ===== at Otahuhu, Auckland. **ANGELA REBECCA ROBERTS** b 25 June 1965 at Te Kuiti. NZ. (daughter of John and Rangimanana Uriku Roberts.)	**JOEL RUSSELL SOWRY** b 23 November 1989 at Hamilton. **MICAH JARED SOWRY** b 30 August 1992 at Hamilton.

ELIZA continued

4th Generation	5th Generation	6th Generation	7th Generation
Horace & Reta continue	Russell & Marilyn cont.	**KEVIN BRIAN SOWRY** b 3 October 1965 at Otorohanga. m 6 August 1988 ==== at Te Kuiti.	**CLAIRE MARIE SOWRY** b 31 May 1991 at Te Kuiti.
		JANINE MARIE OVERALL b 30 April 1967 at Tokoroa. (daughter of Kevin William Overall and Rosalie Ann nee Kirk)	**RACHEL KAREN SOWRY** b 15 June 1995 at Ipswich, Australia.
		KRISTINA MARY SOWRY b 12 March 1980 at Hamilton.	
		JARED HORACE SOWRY b 30 April 1982 at Hamilton. d 24 January 1990 (8) Buried at Te Kuiti.	
	ATHOL NOEL SOWRY b 21 November 1944 at Pahiatua. m 17 June 1967 ===== at Eketahuna.	**CLIVE JOSEPH SOWRY** b 4 November 1967 at Pahiatua.	
	BETTY MARGARET NAGEL b 4 September 1947 at Eketahuna. (daughter of William Henry Nagel & Marjorie Melinda nee Finnie.)	**PRISCILLA RETA SOWRY** b 7 April 1969 at Pahiatua. m 7 April 1990 ===== at Woodville.	**JORDAN KEITH MUDGWAY** b 31 October 1996 at Palmerston North.
		KEITH RUA MUDGWAY b 5 October 1966 at Palmerston North.	**JESSICA PRISCILLA MUDGWAY** b 1 December 1998 at Palmerston North.

ELIZA continued

4th Generation	5th Generation	6th Generation	7th Generation
Horace & Reta continue	Athol & Betty continue	**ELROY HERBERT SOWRY** b 11 August 1979 at Palmerston North.	
HANNAH DORIS SOWRY b 6 May 1903 at Makomako, Pahiatua. d 22 Nov 1984 (81) Bur Eketahuna. m 14 April 1925 ===== at Pahiatua. **ROBERT CHARLES FRANCIS DAGG** b 18 August 1885 Upper Plain, Masterton. d 29 Sept 1964 (79) Bur Eketahuna. (son of Henry John Dagg and Sarah nee Wolton) They had five children.	**HERBERT HENRY DAGG** b 29 June 1926 at Pahiatua. m 30 July 1949 ====== at Masterton. **JOSEPHINE MARJORIE McKELVEY** b 19 March 1929 at Masterton. (daughter of Frederick George McKelvey and Marjorie Anastasia nee Cross)	**COLLEEN FRANCES DAGG** b 21 July 1950 at Masterton. m 27 Nov 1971====== at Masterton. **BRIAN MARTIN TAYLOR** b 29 March 1950 at Wellington. (son of Edward Martin Taylor and Beatrice Annie (Betty) nee Clark)	**MICHELLE FRANCES TAYLOR** b 7 May 1972 at Masterton. partner ========== **JAMES DOUGLAS PARKINSON** *(Michelle & James have* *an 8th generation child* ***RYAN JAMES*** ***PARKINSON*** *b 26 July 1998* *at Masterton.)* **VANESSA ANN TAYLOR** b 1 July 1973 at Masterton. partner = **RICHARD JAMES BUICK** b 27 February 1962 at Woodville. *(Vanessa & Richard have* *an 8th Generation child* ***ASHLEE CASSANDRA*** ***TAYLOR*** *b 31 December 1992* *at Masterton.)* : partner ==== **PETER STEWART WILLIAMS** b 11 July 1967 at Lower Hutt. *(Vanessa & Peter have* *an 8th Generation child* *JADE next page*

4th Generation	5th Generation	6th Generation	7th Generation
Doris & Robert continue	Herbert & Josephine continue	Colleen & Brian continue	*JADE KEITH WILLIAMS* *b 26 May 1997* *at Masterton.)*
			ROY MARTIN TAYLOR b 26 April 1981 at Masterton.
		VERONICA JUNE DAGG b 8 July 1951 at Masterton. m 29 August 1970 ==== at Eketahuna. **JOHN EDWARD HENRY DUCKETT** b 17 May 1947 at Masterton. (son of Leo Duckett and Charlotte Minnie nee Jarvis)	**MATHEW DAVID DUCKETT** b 16 December 1970 at Masterton. partner ==== **JANINE ANNE COULSON** b 9 January 1964 at Lower Hutt. *Mathew & Janine have* *8th Generation child* **RICKY MATTHEW COULSON** *b 17 November 1994* *at Masterton.*
			ROBERT JOHN DUCKETT b 29 August 1972 at Masterton. m 14 August 1999 at Masterton. **ROSEANA NGARIE JOYCE MOUNT** b 20 August 1974 Masterton. *Robert & Roseana have* *three 8th Generation* *children,* *STEFAN* *JOHN CARLOS* *DUCKETT-MOUNT*

ELIZA continued

4th Generation	5th Generation	6th Generation	7th Generation
Doris & Robert continue	Herbert & Josephine continue	Veronica & John continue	*STEFAN b 30 April 1992 at Whakatane.* *and* ***COURTNEY JANE DUCKETT-MOUNT*** *b 13 December 1993 at Whakatane.* *and* ***CASEY NGARIE JUNE DUCKETT-MOUNT*** *b 12 June 1996 at Masterton.*
			JEREMY EDWARD DUCKETT b 26 July 1977 at Masterton.
			AMANDA JUNE DUCKETT b 1 September 1981 at Masterton.
		IAN JOHN CHARLES DAGG b 19 January 1954 at Masterton. m 20 March 1982 ==== at Masterton. **JANICE LYNN MORRIS** b 28 October 1960 at Masterton.	**ADAM ROBERT CHARLES DAGG** b 7 March 1986 at Masterton.
			ROWAN IAN DAGG b 17 July 1990 at Masterton.
			JARROD LINSEY DAGG b 22 August 1993 at Masterton.

4th Generation	5th Generation	6th Generation	7th Generation
Doris & Robert continue	Herbert & Josephine continue	**MARTIN GEORGE DAGG** b 3 May 1955 at Masterton. m 2 May 1992 ====== at Ihuraua, Wairarapa. **KAREN LORRAINE BIRD** b 18 March 1962 at Eketahuna.	**JOEL ALVIN JOHNATHON DAGG** b 13 January 1985 at Palmerston North.
		ANASTASIA CELCILIA DAGG b 2 November 1961 at Masterton. m 16 Feb 1985 ====== at Masterton. **GEORGE ROPATA WORKMAN** b 6 March 1962 at Tasmania, Australia.	**SHARLEEN JANE WORKMAN** b 12 June 1981 at Masterton. **TIMOTHY STANTON WORKMAN** b 21 May 1986 at Masterton.
		ALLISON JOAN DAGG b 4 April 1964 at Masterton. partner ========= **KEVIN THOMAS DAVIS** b 10 October 1950 at Wanganui.	**TRISTIN KEVIN DAVIS** b 15 December 1987 at Masteron. **LISA JOAN DAVIS** b 17 March 1992 at Masterton.
		YVONNE ANNE DAGG b 27 July 1970 at Masterton. Solo Mother =======	**JORDAN MARTIN DAGG** b 27 February 1997 at Masterton.

ELIZA continued

4th Generation	5th Generation	6th Generation	7th Generation
Doris & Robert continue	**BETTY JOY DAGG** b 20 April 1928 at Pahiatua. m 21 Oct 1950 ====== at Masterton.	**ROBERT ZANE PERRY** b 12 June 1953 at Hastings.	
	WILLIAM JOHN PERRY (Jack) b 14 December 1925 at Invercargill. d 7 Dec 1978 (53) Cremated at Nelson. (son of Fred Perry and Alice Johanne nee Higgins) : 2nd m September 1988 on launch at Queen Charlotte Sound, Picton. **PHILIP B CAGNEY** b 11 November 1927 at Oamaru.	**DOUGLAS CRAIG PERRY** b 4 August 1955 at Masterton. m 22 Oct 1977 ====== at Blenheim. **SANDRA JANICE MORAN** b 24 May 1957 at Blenheim. (daughter, John Charles Moran and Marion Katherine nee Hart)	**NATHAN STUART PERRY** b 5 November 1978 at Blenheim. **BRENDON JOHN PERRY** b 8 August 1981 at Blenheim. **ANNA RACHEL PERRY** b 25 November 1984 at Blenheim.
	DULCIE FLORENCE DAGG b 14 January 1932 at Pahiatua. m 5 October 1968 at Masterton. **FREDERICK GEORGE McKELVEY** b 23 October 1904 at Te Wharau, Masterton. d 8 October 1971 (67) Bur Masterton.		
	MAIRE DORIS DAGG b 11 October 1936 at Masterton. partner ========== NOEL next page	**ROBIN MAIRE DAGG** (twin) b 30 July 1966 at Masterton. m 9 Sept 1988 ====== Masterton. ROBERT next page	**CARLOS JARED NICHO** b 19 February 1992 at Masterton. AKESHIA next page

4th Generation	5th Generation	6th Generation	7th Generation
Doris & Robert continue	**NOEL CLIFFORD REYNOLDS** b 8 January 1918 at Masterton. d 6 April 1969 (51) Bur Carterton. (son of Arthur John Reynolds b 5 Aug 1867 at Carterton and died 31 March 1934, and Mabel nee Minifie b1875, d 13 Oct 1967. Both burried Carterton.)	**ROBERT SAMUEL NICHO** b 22 July 1965 at Martinborough, NZ.	**AKESHIA CRYSTAL NICHO** b 22 July 1994 at Masterton.
		BEVERLY RUTH DAGG **(twin)** b 30 July 1966 at Masterton. m 9 Sept 1988 ====== at Masterton.	**KERRY DAGG** adopted to **HIGGINS** b 2 September 1984 at Hamilton.
		HORI KARAKA WIHONE b 9 March 1964 at Martinborough.	**KARA HUIA WIHONE** b 6 May 1989 at Masterton.
			REWA TE PUIA WIHONE b 25 July 1992 at Masterton.
			MAPU RANGI WIHONE b 15 February 1996 at Masterton.
			PIRI HEPETA WIHONE b 5 November 1999 at Masterton.
	JENIFER ROBIN DAGG b 19 May 1941 at Masterton. m 22 May 1965 ===== at Eketahuna. RON next page	**ROBERT JAMES BRANNIGAN** b 10 June 1966 at Eketahuna. LUCINDA next page	

ELIZA continued

4th Generation	5th Generation	6th Generation	7th Generation
Doris & Robert continue	**RONALD PETER BRANNIGAN (Ron)** b 26 November 1938 at Eketahuna. (son of Leonard James Brannigan and Christine Marie nee Jensen)	**LUCINDA** (Cindy) **CHRISTINE BRANNIGAN** b 5 September 1968 at Eketahuna.	
		MAREE ANNETTE BRANNIGAN b 8 January 1970 at Eketahuna. m 20 March 1993 at Totara Reserve, in Pohangiha. **ANDREW HUBBARD** b 1965 at Palmerston North. (divorced)	
ROY ALBERT SOWRY b 10 December 1905 at Makomako, Pahiatua. d 5 February 1977 (71) Bur Kamo, Whangarei. m 2 Dec 1937 ====== at Ngaruawahia. **MILLICENT AGNES ELEANOR MILES** b 18 May 1913 (Millie) at Kioreroa, Whangarei d 23 Oct 1997 (84) Bur Kamo, Whangarei. (daughter of Leonard Miles and Eleanor Harriet Marchant) They had six children.	**NEIL LEONARD SOWRY** b 4 October 1938 at Pahiatua. 1st m 1965 (no issue) at Whangarei. **JENNEANE MARY ROGERS** (Jenny) : 2nd m 6 Jan 1998===== at Whangarei. **DIANE AGNES WARD** b 24 February 1944 at Wanganui. (daughter of Charles Maurice Ward and Althea Toy nee Rogers)	**PAULINE LISA SOWRY** b 28 August 1970 at Whangarei.	
		GAYLENE DIANE SOWRY ========== b 26 November 1972 at Whangarei. : : : : partner ========== **MILES SAMUEL CROWTHER** b 30 June 1970 at Hamilton.	**EATHAN ROSS SOWRY** b 3 February 1992 at Whangarei. d 4 February 1992 Bur Whangarei. **SAMUEL ROBERT CROWTHER** b 9 January 1994 at Whangarei.

ELIZA continued

4th Generation	5th Generation	6th Generation	7th Generation
Roy & Millie continue	Neil & Diane continue	(Miles was son of Neil Crowther & Caroline nee Dowsett)	**SIMON NEIL CROWTHER** b 20 August 1996 at Whangarei.
		ROBERT NEIL SOWRY b 23 May 1974 at Whangarei.	
	JEAN ROSE SOWRY b 30 August 1939 at Kawakawa, Northland. m 27 Jan 1962 ====== at Whangarei. **ANDREW** (Andy) **MALCOLM MILNE** b 5 December 1938 at Huntly. (son of Andrew Colin Milne and Helen Alice nee Phillips)	**COLIN BRUCE MILNE** b 8 October 1962 at Whangarei.	
		SHERYL ROSE MILNE b 9 April 1964 at Hamilton. m 19 April 1987 ===== at Te Awamutu. **MARK ROBERT RODGERS** b 22 September 1963 at Dunedin.	**CAMERON ALLAN RODGERS** b 23 January 1994 at Hamilton. **VANESSA MAREE RODGERS** b 24 October 1996 at Hamilton.
		WENDY ANNE MILNE b 2 January 1967 at Hamilton. m 31 March 1990 ==== at Te Awamutu. **WAYNE DOUGLAS BROWN** b 26 September 1966 at Auckland City.	**JESSE ROBERT BROWN** (twin) b 10 August 1991 at Hamilton. **COREY ANDREW BROWN** (twin) b 10 August 1991 at Hamilton.
	ANNE next page	BRETT next page	

4th Generation	5th Generation	6th Generation	7th Generation
Roy & Milly continued	**ANNE JOY SOWRY** b 27 March 1941 at Whangarei. m 30 March 1962 ==== at Auckland.	**BRETT JOHN McWILLIAM** b 26 September 1962 at Christchurch.	
	JOHN ERNEST McWILLIAM b 15 June 1939 at Christchurch. (son of Ernest McWilliam & Veronica nee Bretton) :	**CORAL ROSE McWILLIAM** b 23 December 1963 at Christchurch. m 18 Dec 1982====== at Tauranga. **MYLES JOHN O'REILLY** b 3 February 1963 at Auckland. (son of Jerard O'Reilly and Stella M F nee Donelly.) (Stella later married a Mr Candler. Myles and his children used this name awhile.)	**DARNELLE JADE RICHARDSON** b 17 March 1981 at Tauranga. partner ========= **PAUL RICCARDO TUANAU** b at : *Darnelle & Paul have two 8th Generation children* **CALEB RUSSELL TUANAU** *b 23 March 1999 at Tauranga. and* **WIPORI PAUL WHARE TUANAU** *b May 2000 at Tauranga.*
			HAYDEN BEN O'REILLY b 13 April 1984 at Tauranga.
			LUKE ADAM O'REILLY b 14 January 1987 at Rotorua.
			VICKY next page

ELIZA continued

4th Generation	5th Generation	6th Generation	7th Generation
Roy & Millie continue	Anne & John continue	Coral & Myles continue	**VICKY JEWELLE O'REILLY** b 13 September 1988 at Rotorua.
	: :	**GLENN ROY McWILLIAM (twin)** b 29 September 1965 at Christchurch. m November 1992 at Rotorua. **JAQUELINE KAAHO** born at Rotorua.	
		No Name Baby Boy McWILLIAM (twin) b 30 September 1965 at Christchurch. d 30 September 1965 Bur Christchurch.	
	Anne remarried on 10 November 1970 at Palmerston North === **RENNIE ALBERT RICHARDSON** b 10 August 1941 at Palmerston North. (son of Furner Richardson and Mina nee Winiata) : Anne married thirdly on 1 March 1986 at Tokoroa. **BRIAN GEORGE RADFORD** b 18 September 1941 at Te Aroha. (son of Neville Radford and Alma nee Conder)	**KERRY FURNER RICHARDSON** b 4 September 1970 at Wanganui.	
		JARROD HESTON RICHARDSON b 15 June 1979 at Tauranga.	

4th Generation	5th Generation	6th Generation	7th Generation
Roy & Millie continue	**MERLE DORIS SOWRY** b 5 July 1942 at Whangarei. married in 1965 at Port Harcourt, Nigeria. **JOE JOHNSON** b 4 August 1940 at Adelaide, Australia. : 2nd partner ======== **GEORGE BARRETT** b 16 August 1938 at Las Vegas, U.S.A. (son of Raymond Barrett & Lilly nee Carter)	**PIA GEORGINA BARRETT** b 21 March 1974 at Auckland.	
	FRANK ROY SOWRY **now LEYLANDER** b 24 August 1944 at Whangarei. m 26 August 1965 at Whangarei. **LYN HANSEN** : Frank married secondly on 10 Oct 1975 ===== at Whangarei. **SHIRLEY ELIZABETH TAYLOR nee Rowley** b 4 October 1936 at Auckland. d 31 May 1988 (51) Bur New Plymouth.	**AARON FRANK LEYLANDER** b 7 April 1974 at Whangarei.	
	PAMELA BETTY SOWRY b 24 October 1947 at Whangarei. d 14 July 1950 Bur Kamo, Whangarei.		

4th Generation	5th Generation	6th Generation	7th Generation
LEO ARTHUR SOWRY b 30 July 1907 at Makomako. d 3 February 1967 (59) Bur Levin. m 27 May 1950 ===== at Pahiatua. **PEARL DARDANELLA MARY STINSON** b 10 May 1916 at Feilding. d 9 Nov 1984 (68) Bur Levin. (daughter of Arthur Burgess Stinson and Emily Sarah nee Rush) They had two children.	**PATRICIA HELEN SOWRY** (Trish) b 30 March 1951 at Pahiatua. m 28 November 1970 at Levin. **MALCOLM BERESFORD SNOAD** b 7 August 1910 at Hastings. d 21 May 1990 (79) Bur Levin.		
	RONALD BRIAN SOWRY b 11 March 1956 at Levin.		
ETHEL ROSE SOWRY b 26 May 1913 at Rose Farm, Makomako. d 18 August 1984 (71) Bur Ballance. m 19 June 1937 ===== at Makomako, Pahiatua. **JAMES LINDOUL FIELDING (Lin)** b 16 January 1915 at Masterton. (son of Alfred Charles Fielding and Gertrude May nee Day.) They had two children.	**CYNTHIA ANN FIELDING** b 20 November 1939 at Palmerston North. m 1 Feb 1964 ====== at Palmerston North. **PETER LESLIE MACPHERSON** b 9 November 1939 at Palmerston North. (son of Leslie Norman James Macpherson and Amy Adelaide nee Saunders)	**COLIN PETER MACPHERSON** b 25 October 1964 at Palmerston North. **WENDY ANN MACPHERSON** b 8 December 1966 at Palmerston North.	
	ALAN next page	NIKKI next page	MEGAN next page

4th Generation	5th Generation	6th Generation	7th Generation
Ethel & Lin continue	**ALAN JOHN FIELDING** b 8 April 1942 at Palmerston North. m 30 Oct 1965 ====== at Palmerston North. **CAROL ANN BELTON** b 22 January 1948 at Huntly, Waikato. (Daughter of Thomas Melling Belton and Noeline nee Ogilvie) : Alan m 2nd May 1985 Greytown, Wairarapa. **MAREE SALTER-HESSON** divorced 1987, no issue.	**NIKKI SANYA FIELDING** b 2 April 1966 at Palmerston North. m 6 Feb 1988 ======= at Whangarei. **ARNOLD HENRY SNELL WEIR** (Arnie) b 20 September 1963 at Whangarei. <u>**KRISTOPHER GEOFFREY FIELDING**</u> b 23 July 1968 at New Plymouth. d 17 July 1995 (26) Bur Ballance.	**MEGAN ROSE WEIR** b 16 November 1998 at Auckland.

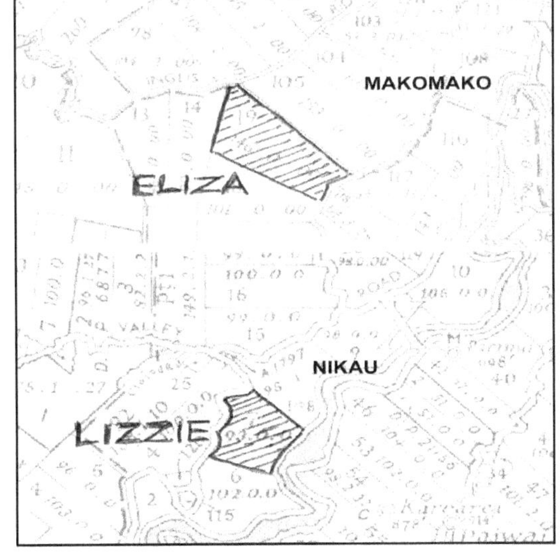

The sisters Lizzie and Eliza lived quite close to each other.

CHAPTER SEVEN

7th Generation (3rd NZ)

JOHN COATES (Jack) THOMAS

(1875-1955)

1875... BIRTH - AUCKLAND:
William and Eliza's third child and first son, JOHN COATES THOMAS was born 6 January at Whau, Auckland. His birth certificate shows his father was a 'Miller' and Eliza gave their residential address as 'Waterview'.

He was named John after his grandfather John Thomas, and Coates was his grandmother Jane's maiden name.

He was known as JACK. On our 'Brief Tree' (p 8/9) he is John Thomas VII.

1881... SCHOOL: Auckland.
The Mt Albert School enrolment registers state that Jack first attended the Whau School (Avondale), but no records prior to 1883 have survived.

> Registers shows Jack (6) was enrolled at Mt Albert School by his father, along with sisters Lizzie and Eliza, on 20 April 1881.

Jack did not sit the 29 March 1882 exams, as he.. *"has not been 11 months at school."* All three children were withdrawn from the school on 26 May 1882, when Jack was aged 7... *"to go to Christchurch".*

1882... ASHBURTON: Jack, aged 7, moved south with his parents and siblings. When the family moved onto their Allenton Nursery at Ashburton, Jack lived near his first cousins, uncle John's children.

1882... SCHOOL: Ashburton.
Jack was enrolled at the Ashburton Borough School by his father on 13 November 1882, and when he left the school on 7 April 1887 aged 12 years and 3 months, they noted on his enrolment card... *"gone to work".*

> When he started his working life, we wonder if he went to work at the Allenton Nursery with uncle John, was involved with his father in carpentry, or at this age was out working on someone's farm.

Soon after September 1887, five months after he left school, Jack's parents and family moved to Ngawapurua, in the North Island near Woodville.

1888.   Woodville.
Although Jack had been 'working' for nine months, he was enrolled at the

Woodville School on 30 January 1888, aged 13. He passed his Standard 3 exam in May, and his last day at school was 21 May 1888... *"to go to work"*.

1898... Jack's parents and some of his younger siblings moved to New Lynn in Auckland, late in 1898 when Jack was nearly 24 years of age.

1889 to 1898. There is nothing remembered of Jack's life during these nine years when aged between 14 to 23. He was probably working at whatever he could find in the Levin, Palmerston North and Woodville districts. Jack gave his occupation as *'farmer of Levin'* when he married in December 1899.

1899... MARRIAGE - LEVIN:

Jack was married to **ALICE MARY JAMES** (aged 26), on 25 December at the residence of her parents in the Horowhenua Village Settlement, Levin, by the Rev. H.E. Bellhouse of the Wesleyan faith.

Two items recorded on the wedding certificate are confusing... (a) Jack's age as 23, when he was a couple of weeks off his 25th birthday, and (b) his mother's maiden name, was recorded as Carrie when it was actually McKay. In the latter case, McKay was her birth name, but in New Zealand she lived with her uncle Isaac Carrie and grandmother Isabella Carrie, and she may have been known by this name to save confusion and explanation generally.

At their wedding Alice was attended by her sister Amy R. James, and Jack's best man was his first cousin Frederick William Thomas, then a 'Labourer' in Levin. They must have become good mates in the Allenton days.

> Perhaps around this time Jack disliked his middle name of Coates, as this marriage certificate records him as only John Thomas and he also signed his name without the name Coates ! (T)

Alice was known as Alice Mary, however Roland's daughter Alice Mary Thomas, named after her grandmother, was known only as Alice. (AG)

The JAMES family.

Alice Mary James was born at Taranaki Street, Wellington on 29 April 1873, one of seven children of Ivor James (b1841) and Mary Ann nee Howe (b1843) who were married at the Wesleyan Chapel in Wellington on 1 January 1866. Ivor's occupation at this 1866 wedding was given as 'carpenter', at Alice's birth in 1873 it was 'carter', at Alice's wedding in 1899 he was a 'farmer' and on his death certificate he was a 'builder'.

> Witnesses at Ivor and Mary's wedding were John Howe, a farmer of Wellington (and probably Mary's father) and Victoria Rowett.

Ivor died 8 June 1913 (72) and Mary died 7 January 1914 (71). They died within 7 months of each other and are buried at Levin's 'Tiro Tiro Road Cemetery', Block 12, Plots 15 and 16. There is no headstone. There were four sons and three daughters, aged from 45 to 28, alive, when they died.

Ivor's death certificate advises he was born in Monmouthshire in Wales, his parents were William James and Eliza nee Phelps and he had been in New Zealand 51 years (therefore arrived about 1862). Mary's death certificate notes her birth in Wellington 1841-2, to John Howe (a farmer) and Elizabeth nee Mace, and she died of a heart attack after a fall.

CHILDREN: Jack and Alice had five children they named...........
Irene (1901), Roland (1902), Gwen (1904), Ivy (1906) and Edna (1907).
Irene and Roland were born at Levin where father Jack was a 'farmer'.
Gwen, Ivy and Edna were born while their parents were living in New Lynn.

1900/2... FINGERS: About this time Jack was working at a sawmill in the Levin area, when a work mate bumped him, and the saw removed nearly all his left hand thumb and fingers except the little one. While he was in hospital he was regularly visited by Salvation Army members. Jack was very impressed and soon after joined the "Sally" organisation. (GW, ZK, AG)

1902... ELECTIONS:
The Otaki rolls list brothers Harry Thomas, Jack and Jack's wife.........

John Thomas	Horowhenua VS	Engine Driver
Alice Mary Thomas	Horowhenua	Domestic Duties
William Henry Thomas	Horowhenua VS	Sawmill Hand

AUCKLAND:
1903-8... Jack and Alice moved to live in New Lynn, Auckland soon after son Roland's birth in October 1902, and Jack was immediately involved in the brickworks on his father's farm, with his brothers Harry and Albert. His carpentry and engineering skills would have been put to valuable use, not only in the erection of the building, but also in the mechanisation of brick making. Jack's father closed down his brick making activities in 1908.
Jack and family lived on the 52 acre block's, section 5, plan 1037 situated on Nikau Road and opposite the southern end of Queen Mary Avenue.

1909... ALICE DIED: Jack and Alice were living in Queen Mary Avenue in New Lynn, Auckland when Alice died on 6 December 1909 aged only 36.

Her memorial card describes her as an..."*affectionate and devoted wife of John Coates Thomas*". At this time her children were aged 10, 8, 6, 5 and 3, and husband Jack was 35. Alice was interred at Waikumete Cemetery, Auckland. There is no headstone on her grave in the 'Non Conformist' section D.. Row 1.. Plot #47.

Was Alice having a sixth child ?

Many of Alice's grandchildren believe she 'died in childbirth'. As her fifth child was over two years of age in 1909, she could have been expecting a sixth child. Jack had many long chats later in his life with daughter Violet's husband George Wright, and during one of these Jack told him *"Alice was pregnant and the baby died inside her. Nobody knew it had died and it poisoned her system and she died."*

Research supports this story, as no Thomas child was recorded as born and then died, in the Auckland district, within a year either side of Alice's death.

Memorial Card ... Phoebe Ching of Ashburton (Jack's first cousin) in 1988 still had her mother's handbag, in which was the 1909 memorial card for Alice Mary Thomas. It is from this small item that we found the initial knowledge of Jack, and his parent's William and Eliza Thomas, for the printing of William's brother John's book... *'The Thomas Family'* in 1993.

Maori Blood ... a number of grandchildren wondered if there was any fact in the comments which they had heard, of 'Alice had Maori blood.'

We have purchased her Marriage Certificate, her Birth Certificate, her parent's Marriage Certificate and both her parent's Death Certificates.

No Maori names or Tribal affiliations were detailed on any of these five documents and we find that 'Degree of Maori Blood' and 'Tribe of Parents' was not required compulsively to be recorded on death certificates until 1961. We have been unable to gain birth details for Mary Ann Howe (est 1842) as her birth was not recorded in New Zealand between 1840 and 1854. Her parents may just have forgotten to register the birth. There is no record of her parents John Howe and Elizabeth

ALICE MARY THOMAS nee JAMES

Mace's marriage, which may have been between 1840 and 1854 in New Zealand. These may have been a better source for an answer to this question.

JACK and ALICE'S CHILDREN

at back...   Rene and Roland...........   at front...Gwen, Ivy and Edna.

1911... ELECTION: The Eden - Auckland roll records Jack as.....
John Thomas...   New Lynn...   Brickmaker.

1912... 2nd MARRIAGE: On 16 November 1912, at St Matthew's Church in Auckland City, Jack now aged 37, married **VIOLET EMILY ADA MARIA EARL** aged 25. Jack was living in New Lynn and gave his occupation as builder, and Violet was a spinster living in nearby Avondale.

The EARL Family.

Violet was born in London on 3 February 1887 at their home, 5 Blomfield Place, Paddington. She was the youngest daughter of John Cherrington Earl, (coachman) and Mary <u>Jane</u> nee Money, who married at Whaplode, in Lincolnshire, England circa 1879.

Violet had a sister named Elizabeth Gertrude Earl, 'Gertie" (born c1880) who later married Harry E. Stenner, and a brother James Robert (Bob) Earl (born c1882) who we think married a lady named May. (GW)

Violet's father, John Cherrington Earl was born c1857 at Holbeach Drove, Lincolnshire, to Christopher Earl (bootmaker) and wife Elizabeth nee French.

Violet's mother, Mary Jane nee Money was born c1855 in Wood Green, north London, to Robert Money (builder) and wife Rebecca nee Donington. (Details from death certificates purchased by Violet Wright.)

The whole Earl family came to New Zealand.

Violet and sister Gertie came first, approximately 1909 to 1911.

After Violet married Jack, he arranged for her parents to come to New Zealand too. They arrived around 1920.

Jack gave Violet's father a job at J. J. Craig's brick works. It seems the gentle-man who employed her father in England as his coachman, retired the horses and purchased a car and therefore her father became unemployed. (GW)

In New Zealand, Violet and Gertie worked for 'Milne & Choyce as hat makers. (GW)

Their home at 92 Rosebank Road, Avondale was known as *"Cherrington Villa"*.

1926... **JOHN and JANE EARL with granddaughter VIOLET** (GW)

It would appear that Violet loved children, for she accepted a ready made family of five aged from 5 to 12 years, and went on to have five children of her own.....

Marjorie (1914), Ivan (1915), Lesley (1917), John (1919), Violet (1921).

1913-14... LAND SALES:

The 30 October 1909 Deed of Sales from William Thomas to his three sons of 52 acres has a plan showing 'private' roads, and suggested division of this land into seven large parts. (pages 93 + 94) In 1912 the sons decided to subdivide and sell up this land, and the years 1913 and 1914 were very busy times. There were a great number of land transactions, between the brothers and to new owners. Some pieces sold as large blocks, and others were subdivided and later re-subdivided.

Late in 1914 a Mr Alfred W. Bussey wanted to buy a seven acre block of the New Lynn property, and Jack and Harry agreed to swap their more valuable 'residential' land for 121 acres of farm land at Brigham's Creek. They agreed to pay Mr Bussey £ 40 for 'equality of exchange'.

1914... MASSEY: Daughter Marjory was the last of Jack and Violet's children to be born while they lived at Queen Mary Avenue, New Lynn. Shortly after this the family moved onto a farm at Brighams Creek, Massey.

TITLE 220/133:   Transfer #84725.   On 22 December 1914 Jack bought Lots 31 and 32 totalling 121 acres (from A. W. Bussey, a baker), situated on the western side of State Highway 16 running down to Brighams Creek. (In 2001 this farm is near the end of the North Western motorway.) Jack owned this jointly with brother Harry until 18 September 1918 when Harry sold him his half. A busy title with numerous mortgages, caveats, etc.
        Transfer #245731   Later on 15 December 1930, Jack sold 18 acres of Lot 31 to brother Harry who, by this date, owned Lot 30 next door to Jack. He agreed to sell the balance of 103 acres to Rosamond May Proude and Wallace Casters Berry for £ 3,100 on 15 December 1930, and held a mortgage (#212251) over the 103 acres (CT623/139) dated 10 February 1931, which was discharged 20 May 1935.

January 1915... Jack (40) and his family at this time, from left...
Ivy, Irene, Violet with Marjorie, Gwen, Jack, Edna & Roland. (FT)

Another family photo taken on this day is printed on page 97.

Jack then moved his family to a larger farm at Donnellys Crossing which he had purchased from Mrs Rosamond M. Proude mentioned previously.

While at Massey, Jack lent money (by mortgage) to Robert Dunlop and William P. Dunlop who owned Lots 33, 34 and 46 to the south and next to his farm. (CT606/250 dated 12 February 1930. Discharged 12 May 1936.)

1916-21... While living on the Massey farm, Jack became foreman at J.J. Craig's quarry at the foot of Mt Eden (site now of Eden Gardens), and when they closed operations Jack went back to brick making at J. J. Craig's Avondale works in St Georges Road. He travelled there daily from the farm in his seven seater car, a Chandler tourer. (GW)

Jack was a good steam-engine engineer and operator and on one occasion Craig's sent him to Huntly to find out why production levels were so erratic. The finding was that nothing was wrong with the machines, and also that the staff could work at normal speed only when strongly supervised. (GW)

1921... WINSTONES:

Around 1921 Jack was working on the Te Atatu peninsula, making bricks and delivering crushed shells. He gained a Winstone's contract to supply four million bricks at so many per month. Then the 1921 depression hit Auckland's building activity, and after only three months he was told to cease production.

Some months later Winstones had not taken delivery of the bricks he had produced and refused to pay him, saying he was in default of the contract.

They won, and Jack lost his Avondale house and a shop property he rented to Nobles the bakers, in Railway Street, Henderson. (GW)

1921... VIOLET DIED:

Violet, aged 34, died on I July 1921 whilst they lived at Brighams Creek. She died shortly after giving birth to their fifth child and was laid to rest at Waikumete Cemetery, Anglican plot 2500.

VIOLET EMILY ADA MARIA THOMAS nee EARL

In 1930 and in 1939 her parents joined her. The headstone reads......
"In loving remembrance of our Violet, beloved wife of JC Thomas,
Youngest daughter of MJ & JC Earl, born Feb 3-1887, died July 1-1921.
In ever loving memory of John Cherrington Earl beloved husband of
M J Earl, late of London, England who went home Sept 3-1930 aged 73.
Also Mary Jane Earl died January 28-1939 aged 84."

JACK and VIOLET'S CHILDREN
at back...
Marjory, Lesley, Ivan,
at front...
John and Violet.
(KA-R)

VIOLET'S BIRTHDAY BOOK. This book, now with granddaughter Betty Flexman, has many entries in Violet's handwriting.

1922... 'Eden-Auckland' Electoral Roll records...
       John Coates Thomas   of Massey, Henderson Farmer.
also listed is...   Irene Thomas   of Massey, Henderson. Spinster.

1923... Jack's father William Thomas died on 26 February 1923 aged 75.

1924... MAIL RUN: About this time Jack also operated a mailrun in the Henderson / Massey area, and daughter Violet recalls accompanying him in the horse and gig. He had this mail run for a number of years. (VW)

1925... MASSEY SCHOOL: The book *'Henderson's Mill'* by Anthony G. Flude records, (p 100) that the Massey School opened in 1925, the teacher was Mr W. Strong, and the first day pupils included Ivan Thomas, Lesley Thomas and John Thomas. These were the three sons of Jack and Violet.

1927... PHONE: *'Henderson's Mill'* also lists Henderson phone numbers for the year 1927, and included.......
      J. C. Thomas ... Massey, residence ... phone number 106M.

1927... IRENE: Jack's eldest daughter Irene married Ernest Sanford on 22 December, and we are advised grandmother Eliza paid all the costs. (GW)

1930... DONNELLYS CROSSING:
Jack sold up at Massey, and moved himself and six of his children onto a 318 acre dairy farm at Donnellys Crossing, towards the western coast from Whangarei. With Jack went son Roland 26, Marjory 14, Ivan 13, Lesley 11, John 9 and Violet 7. (GW) Roland married later in 1931 and he stayed to work on the farm and lived in the second farmhouse. (AG)

TITLE 342/86 & 87. Transfer #245456. On 15 December 1930 Jack bought from Rosamond May Proude, 318 acres of farm land of 5 lots #18, 18A, 19, 20 and 21 on both sides of Proudes Road. He paid £ 3,250 and carried a mortgage until 14 January 1941. Rosamond Proude and Jack seem to have 'exchanged' properties, as she became owner of the Massey farm.

Transfer #389928 shows Jack sold this farm to Leonard Arthur Stenersen of Aranga on 5 July 1945. Stenersen paid £ 530 cash and Jack held a mortgage for the balance until 14 July 1950.

GRASS SEED: Jack was not a man to rely on one source of income, and while at Donnellys Crossing he purchased a 'Case' tractor and a thrasher, to thrash grass seed. Jack operated the thrasher, while son Roland drove the tractor, and he was contracted for work all around the district. (GW)

SCHOOLS: This farm was situated between three small schools at Katui, Aranga and Donnellys Crossing, and Jack's youngest children attended them all... more than once. Jack would have an argument with the teacher, remove his children and enrol them at the next school. The arguments centred around Jack's desire for his children to milk the cows before they went to school, and after they returned home. He wanted them home at a specific time, and if they did not get home by this time... perhaps having been kept late at school... he would 'blast' the teacher and take them out of that school. Son John advises that for every minute they arrived home after the set time, they received a slap around the backside with a switch stick. (JCET)

PIT-SAWN: Jack's house on Lot 18 on this farm was made of pit-sawn timbers, as was the original cowshed Jack and son Roland erected. Doug Gillespie later built a new cowshed on this farm. When son Roland married, a new house was erected on Lot 20 for him and his family. (AG)

HORSES: There were two horses on the Donnellys Crossing farm named 'Heather' and 'Warrigal'. One day Heather got a leg caught in a hole left by the gum diggers. While trying to get her out of the hole, Jack was kicked by the horse and nearly died. He was laid up in bed for a long time. (AG)

PARROT: Jack kept a parrot in the house and he often threatened to "do it in". One particular occasion really upset him. He was working some sheep with his dogs in a paddock near the house, when his dogs raced off. The parrot, which had learnt to imitate Jack's whistle, had panicked when a cat entered the room it was in, whistled for help and the dogs immediately responded. Jack gave the bird a few choice words. (GW)

Another time Jack became most upset with the parrot, was when he found it had pecked out all the metal eyelets in his work boots. (VW)

KAURI LOG: While living at Donnellys Crossing, Jack noticed a large kauri log lying at the side of the road. After a while he enquired as to whom may own it, and found nobody knew. So he had it sawn up and made an addition to his home. Soon after the owner noticed it had vanished and complained to the police. Jack was fined £ 50 or go to gaol for one week. He decided on gaol, and spent one week at the police residence in Dargaville. While there he used his carpentry skills and also did some painting. Jack was most upset when his next cream cheque arrived, because the £ 50 for the log had been deducted. He felt he had paid twice for his timber. (VW)

1931... KEN: Jack's first grandchild, Kenneth Sanford, was born 3 March.

1921 - 1937. Son John recalls that during the sixteen years between wife Violet's death, and Jack's marriage to Myrtle, Jack had a number of live-in female housekeepers. He also recalls his father as a very versatile fellow, able to do all manner of things. As well as farming, Jack also did carpentry and painting jobs on neighbouring farms, built new homes and made alterations to homes, outbuildings and local schools. At this time he left a lot of the farm work to his sons Ivan, Lesley and John, and went off to operate steam engines at various sawmills. At some time he and brother Harry worked near Whakatane and helped build the paper mills there. It is thought this is where he met Myrtle, who was employed as a cook. When he returned to the farm Myrtle came too. Everybody assumed they had married, but a local post office employee found out that they had not. They tolerated the gossip for some time, then went and got married at a registry office. That settled the gossip. (JCET+VW+AWT)

1935... Jack's mother Eliza Thomas died 7 March 1935 aged 84.

1938... 3rd MARRIAGE: Jack (63) married on 24 March at the Whakatane Registrar's Office to **ROSE <u>MYRTLE CAMERON</u>** (41). Myrtle's divorce was issued on 7 December 1937. They had no children together, but Myrtle did have three children from her first marriage, to join with Jack's ten.

WWII... Son Leslie joined the Merchant Navy serving at Tabrook and near Russia. Son Ivan became a member of the Military police and died in Egypt. Son John volunteered and spent four years in the Middle East, and a period of that was a prisoner of war.

1945... 70th BIRTHDAY:
In January 1945 Jack turned 70 and a huge family gathering on Orewa beach was organised. Everyone attended except son Ivan who had died. Daughter Edna's husband Bill Taylor drove a bus and picked up family members from Auckland, New Lynn and Henderson. There was a huge sign on the front of the bus........   **"The THOMAS GANG   Orewa or bust."**
There are still many happy memories of these gatherings.   (DT+V&GW)

<u>**The photo on page 190 records Jack's family at Orewa**</u>. (BF)

1945... RETIREMENT: Jack and Myrtle left Donnellys Crossing in July, and lived a short time in Mangatoroto. Then he erected a new 'Spanish' type bungalow in The Terrace at Orewa, (used to be the old Main Rd north), on the hill looking south over Orewa town's main street and the beach. They painted the house yellow. Here they retired. (AG)

JC (Jack) THOMAS' 70th Birthday at Orewa Beach, Auckland. January 1945.

<u>back left to right</u>... Lionel Marshall, George Wright & Bobby, Arthur Haslam, Reg Gatfield, Bill Taylor, Reg Mason, Myrtle Thomas, Les Thomas, Jack Thomas, John Thomas, Rex Taylor, Roly Thomas, Des Taylor, Ray Haslam, Arthur Dove, Ken Sanford and Allen Thomas.   <u>center left to right</u>... Violet Wright, Gwen Marshall, Ivy Haslam, Marj Gatfield, Joyce Thomas, June Thomas, Bunty Thomas, Delcie Dove, Winnie Cameron, Edna Taylor, Pearle Thomas, Rene Mason, Edie Dove.   <u>front left to right</u>... Bryan & Ian Haslam, Keith Marshall, Joy Wright, Colin Haslam,   ?   , Patricia Thomas, Zita Sanford, Betty Marshall, Zelma Marshall, Heather Thomas, Alice Thomas, Dorothy Thomas, Richard Thomas and June Thomas.

JACK and MYRTLE in 1946 (KA-R)

1950... 75th BIRTHDAY:
There were at least three occasions when the family decided to get together, and one was at daughter  Rene Sanford's farm at Massey in January 1950, for Jack's 75th birthday. A photo of those attending was taken by Rene's step-son Trevor Mason, with everyone standing under Rene's large apple tree. (ZK) We are sorry are unable to reproduce it here. (T)

MEMORIES:

PORRIDGE: Jack had a bowl of porridge each morning for breakfast. However, he would only eat about three quarters of it, then rap his spoon on the table and his big cat would come to him and eat the rest of it. His children and grandchildren have fond memories of the cat which they named *'Porridge'*. (MG+ZK)

HAND WRITING: Many members of the family, recall Jack's 'beautiful neat hand writing', which some described as almost calligraphic.
His signature on the Massey farm's sale papers clearly shows his style.

WHO IS IT? Step-daughter Winifred has fond memories of her 'Dad' Jack, and recalls he would answer the phone with either *"Hello,Hello,Hello!"* or *"Who is it? Who is it?"*. This caused much laughter amongst the children.

HOBBY: If Jack had a hobby, it was working with wood. He loved to make things, be they houses or furniture. When he died he left a Grandfather clock to Myrtle. He had bought the clock parts but built the cabinet. (AG)

1955... JACK DIED:

John Coates Thomas (Jack) died on 4 July aged 80 years.
At this time Myrtle was 58.
His Waikumete Cemetery card states that he was a *'retired carpenter'* and his last address was Old Main Road, Orewa.
He is not buried with either of his three wives ... but interred alone in the 'Protestant' Section A... Row 6... Plot 57, without a headstone.
The Cemetery records show that there is only one person in Jack's grave and only Alice in her grave.
Jack (*a retired farmer*) signed his Will on 12 April 1955 and left all of his estate of £ 3,500 ($7,000) to Myrtle. None of his ten children, three step-children or grandchildren were mentioned in his Will, or on his death certificate.

BEDSIDE TABLE made by Jack (AG)

HEIRLOOMS:

Amongst Alice's family treasures are a bed-side

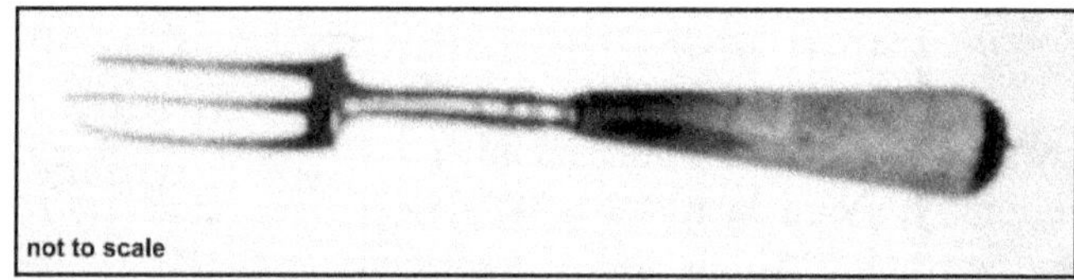

table made by Jack and the small fork (pictured) he used to hold between his left hand's little finger and thumb base. (AG)

1976... MYRTLE DIED:

On 22 March Myrtle died aged 79. Her Will left a Grandfather Clock and all personal items (including rings) to her friend Martha Banks of Main Road, Orewa. The balance of her estate valued at $3,900, went to her children from her first marriage, Mary Frances Ryan, Winifred Myrtle Bayes and Morton Kennedy Cameron. Her second child Violet May Cameron died at an early age. Myrtle was buried at the Silverdale Cemetery.

JOHN COATES (Jack) THOMAS FAMILY TREE:

3rd Generation

JOHN COATES THOMAS..1st married............. **ALICE MARY JAMES**
b 6 January 1875 (JACK) 25 December 1899 b 29 April 1873
at Waterview, Auckland.   at Levin, NZ.   at Wellington.
d 4 July 1955 (80)   d 6 December 1909 (36)
Bur Waikumete, Auckland.   Bur Waikumete, Auckland.

                 2nd married............ **VIOLET EMILY ADA MARIA EARL**
                 16 November 1912 b 3 February 1887 at her parent's home
                 at Auckland City. 5 Blomfield Place, Paddington, London.
                                      d 1 July 1921 (34)
                                      Bur Waikumete, Auckland.

                 3rd married............. **ROSE <u>MYRTLE</u> CAMERON**
                 24 March 1938   b 25 January 1897
                 at Whakatane.   at Wellington.
                                     d 22 March 1976 (79)
                                     Bur Silverdale, Auckland.

Jack and Alice had five children known as Irene, Roland, Gwen, Ivy and Edna.

Jack and Violet had five children known as Marjorie, Ivan, Lesley, John and Violet.

Jack and Myrtle had no children together. Myrtle bought four children to the family.

4th Generation	5th Generation	6th Generation	7th Generation
IRENE THOMAS b 19 Jan 1901 (Rene) at Levin. d 19 May 1965 (65) Cremated Waikumete. 1st m 22 Dec 1927 === at Auckland City. **ERNEST SANFORD** b 29 June 1897 at Grange Road, Soothill Upper, Batley, Yorkshire, England. d 31 October 1939 (42) Cremated Waikumete Cemetery, Auckland. (son of Fred Sanford & Sarah Ellen nee Wood) They had 2 children. :	**KENNETH TREVOR SANFORD** (Ken) b 3 March 1931 at Auckland City. m 25 Feb 1956 ===== at Auckland City. **PATRICIA ANN HOLT** b 23 February 1936 at Auckland City. (daughter of Edward Holt and Winifred nee Nomm) They had 3 children.	**CLINTON ERNEST SANFORD** b 11 April 1959 at Auckland City. m 28 Jan 1984 ===== at Blenheim. **KERRYN LEE TOWNSEND** b 27 May 1958 at Gore, Southland.	**JESSSICA OLIVIA SANFORD** b 22 November 1988 at Auckland City. **JOSHUA TREVOR JAMES SANFORD** b 25 February 1990 at Auckland City. **RUTH NAOMI SANFORD** b 24 November 1992 at Auckland City. d 27 May 1993 Bur Puhoi, Northland.

JACK continued

4th Generation	5th Generation	6th Generation	7th Generation
Irene & Ernest cont....	Ken & Patricia cont....	Clint & Kerryn contin..	**ELIZABETH GRACE SANFORD** b 19 November 1994 at North Shore City.
			ABIGAIL LUCRETIA ELLEN ANN SANFORD b 9 November 1997 at North Shore City.
		LUCINDA ANN SANFORD b 16 November 1961 at Auckland City. m 28 Nov 1981====== at Te Atatu, Auckland. **ROBERT VANNISSELROY** b 1 February 1958 at Auckland City.	**BRENTON JOHN VANNISSELROY** b 17 November 1985 at Auckland City.
			TRENT ALEXANDER VANNISSELROY b 5 October 1988 at Auckland City.
			JORDAN VAUGHAN VANNISSELROY b 26 February 1993 at Auckland City.
			RHIANNON AMBER VANNISSELROY b 18 September 1997 at Auckland City.
		VAUGHAN next page	

194

JACK continued

4th Generation	5th Generation	6th Generation	7th Generation
Irene & Ernest continue : : : : : : : : :	Ken & Patricia continue	**VAUGHAN EDWARD SANFORD** b 1 December 1965 at Auckland City. m 17 February 2001 at Cronulla, Sydney, Australia. **MELISSA LEA MANGAN** b 5 July 1974 at Randwick, Sydney, Australia.	
: : : : : : : : :	**ZITA VALERIE SANFORD** b 15 November 1934 at Auckland City. m 16 March 1957 ==== at Auckland City. **GORDON DAVID KAY** b 7 March 1931 at Te Puke. (son of Robert Kay and Amy Kathleen nee Sherry) (3 children)	**LEANNE RAEWYN KAY** b 16 July 1961 at Helensville. m 16 March 1985 ==== at Auckland City. **BRIAN ROBERT KARL** b 20 February 1959 at Matamata.	**STEVEN JOSEPH KARL** b 1 October 1990 at Otahuhu, Auckland. **DARRYN ROBERT KARL** b 2 August 1992 at Papakura, Auckland.
: : : : : :		**BRYCE ROBERT KAY** b 28 March 1963 at Helensville. m 20 June 1987====== at Auckland City. **WENDY FRANCES McGIVERN** b 28 December 1960 at Auckland.	**ANYA ZITA KAY** b 14 August 1993 (a) in Russia. **DENIS BERNARD KAY** b 25 April 1995 (a) in Russia.
2nd m 25 June 1942 at Auckland City. **REGINALD WILLIAM MASON=** b 9 April 1896 at Auckland. d 6 April 1962 (65) Cremated Waikumete.	Irene became step-mother to **TREVOR MASON** and **KEITH MASON**	**SHARON ANGELA KAY** b 5 November 1964 (a) at Auckland City.	

JACK continued

4th Generation	5th Generation	6th Generation	7th Generation
ROLAND JOHN THOMAS b 19 October 1902 at Levin. d 3 April 1972 (69) Cremated Waikumete. m 8 July 1931======== at Howick, Auckland. **PEARLE EILEEN NICHOLSON** b 16 November 1908 at Ashhurst, Wellington. d 5 July 1987 (78) Cremated Waikumete. (daughter of Frederick Nicholson born Halifax 24 Oct 1876 and died Hamilton 19 July 1950 and Mary nee Allen, born 1879 and died at Hamilton 13 April 1968) They had 6 children.	**ALLEN JAMES THOMAS** b 15 July 1932 at Te Kopuru, Northland. d 23 October 1972 (40) Bur Waikumete, A. m 1954 ==== at **NORMA MAY**	**SHIRLEY MAY THOMAS** b 1955 at Auckland. **BARRY JAMES THOMAS** b 1956 at Whangarei.	
	ALICE MARY THOMAS b 15 August 1933 at Te Kopuru, Northland. 1st m 1 Aug 1953 ==== at Auckland City. **JOHN ROBERT HAMILTON MOSS** b 16 April 1933 at Te Aroha. NZ. (son of George Albert Moss and Ellen Maude Evelyn nee Eaves) They had 5 children. : : : : : : : : : : : : : :	**KEVIN JOHN MOSS** b 7 October 1954 at Auckland City. m 6 Dec 1980======= at Auckland City. **JOAN ELLEN ROOKES** b 4 October 1960 at New Plymouth.	**JOELENE ELLEN MOSS** b 29 May 1984 at Hamilton. **BILLY-JOE KEVIN MOSS** b 4 December 1985 at Hamilton. **TIMOTHY LAWRENCE JOHN MOSS** b 22 June 1990 at Dargaville, Northland. **STEPHEN JAMES MOSS** b 24 August 1993 at Dargaville, Northland. **MARY-DE SUSAN MOSS** b 7 November 1997 at Hamilton.
	:	DIANNE next page	

JACK continued

4th Generation	5th Generation	6th Generation	7th Generation
Roland & Pearle cont..	Alice & John continue	**DIANNE CAROL MOSS** b 4 November 1955 at Auckland City. m 14 Feb 1976 ====== at Dargaville. **MALCOLM GEORGE SINCLAIR** b 3 April 1952 at Te Kopuru, Northland.	**TANYA MARIE SINCLAIR** b 26 September 1977 at Whangarei.
	:		**JODIE ANN SINCLAIR** b 7 September 1979 at Whangarei.
	:		**ROBERT SCOTT SINCLAIR (Bobby)** b 1 October 1980 at Whangarei.
	:	**ROBIN GEORGE MOSS** now Gillespie b 26 December 1957 at Papakura, Auckland.	
	:	**GEOFFREY MICHAEL MOSS** now GILLESPIE x Deed b 17 September 1960 at Auckland City. 1st m 22 Aug 1981==== at Pukekohe, Auckland. **CARLENE JOANNE NEEDHAM** b 17 October 1962 at Auckland City. : 2nd m 27 Nov 1993 at Whangarei. **GLENDA JOY OLSEN** b 16 June 1955 at Kawakawa, Northland.	**MELANIE ANNE GILLESPIE** b 19 May 1984 at Pukekohe, Auckland.
	:	DEBRA next page	

197

4th Generation	5th Generation	6th Generation	7th Generation
Roland & Pearle contin..	Alice married 2nd m 11 Dec 1975 at Dargaville, Northland. **DOUGLAS PERCIVAL GILLESPIE** b 20 April 1933 at Papakura, Auckland. d 31 Aug 2000 (67) Bur Dargaville. (son of Percival Perrott Gillespie and Isabella Mary nee Hampton) Alice and Doug had no children together, but Doug bought 7 children to the family.. Margaret, Alan, Shirley, Jocelyn, Lynn, Cynthia & Valerie	**DEBRA HELEN MOSS** b 9 August 1966 at Auckland City. m 23 Feb 1985 ====== at Auckland City. **CHRISTOPHER CHARLES HOUGHTON** b 24 January 1959 at Auckland City.	**MARK CHARLES HOUGHTON** b 2 July 1986 at Whangarei. **GRANT CHRISTOPHER HOUGHTON** b 24 June 1988 at Auckland City. **LETICIA LEIGH HOUGHTON** b 23 May 1991 at Papakura, Auckland.
	DOROTHY SHIRLEY THOMAS (Dolly) b 13 January 1935 at Te Kopuru, Northland. d 11 October 1983 (48) Bur Albany, NSC. m 1 August 1953===== at Auckland City. **KENNETH GEORGE MOSS** (Ken) b 12 March 1930 at Te Aroha. (son of George Albert Moss and Ellen Maud Evelyn nee Eaves) They had 6 children.	**EVELYN PEARLE MOSS** b 15 July 1954 at Greenlane, Auckland. 1st m 19 June 1974 === at Greenhithe, NSC. **ERNEST <u>BRUCE</u> CLEGHORN** b 3 May 1952 at Auckland City. : 2nd m 21 June 1997 at Chesterfield, England. **GEOFFREY MELVIN WHITEHEAD** b 21 June 1951 at Skegness, England.	**ALICIA JOY CLEGHORN** b 4 January 1977 at Takapuna, NSC. **ANTONY BRUCE CLEGHORN** b 3 April 1979 at Takapuna, NSC.
		DAVID next page	TANIA next page

JACK continued

4th Generation	5th Generation	6th Generation	7th Generation
Roland & Pearle contin..	Dolly & Ken continue	**DAVID MOSS** b 4 May 1956 at Auckland City. m 3 Dec 1977======= at Te Aroha.	**TANIA ANN MOSS** b 4 September 1981 at Southport, Australia.
		KAYE MERLE BINGHAM b 20 June 1960 at Kati Kati.	**HAYLEE LOUISE MOSS** b 7 August 1983 at Tauranga.
			KARA JEANNE MOSS b 17 May 1986 at Tauranga.
		GARY MOSS b 11 May 1959 at Takapuna, NSC. m 1979 === at Torbay, NSC. **DONNA LOUISE COOKE** b at	**ADAM MOSS** b 25 March 1980 at Takapuna, NSC.
		JANET MOSS b 25 March 1957 at Auckland City. m 23 Oct 1976 at ==== Mullabrack, County Armagh, Ireland. **SAMUEL JOHN TWEEDIE** b 18 January 1951 at Portadown, County Armagh, Ireland.	**TROY JOHN TWEEDIE** b 19 December 1977 at Parramatta, NSW, A.
			JANELLE ANN TWEEDIE b 25 September 1979 at Parramatta, Sydney, NSW, Australia.
		MARGARET next page	KENDALL next page

4th Generation	5th Generation	6th Generation	7th Generation
Roland & Pearle contin..	Dolly & Ken continue	**MARGARET MOSS** b 19 September 1962 at Takapuna, NSC. m 22 Nov 1985 ===== at Takapuna, NSC.	**KENDALL FAIRLIE HEFFERNAN** b 27 March 1987 at Greenlane, Auckland.
		VINCENT JOHN WILLIAM HEFFERNAN b 23 August 1951 at Invercargill. d 30 Sept 2000 (49) Bur	**ASHLEY DOROTHY HEFFERNAN** b 19 March 1988 at Greenlane, Auckland.
			TAYLOR ELLEN MARGARET HEFFERNAN b 22 December 1990 at Takapuna, NSC.
		MICHAEL MOSS b 11 May 1970 at Takapuna, NSC.	
	HEATHER DAPHNE THOMAS b 27 October 1936 at Te Kopuru, Northland. m 5 March 1955 ===== at Auckland City. **KEITH FRANCIS REYNOLDS GILBERT** b 30 October 1930 at Auckland City. (son of George Edward Reynolds Gilbert and Rita Gladys nee Titter) They had 4 children.	**ROSEMARIE REYNOLDS GILBERT** b 30 November 1955 at Auckland City. m 29 Aug 1981===== at Auckland City. **LANCE GEORGE EDLIN** b 2 November 1957 at Thames.	**SAMUEL GEORGE EDLIN** b 20 January 1984 at Hamilton.
			ROBERT FRANCIS EDLIN b 29 November 1985 at Morrinsville.
			JOHN DAVID EDLIN b 6 January 1989 at Thames.
		LEONIE next page	SARA next page

JACK continued

4th Generation	5th Generation	6th Generation	7th Generation
Roland & Pearle contin..	Heather & Keith contin..	**LEONIE MAY REYNOLDS GILBERT** b 11 March 1957 at Auckland City. 1st m 12 April 1975=== at Henderson, Auckland. **PETER JOHN BLOM** b 18 May 1953 at Huntly. : : : : : : : : : : : : : : 2nd m 5 Dec 1981==== at Glen Eden, Auckland. **GEOFFREY PAUL BRUNKER** (Geoff) b 27 March 1954 at Sydney, Australia.	**SARA LOUISE BLOM** b 26 February 1976 at Kaitaia, Northland. partner ========= **CLAY PETER BOWSHER** b 23 September 1976 at Hamilton. : *Sara and Clay have* *8th Generation* ***RHAIN WATEA HENRY BOWSHER*** *b 2 May 2000* *at Huntly.* **REBECCA LISA BLOM** b 21 October 1977 at Sydney, Australia. **MATHEW PAUL BRUNKER** b 4 December 1980 at Te Kuiti.
		PAUL DUANNE REYNOLDS GILBERT b 17 March 1959 at Auckland City. m 1979 == at **JOCELYN BRIGHT** (Joss) b at	**SANDY REYNOLDS GILBERT** b 27 July 1977 at Auckland City. **JASON REYNOLDS GILBERT** b 18 August 1980 at Auckland City.

4th Generation	5th Generation	6th Generation	7th Generation
Roland & Pearle contin..	Heather & Keith contin..	Paul remarried	
		2nd m === at **JULIA MARY DOUGLAS** b at	**MELISSA REYNOLDS GILBERT** b 18 January 1983 at Auckland City.
		ANNETTE REYNOLDS GILBERT b 6 November 1961 at Auckland City. m 4 April 1981 ====== at Auckland City. **WARREN ERIC GREEN** b 21 August 1959 at Auckland City.	**CHARMAINE RUTH GREEN** b 4 August 1982 at Henderson, Auckland. **JESSICA FRANCES GREEN** b 5 May 1984 at Henderson, Auckland. **LAURA JANE GREEN** b 24 November 1987 at Mt Albert, Auckland.
	JUNE ADELE THOMAS b 7 June 1938 at New Lynn, Auckland. m 3 Sept 1960 ====== at Birkenhead, NSC. **DENIS RITCHIE McMILLAN** b 29 August 1939 at St Kilda, Dunedin. (son of and They had 3 children.	**SCOTT WAYNE McMILLAN** b 12 December 1965 at Avondale, Auckland. m at **SANDRA GAZZARD** b 4 March 1963 at **CRAIG JOHN McMILLAN** b 17 June 1967 at Avondale, Auckland.	

JACK continued

4th Generation	5th Generation	6th Generation	7th Generation
Roland & Pearle contin..	**RICHARD LESLIE THOMAS** (Dick) b 23 April 1943 at Paparoa, Northland. m 2 March 1966 ===== at Titirangi, Auckland. **SUSAN NELDA COTTERILL** (Sue) b 25 March 1946 at Whangarei. (daughter of Daniel Henry (Blue) Cotterill and Narine Heather nee Swinbourn) They had 2 children.	**SHARON LEE THOMAS** b 7 June 1967 at Henderson, Auckland. m 25 May 1991====== at Pukapuka, Northland. **MARK WAYNE HALLETT** b 1 January 1960 at Warkworth, Northland. (son of Laurence (Mick) Charles Hallett and Thelma Christina nee Sanderson)	**CHANIKA HALLETT** b 17 June 1992 at Warkworth, Northland. **BEN HALLETT** b 24 March 1994 at Auckland. d 2 August 1994 Crem North Shore City. **MELISSA HALLETT** b 1 June 1996 at Warkworth, Northland.
		MARK WAYNE THOMAS b 11 August 1968 at Whangarei. m 18 November 1995 at Wenderholm, Hibiscus Coast, Auckland. **ANGELA CHRISTINE SMITH** b 13 October 1975 Warkworth, Northland. (daughter of Brian Trevor Smith and Rita Theresa nee Harris)	
GWENYTH MARY THOMAS (Gwen) b 15 October 1904 at New Lynn, Auckland. d 20 February 1985 Bur Orewa. continued next page	**BETTINA JOY MARSHALL** (Betty) b 17 September 1934 at Te Kopuru, Northland. m 16 Oct 1954 ====== at Orewa, Auckland. continued next page	**DAVID JOHN FLEXMAN** b 3 May 1956 at Narrow Neck, NSC. m 21 January 1989 at Te Kuiti. continued next page	

JACK continued

4th Generation	5th Generation	6th Generation	7th Generation
Gwen married m 26 Aug 1933 ===== at Dargaville, Northland. **LIONEL** **MARSHALL** b 12 February 1906 at Johnsonville, Wgtn. d 10 August 1966 (60) Crem Waikumete. (son of John Boyd Marshall and Clara nee Fogarty) They had 4 children.	Betty married **PETER WATERS** **FLEXMAN** b 7 May 1933 at Waiuku, Auckland. (son of Ronald Ernest Flexman and Lillian Teresa nee Waters) They had 3 children.	David married **KAREN FRANCES** **DONOVAN** b 22 July 1959 at Putaruru.	
		IAN BRUCE **FLEXMAN** b 10 December 1957 at Narrow Neck, NSC. m 21 July 1979 ====== at Te Kuiti. **RAEWYN JANICE** **HEINE** b 8 October 1957 at Motueka.	**RICKY ANDREW** **FLEXMAN** b 23 February 1981 at Te Kuiti. **SIMON LEIGH** **FLEXMAN** b 17 November 1982 at Te Kuiti. **BRYCE PAUL** **FLEXMAN** b 12 July 1987 at Te Kuiti.
		CHRISTINE GAY **FLEXMAN** b 16 July 1961 at Te Kuiti. m 13 Oct 1984 ====== at Te Kuiti. **COLIN JAMES** **McQUILKIN** b 28 July 1959 at Te Kuiti.	**ERIN CHRISTINA** **McQUILKIN** b 5 June 1986 at Te Kuiti. **LAURA JAYNE** **McQUILKIN** b 29 May 1988 at Hamilton. **ABBY ELIZABETH** **McQUILKIN** b 8 October 1990 at Hamilton. BRIAR next page

4th Generation	5th Generation	6th Generation	7th Generation
Gwen & Lionel continue	Betty & Peter continue	Christine & Colin contin	**BRIAR KATE LILLIAN McQUILKIN** (twin) b 31 December 1992 at Hamilton.
			BEN JONATHAN THOMAS McQUILKIN (twin) b 31 December 1992 at Hamilton.
	ZELMA ROSE MARSHALL b 30 November 1935 at Te Kopuru, Northland m 1 Oct 1955======= at Orewa. **BRIAN CLEVERLEY TARRANT** b 26 November 1933 at Te Kuiti. (son of Phillip Cleverley Tarrant & Elsie Marion nee McSweeney) They had 3 children.	**LEONE GAY TARRANT** (a) b 10 December 1962 at Auckland City. m 3 Nov 1992 ====== at Auckland. **ALAN FREDERICK KENNEDY** b 1 June 1951 at Albany. NSCity.	**SAMUEL BRIAN KENNEDY** (Sam) b 16 June 1992 at Auckland City. **HOLLY ROSE LOUVAINE KENNEDY** b 28 July 1994 at Auckland City.
		KEVIN BRIAN TARRANT (a) b 11 June 1964 at Auckland City.	
		WAYNE CLEVERLEY TARRANT b 10 July 1968 at Auckland City. partner ========== **SARAH KIRK** b	**HANNA ROSE TARRANT-KIRK** b 14 July 1991 at Waitakere City. Auckland.

JACK continued

4th Generation	5th Generation	6th Generation	7th Generation
Gwen & Lionel continue	**KEITH THOMAS MARSHALL** b 14 May 1939 at Te Kopuru, Northland m 1967 ==== at **MARGARET CATHERINE BREUER** b 1 February 1944 at Hastings. daughter of Colin Breuer and Margaret nee	**SCOTT THOMAS MARSHALL** b 6 September 1968 at Auckland City.	
		CRAIG ANDREW MARSHALL b 25 September 1970 at Auckland City.	
		GLENN DAVID MARSHALL b 19 June 1973 at Auckland City.	
	GARY ROSS MARSHALL b 28 November 1951 at Te Kopuru, Northland m 15 October 1976 === at Orewa, Auckland. **MARIAN HELEN WRIGHT** b 26 December 1954 at Whangarei. daughter of Rev Leonard Cecil Wright & Rosalie Margaret nee Edwards.	**ALEXANDER GARY MARSHALL** b 29 November 1983 at Auckland City.	
		MICHAEL JAMES MARSHALL b 19 January 1987 at Auckland City.	
IVY GLADYS THOMAS b 5 March 1906 at New Lynn, Auckland. d 29 July 1968 (62) Cremated Waikumete. m 1933 =========== at ARTHUR next page	**RAYMOND ARTHUR HASLAM** b 7 October 1932 at Hastings. 1st m 1952 ========= at Auckland City. **DAWN MONICA VIRTUE** ⦂	**DENISE RAEWYN HASLAM** b 6 November 1953 at East Coast Bays, NSC. m 27 Feb 1970 ====== at New Lynn, Auckland. **GRAHAM JOHN GILL** continued next page	**STEVEN RAYMOND GILL** b 28 July 1970 at Mt Albert, Auckland. **TANYA DAWN GILL** continued next page

JACK continued

4th Generation	5th Generation	6th Generation	7th Generation
Ivy married **ARTHUR JOHN** **EDWARD HASLAM** b 1906 at Auckland City. d 20 June 1982 (76) Cremated Waikumete. son of and They had 4 children.	Ray married 2nd m 19 Nov 1971 at Auckland City. **JOAN ISOBEL** **LEMON** b 26 February 1930 at Kawakawa, Northland. (daughter of Major Alfred Lemon and Jessie Tait nee Stewart)	Graham was born in 1948 at Auckland City. : : partner =========== **LESLIE GORDON** **McLIVER** b 1952 at Auckland City.	Tanya was born b 15 November 1972 at Hamilton. **REGAN HECTOR** **HASLAM- McLIVER** b 16 February 1977 at Greenlane, Auckland.
	IAN TERENCE HASLAM b 25 January 1937 at Dargaville. d 23 June 1956 (19) Cremated Waikumete.		
	BRYAN JOHN **HASLAM** b 17 October 1938 at Auckland. m 18 Oct 1968 ====== at Auckland. **BEVERLEY ANNE** **FRENCH** b 26 November 1941 at Auckland. (daughter of Leonard Stanley French and Lorna nee Moss)	**TERRY DEAN** **HASLAM** b 21 April 1967 at Auckland. : : m 2 March 1996 ===== at Auckland City. **LINDA JEAN** **NEWING** b 9 April 1962 at Auckland City.	**ALISHA JADE** **HASLAM** b 7 April 1990 at Auckland City. **CORY ADAM** **HASLAM** b 4 February 1998 at Waitakere City.
		PAUL ANTHONY **HASLAM** b 1969 at Henderson, Auckland. at partner ========= x x b at	x **HASLAM** b at

JACK continued

4th Generation	5th Generation	6th Generation	7th Generation
Ivy & Arthur continue	Bryan & Beverley cont..	**JANINE IVY** **HASLAM** b 1971 at Avondale, Auckland. m 1990 ═════ at **SIMON AVRO** **MILLAN** b 1969 at Auckland City.	x **MILLAN** b at
	COLIN ROSS **HASLAM** b 1941 at Auckland City. m 1966 ═══ at **SHARRON DALE** **HUTCHINSON** b 1946 at Auckland City. (daughter of and nee	**DEAN** **HASLAM** (a) b at **TONY** **HASLAM** (a) b at **RYAN JAMES** **HASLAM** b 1978 at Henderson, Auckland.	
EDNA MAY **THOMAS** b 15 July 1907 at Auckland. d 18 July 1998 (91) Burried Westharbour Gardens, Hobsonville. m February 1931 ═════ at Auckland City. **WILLIAM JOHN** **TAYLOR** (Bill) b 18 June 1904 at Auckland City.	**DESMOND JOHN** **TAYLOR** (Des) b 13 November 1931 at Auckland City. m 23 Feb 1957 ══════ at Auckland City. **JOAN NANCY** **McLEOD** b 11 November 1934 at Auckland City. (daughter of James McLeod and Florence Beatrice nee Loiring)	**MARK DESMOND** **TAYLOR** b 7 July 1958 at Henderson, Auckland. m 4 March 1995 at Mt Eden, Auckland. **LYNNE MAREE** **WOODALL** b 8 October 1962 at Paparoa, Northland. ANDREA next page	

4th Generation	5th Generation	6th Generation	7th Generation
Bill Taylor died d 6 June 1977 (72) Crem Waikumete. (son of Albert Taylor and Jane nee James) They had 2 children.	Des & Joan continue	**ANDREA LIN TAYLOR** b 20 August 1961 at Henderson, Auckland. m 5 September 1998 at Auckland City. **MICHAEL CHARLES WILSON** b at	
	REX WILLIAM TAYLOR b 16 September 1933 at Auckland City. m 1 Nov 1961 ===== at Mt Albert, Auckland. **GERALDINE WALTERS WARREN** b 12 August 1941 at Auckland City. (daughter of Allan Walters Warren and Edna Beverley nee Thomas ....no relation.)	**PAUL JAMES TAYLOR** b 4 July 1964 at Takapuna, NSC. partner =========== **PENELOPE HALL** b 12 June 1962 at Ashburton. **MEGAN JANE TAYLOR** b 8 December 1966 at Takapuna. NSC. d 4 May 1997 Crem Schnapper Rock North Shore City. m 5 Nov 1988 ====== at Piha, Auckland. **DAVID MacGREGOR** b 29 December 1962 at Paisley, Scotland.	**LUCIA JANE TAYLOR** b 16 June 2000 at Auckland City. **TAYLOR OGILVY MacGREGOR** b 27 February 1992 at Takapuna, NSC.
MARJORIE JOYCE THOMAS b 26 January 1914 at Auckland City. d 22 July 1996 (82) Crem Waikumete. continued next page	**ROSS** (a) **GATFIELD** b at		

4th Generation	5th Generation	6th Generation	7th Generation
Marjorie married in 1945 === at Auckland City. **REGINALD** (Reg) **ROSSITER GATFIELD** b 1907 at Eltham, Taranaki. d 21 June 1985 (78) Bur Victoria Valley, Kaitaia, Northland.			
IVAN MALCOLM THOMAS b 31 August 1915 at Auckland. (War Dead ref #9745) at Egypt, WW2. m 1942 (ref #9486)=== at Auckland City. **LAVINA JOYCE KELLY** b at (daughter of and nee	**PATRICIA AGNES THOMAS** b at		
LESLIE WALTER THOMAS b 29 June 1917 at Auckland City. d 6 February 1972 (54) Bur Wellsford RSA. m 16 Nov 1946 ===== at Auckland City. **RUBY SIMONA SIM** b 21 June 1925 (Buntie) at Auckland City. d 28 Sept 1999 (74) Cremated Waikumete. continued next page	**BARBARA ANNE THOMAS** b 14 October 1947 at Auckland City. m 6 May 1967 ====== at Auckland City. **ROY ERNEST HAMMOND** b 2 July 1942 at Balmoral, Auckland. (son of Ernest Hammond and Victoria nee Davis)	**KERRY LEIGH HAMMOND** b 21 December 1974 at Mt Albert, Auckland. d 29 December 1974 Bur Waikumete. **MEGAN HAMMOND** b 2 August 1976 at Mt Albert, Auckland. d 5 August 1976 Bur Waikumete.	

4th Generation	5th Generation	6th Generation	7th Generation
(Ruby was the daughter of Edmund Grieg Sim and Robina Philip nee Bunce) They had 4 children.	Barbara & Roy continue	**BETH HAMMOND** b 17 January 1979 at Mt Albert, Auckland. d 19 January 1979 Bur Waikumete.	
		KIM ERIN HAMMOND b 28 October 1981 (a) at Mt Albert, Auckland.	
	GRAEME MILTON THOMAS b 30 April 1949 at Auckland City. m 24 Oct 1970 ===== at Wellsford. **HEATHER MARGARET SHEARER** b 13 October 1948 at Te Puke. (daughter of Kenneth Shearer and Margaret nee Stuart)	**ROBERT LESLIE THOMAS** b 13 January 1973 at Warkworth. m 13 Sept 1997 ===== at Cambridge. **SHARON LEANNE GRINTER** b 26 December 1973 at Cambridge. (dau of Trevor Grinter and Colleen nee Harvey)	**CHELSIE LEIGH THOMAS** b 22 November 1998 at Kaitaia, Northland.
		STEPHEN GRAEME THOMAS b 20 December 1976 at Hamilton. m 7 March 1997 ===== at Waimauku. **REBECCA ISOBEL ALLEN** b 16 May 1977 at Auckland. (daughter of Ron Allen & Janice nee Pearce)	**SOPHIE ISOBEL THOMAS** b 5 August 1997 at Hastings. **DEVON RUBY THOMAS** b 23 December 1999 at Hamilton.
		RICHARD DAVID THOMAS b 13 October 1981 at Hamilton.	

JACK continued

4th Generation	5th Generation	6th Generation	7th Generation
Leslie & Ruby continue	**JOCELYN KAYE THOMAS** b 9 March 1953 at Paparoa, Northland. m 4 Jan 1975 ======= at Wellsford. **MURRAY DENIS NEAL** b 21 April 1953 at Waiuku. (son of Gordon Neal and Eunice nee Hull)	**REBECCA JAYDE NEAL** b 11 November 1982 at Bunbury, Western Australia. **ANDREW MICHAEL NEAL** b 3 December 1985 at Perth, Western Australia.	
	IAN CHRISTOPHER THOMAS b 22 March 1963 at Warkworth. 1st m 14 Feb 1988 at Morrinsville. **MARION MARY ANSLEY** b 9 October 1963 at Morrinsville. : 2nd m 2 Nov 1996 at Auckland City. **KAYE ROSEMARY OLIVER** b 13 September 1964 at Auckland City. (daughter of Trevor Oliver & Susan nee Preston-Thomas)		
JOHN CHERRINGTON EARL THOMAS b 18 July 1919 at Avondale, Auckland. d 25 January 2000 (80) Cremated at Melbourne, Australia. (continued)	**LINDA KAY THOMAS** b 29 March 1947 at Auckland City. 1st m 9 Aug 1969 ==== at Christchurch. GURKA next page	**BRENDA LEE BELLING** b 6 March 1971 at Taupo. JOEL next page	

JACK continued

4th Generation	5th Generation	6th Generation	7th Generation
John married m 22 Nov 1944====== at Auckland. **FLORENCE <u>JUNE</u>** **CAMPBELL** b 29 June 1924 at Greymouth, NZ. (daughter of Claude Arthur Campbell and Elsie nee Duff) They had 6 children. :	**GURKA SINGH** **BELLING** b 24 August 1938 at Taumarunui. NZ. (son of Nasib Kaur & Jawala Singh Belling, both of the Punjab, India : 2nd m 4 May 1979==== at Christchurch.	**JOEL GURKA BELLING** b 2 January 1974 at Taumaranui.	
:	**GUTUTALA** **HAKEAGAIKI** **KERESOMA** (Hake) b 3 January 1949 at Namukulu. Niue Island. d 17 January 1997 Drowned at Niue Island. (son of Nofoagamata & Gututala Hakeagaiki Keresoma.)	**KARL GUTUTALA** **KERESOMA** b 29 Oct 1979 (twin) at Christchurch.	
:		**CHEYNE** **HAKEAGAIKI** **KEKESOMA** b 29 Oct 1979 (twin) at Christchurch.	
:		**JUNE NOFO** **KERESOMA** b 30 September 1982 at Christchurch.	
:	**KERIN MARIA** **THOMAS** (Keri) b 18 September 1948 at Auckland City. 1st m 20 Dec 1967==== at Auckland City. **DAVID MAX** **HOOPER** b 29 March 1948 at Auckland City. (son of Francis Hugh Hooper & Katherine Elizabeth nee Jackson) :	**REBEKAH JANE** Hooper / Reid known as **ASHTON** b 7 September 1969 at Takapuna, NSC.	
June remarried to *GETHIN ALAN* *PARKINSON* *(died, no issue)*	2nd m 18 Feb 1972 === at Palmerston North.	**ADAM GORDON** **REID** b 23 June 1973 at Palmerston North.	
June remarried to *CYRIL RAYMOND* *McCALLISTER* *(died, no issue)*	**STUART GORDON** **REID** b November 1932 at Pahiatua.		

4th Generation	5th Generation	6th Generation	7th Generation
John & June continue	Stuart was the son of Gordon Robert Reid & Leta Margaret nee Hope)		
:	**JOSE THOMAS** b 14 January 1952 at Epsom, Auckland. m 21 Dec 1970 ====== at Christchurch. **WILLIAM <u>JOHN</u> NORFOLK WATKINS** b 3 April 1942 at Grenock, Scotland. (son of Kenneth Watkins and Annie Laurie nee Hoey) (Jose uses Thomas)	**JASON WATKINS** b 23 December 1972 at Papanui, Christchurch. **SARA WATKINS** (Surname changed by Deedpoll to Thomas.) b 30 March 1975 at Papanui, Christchurch. **JENNIFER ANNE WATKINS** (Jenny) b 19 November 1979 at Christchurch City. partner ============ **TIMOTHY DAVID THORNE** (Tim) b 6 February 1979 at Christchurch.	**JOSHUA CALEB TIMOTHY THORNE** b 30 January 2000 at Christchurch.
:	**NAOMI THOMAS** b 10 November 1954 at Palmerston North. m 22 Feb 1974 ====== at Christchurch. **RUSSELL JOHN FULTON** b 23 September 1949 at Dunedin. (son of Frederick Andrew Fulton and Makareta Parks nee Parata)	**JAMES FULTON** b 5 September 1975 at Linwood, ChCh. **STEFAN FULTON** b 4 April 1978 at New Brighton, ChCh. m 2 September 2000 at Wellington. **WENDY ILLAINE HAGUE-SMITH** b 29 April 1976 at Wanganui.	

JACK continued

4th Generation	5th Generation	6th Generation	7th Generation
John & June continue	Naomi & Russell cont..	**GARETH DAVID FULTON** b 2 September 1980 at New Brighton, ChCh.	
:		**DANIELLE SARAH FULTON** b 1 November 1986 at New Brighton, ChCh.	
:		**ROBBIE FREDERICK ARI FULTON** b 6 February 1990 at New Brighton, ChCh.	
:	**ELISE JUNE THOMAS** b 20 February 1957 at Palmerston North. 1st m 30 May 1975 === at Christchurch. **ALAN WILLIAM McLEOD** b 20 March 1955 at Mosgeil, Otago. (son of Harry Benjamin McLeod and Eileen Patricia nee Maitland) (Elise uses Thomas)	**SAMUEL JOHN McLEOD** b 21 December 1977 at Christchurch.	
:	:	**ROSS ALAN McLEOD** b 10 December 1980 at Christchurch. d 21 June 1996 (15) Cremated at Timaru.	
:	:	**DIANNA ROSE McLEOD** b 12 December 1982 at Christchurch.	
:	2nd m 5 Nov 1988==== at Picton. **CARL WILLIAM PARNELL** continued next page	**KATE VICTORIA PARNELL** b 25 October 1989 at Blenheim, NZ.	

4th Generation	5th Generation	6th Generation	7th Generation
John & June continue	Carl born 28 Aug 1964 at Howick, Auckland. (son of Kenneth John Parnell and Constance Irene nee Weaver)	**HANNAH ELISE PARNELL** b 16 September 1994 at Christchurch.	
:	**KATHY-ROSE THOMAS** (Kathy) b 11 March 1960 at Christchurch. m 11 Nov 1978 ====== at Christchurch. **GLEN ADRIAN HARLEY** b 21 August 1958 at Nelson. (son of Peter Brian Harley and Florence <u>Janine</u> nee Levitt) (Kathy uses Thomas)	**RHYS HARLEY** b 23 June 1979 at Christchurch. d 8 October 1979 Crem Christchurch. **ELLIOTT MAURICE HARLEY** b 21 December 1982 at Christchruch. **THOMAS BAILEY HARLEY** b 24 May 1985 at Christchurch. **JUDE JAMES HARLEY** b 17 June 1987 at Christchurch.	
2nd m 21 Dec 1970 at Christchurch City===== **EILEEN ELIZABETH WILLS** b 12 November 1944 at Norfleet, Kent, England. (daughter of Henry Richard Joseph Wills and Evelyn Joyce nee Stevens)	**MELISSA EILEEN THOMAS** b 13 January 1971 at Christchurch. m 13 March 1993 ==== at Melbourne, Australia. **JOHN SIMENCIC** b 10 April 1970 at Melbourne, Australia. (son of Frank Milan Simencic and Paula nee Gelob, from Slovenia.)	**DAKOTA ALYSSA DOVE SIMENCIC** b 29 July 2001 at Melbourne, Australia.	

JACK continued

4th Generation	5th Generation	6th Generation	7th Generation
VIOLET ETHEL THOMAS b 1 July 1921 at Auckland City. m 15 July 1940====== at Auckland City. **GEORGE HENRY WRIGHT** b 22 November 1917 at Whangarei. (son of George Robert Wright and Maria Evelyn nee Russek)	**EVELYN JOY WRIGHT** b 2 April 1941 at Auckland City. 1st m 9 July 1960===== at Papakura, Aauckland. **MALCOLM JAMES WAUGH** b 22 November 1940 at Whakatane. (son of Malcolm Angus Waugh and Lillian May nee Daken)	**WENDY LORRAINE WAUGH** b 19 December 1960 at Auckland City. m 1 Feb 1992 ====== at Auckland City. **DEAN ALEXANDER CLARK** b 27 December 1961 at Auckland City.	**ALICIA LOUISE CLARK** b 12 December 1995 at Greenlane, Auckland. **JACOB ALEXANDER CLARK** b 23 August 1999 at North Shore City.
(grandson of John Wright 1853-1926, m 1882 to Jessie nee Thomson 1862-1972)	:	**MICHAEL BRUCE WAUGH** b 20 March 1962 at Auckland City.	
(great grandson of George Wright 1811-- 1901, m 1842 Hobart, Australia to Sarah nee Green 1817-1865)	: : : :	1st m 4 Sept 1982 at Tamaki, Auckland. **RAEWYN ANN-MARIE POULSON** b 5 February 1964 at Taihape.	
Violet and George had 5 children.	: : : : : : : : : : : : : :	: Michael changed name by Deed Poll 1999 to **MICHELLE ANNE MARIE PAINTER** Commitment ceremony held 6 February 1999 **ELIZABETH SANDRA PAINTER** b 13 December 1965 at Auckland City.	
	: : : : : :	**FIONA LEE WAUGH** b 13 September 1972 at Papakura, Auckland. m 2 Nov 1996====== at Manurewa, Auckland. JEFFUREY next page	**KATHLEEN EVELYN PULLEN-BURRY** b 31 January 1999 at Papakura, Auckland.

4th Generation	5th Generation	6th Generation	7th Generation
Violet & George cont..	Joy continued 2nd m 30 October 1981 at Papakura, Auckland. **ERIC RAMSBOTTOM** b 27 September 1949 at Sheffield, England. (son of Frederick Ramsbottom and Mabel nee Gregory)	Fiona married **JEFFUREY WARREN PULLEN-BURRY** b 9 July 1967 at Green Lane, Auckland.	**DANIEL JEFFUREY PULLEN-BURRY** b October 2001 at Papakura, Auckland. **DARREN EDWARD PETER MURRAY** b 23 May 1993 at Middlemore, Auckland.

ROBERT JOHN WRIGHT
b 26 May 1944 (Joe)
at Auckland City.
m 4 February 1978
at Rotorua.
ROBYN PHYLLIS BAKER
b 30 November 1949
at Hamilton.
Daughter of Seager Bertram Baker
(died 14 Feb 2001 buried at Rotorua)
and Evelyn Mary nee Scott.

5th Generation	6th Generation	7th Generation
PAMELA MAY WRIGHT b 21 July 1947 at Auckland City. m 10 May 1969===== at Papakura, Auckland. **ALLAN JOHN FIELDING** b 15 October 1946 at Papakura, Auckland. (son of Robert Maxwell Fielding and Thelma Hazel nee Fogden)	**LINDA ANN FIELDING** b 6 August 1970 at Papakura, Auckland. m 8 Feb 1997 ====== at Waiuku, Auckland. **GLEN FREDERICK HATTON** b 18 August 1969 at Waiuku, Auckland. **BRIAN JOHN FIELDING** b 23 October 1971 at Papakura, Auckland. continued next page	**JOSEPH JOHN HATTON** b 7 July 1991 at Pukekohe, Auckland. **RHYS CLAY HATTON** b 31 January 1998 at Pukekohe, Auckland.

continued next page

JACK continued

4th Generation	5th Generation	6th Generation	7th Generation
Violet & George cont...	Pamela & Allan continue	Brian married m 13 April 1994 at Capital Hill, Denver, Colorado, USA. **ERICA VAUGHN** b 13 February 1970 at Grand Junction, Colorado, USA.	
	GLENYS ANN WRIGHT b 9 November 1950 at Auckland City. m 25 March 1978 ==== at Papakura, Auckland. **ROBERT WILLIAM ALLEN** b 4 September 1951 at Wanganui. (son of Alister Robert Allen and Patricia May nee Price)	**ANTON PHILIP ALLEN** b 7 June 1980 at Napier. **BADEN JAMES ALLEN** b 21 December 1981 at Papakura, Auckland.	
	FAY KATHRYN WRIGHT b 15 February 1952 at Auckland City. m 1 Dec 1979======= at Windsor, NSW, Australia. **KEIRAN REX COULTER** b 23 August 1953 at Bowraville, NSW. (son of William Rex Coulter and Mary Margaret nee Ahern)	**MICHAEL REX COULTER** b 8 July 1982 at Perth, Australia. **KRISTY MARIE COULTER** b 19 January 1984 at Perth, Australia.	

CHAPTER EIGHT

7th Generation (3rd NZ)

W. H. (HARRY) THOMAS

(1877-1958)

1877... BIRTH - HASTINGS:

On 13 August 1877, William and Eliza Thomas' second son and fourth child was born at Hastings. Eliza registered him as William Henry Thomas but he was known as Harry. His father's occupation was 'carpenter'.

1880... AUCKLAND:

Before his 3rd birthday, and before sister Annie was born in August 1880, Harry travelled with his family to live in Waterview, Auckland.

1882... ASHBURTON:

Soon after 28 May 1882, Harry was on the move again. His parents took the family to Ashburton in the South Island. It is possible that he may have celebrated his 5th birthday enroute.

1882... SCHOOL: <u>Ashburton.</u>

Harry was five in 1882 but was not enrolled at Ashburton Borough School until he was nearly 9½, on 24 January 1887. His father told them Harry had been in 'Infant School'. We have not found this recorded yet.

> Harry left this school on 7 September 1887 (after 7 ½ months attendance) and travelled to live at Ngawapurua in the North Island with his parents and siblings. He was now 10 years old.

<u>Woodville.</u>

Harry's brother Jack was enrolled by his father at the Woodville School on 30 January 1888, and we think Harry was as well. He did attend this school but, apart from passing Standard 2 exams in 1888, we do not know when Harry's education was considered complete.

1889 to 1902: There is nothing factual remembered about Harry's life between the ages 11 to 28. His family believe he was a 'bushman' during his younger years. Harry spent a lot of his adult years doing carpentry work, so he could have spent some time with his father learning this trade. (M+TC)

> Harry's parents and younger siblings moved to a farm in New Lynn, Auckland, late in 1898 when Harry was aged 21.

**1902... OTAKI
Electoral Roll.**
Along with brother Jack
and wife Alice was...
*William H. THOMAS,
a sawmill hand in the
Horowhenua district.*
It is possible these two
brothers worked together
for some years doing a
combination of carpentry,
bush work, and farm
labouring in the area.

Harry's brother Jack
married at **Levin** in 1899
and in 1905 so did Harry.

SALVATION ARMY:
The Close family were
also members of the
Salvation Army and it was
here Harry probably met
Mary. They continued
their membership after
they married, and Harry
played the euphonium.

HARRY wearing Salvation Army Uniform
(RH)

1903-8: Harry's father and brothers built a brickworks in New Lynn and operated it from 1903 to 1908. He was one of those who made the bricks.

1905... MARRIAGE:
Harry aged 27, married MARY ELIZABETH CLOSE aged 22, in Levin on 26 July 1905 at the Salvation Army Barracks. He gave his occupation as 'brickmaker' and his usual address as New Lynn, Auckland. Witnesses were William John Close and Laura Gertrude Close... Mary's siblings.

After the wedding Harry and Mary returned to Rimu Street, to live next door (but across the gully), to his parent's home on the New Lynn farm.

The CLOSE family.

Mary Elizabeth Close was born 18 December 1882 in O'Kains Bay, Akaroa near Christchurch. She was the first child of William Close (farmer) and his wife Elizabeth nee Harrison, who had married in Duvanchelle, Banks Peninsular on 22 December 1881.

William and Elizabeth had six children. Mary Elizabeth b1882 registered at Akaroa, William (Will) John b1885 at Woodville, Albert Arthur (Tim) b1888 at Woodville, Laura Gertrude b1889 at Pahiatua, Robert Henry (Rob) b1891 and Emily born 21 January 1893. Will and Laura were witnesses at sister Mary's wedding.

School records for Pahiatua show Mary attending in 1893 and 1896, Will 1893 to 1899 and advises... *"lives some distance away and has just come to school".* Albert 1896 to 1899, Laura 1897 and 1898 and Robert 1899. Finally, the family moved to Levin... (possibly via Mangarama and Sawyers Bay.) Father William enrolled Albert, Laura, Robert and Emily at Levin School on 17 September 1900.

CHILDREN:

Harry and Mary had four children....Athol b1906, Eileen b1911, Gilbert b1916 and Melva b1919.   Their first grandchild was Barry born in 1935.

A full list of Harry and Mary's descendants starts on page 226.

1913-14... Land Sales: The 30 October 1909 'Deed of Sale' from William Thomas to his three sons Jack, Harry and Albert, of 52 acres has a plan showing 'private roads' and suggested division of this land into 7 large parts. (pages 93+94) In 1912 the sons decided to subdivide and sell up this land and the years 1913 and 1914 were very active times. There were many land sales between the brothers and to new owners.

Some pieces sold as large blocks whereas others were subdivided and later re-subdivided. There were a great number of land transactions.

The Rimu Street house, New Lynn. (GC)

On 25 May 1918 Harry became sole owner of 8 acres, (Vol 277/248) helped by a loan and mortgage held by his father-in-law William Close, and which was discharged on 26 April 1921. This property title details much activity of subdivision and sale over the next 10 years.

MASSEY: 6 October 1919. (Vol 208/141) After most of their land at New Lynn was sold, Harry purchased Lot 30 of 77 acres of farmland at Massey, and worked it from New Lynn. He never lived on this land, which adjoined farm land owned by brother Jack. (GW+AWT)

Harry sold this Massey farm land in two pieces, but first, on 15 December 1930 he purchased 18 acres of the adjoining land from brother Jack, bringing his total farm to 95 acres. Jack's daughter Rene had won £ 750 in a Tats sweep-stake and bought 40 acres of Harry's farm in April 1931. It is thought that Harry exchanged the balance for their Devonport home. (GW)

OCCUPATION: Sometime after the brick-works activity ground to a halt, and Harry had tired of farming at Massey, he placed a share-milker on the farm and found work at Parker & Lamb's timber mill in Freeman's Bay, Auckland. He worked here for a number of years. Their Kauri logs were floated down from Great Barrier Island and from Northland, guided by tug boats. Most of the Kauri, Rimu and Kahikatea was exported to Britain. (AWT+TC)

When the timber mills closed, Harry and Jack worked at Whakatane, and, helped to build the paper mill. (AWT)

Harry then found work as a carpenter for the New Zealand Navy, in Devonport on Auckland's North Shore. (TC)

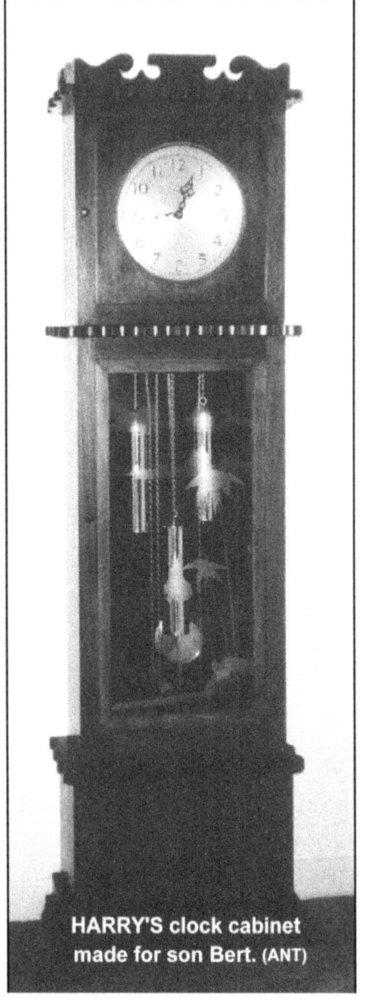

WOOD: Throughout his life Harry enjoyed working with wood. He did carpentry and cabinet making as a hobby. His four children each received a 'grandfather' clock for which Harry made the cabinets. This activity was also enjoyed by his brothers Jack and Arthur.

Harry also made wooden standards for lamp shades, and his granddaughter Jan Hoverd has a bedroom suite he made from mottled Kauri comprising double bed, dressing table, commode and sideboard.

Delcie Twizell has a small inlaid wooden trinket bowl with lid which was made by Harry, and numerous other inlaid examples exist within the family. Grandson Gary recalls seeing a ship-in-a-bottle that Harry had made.

1954 ... 3 GENERATIONS.   Mary and Harry, with grandson Gary and daughter Melva.   (ANT)

MARY: Mary was very good with her hands and was always busy knitting, needle-working or crocheting items for her family. (MC)

HOUSE: All their children were born in New Lynn, and after selling this home about 1929, they moved to High Street in Devonport. A home with a turret on top, which Harry soon removed. Later, about 1950, they moved for the last time, to live at 7 St Leonards Road, Devonport, Auckland. (GC)

1958... HARRY DIED: Harry passed away on 21 December 1958, aged 81, and was buried at Glenfield Cemetery, North Shore City.

Harry's Will was signed 2 July 1951, and his trustees were his sons Athol and Gilbert, and E.W. Henderson, a solicitor.

He left an estate of under £ 5,000 and asked for his wife Mary... *'.....to receive all his furniture, plate, plated goods, glass, china, books, pictures, prints, statutory musical instruments and all other personal and domestic use or ornament of which I might die possessed'...*

.... 'Subject to the above the whole of the estate into trust for Mary's free use and occupation and enjoyment, providing she maintains it.' (Nat Arch)

Later, Athol received the house and land, and the balance of the estate was divided equally between Harry and Mary's children.

1971... MARY DIED: Mary died 29 July 1971, aged 88, having lived her final days in hospital. Before this, she had been cared for by daughter Melva and Trevor Cooke in their home for about 6 months. (MC)

No Will has been found for Mary, but Harry's Will seems to cover this area as well. There is no evidence that Mary objected to Harry's wishes for the disposal of their estate after her death.

Mary was buried at Glenfield with Harry in plot #1011, and their headstone carries their names and dates and the words *"AT REST"*.

--oo0Ooo--

We are grateful to Harry's son Athol for confirming our cover photo as that of his grandfather William Thomas, also to Jack's granddaughter Ivy and her son Ray Haslam, for keeping this photo safe for us.

W. H. (HARRY) THOMAS FAMILY TREE:

3rd Generation
WILLIAM HENRY THOMAS....... married................ **MARY ELIZABETH CLOSE**

b 13 August 1877 (Harry)	26 July 1905	b 18 December 1882
at Hastings, NZ.	at Levin, NZ.	at Akaroa, Canterbury, NZ.
d 21 December 1958 (81)		d 29 July 1971 (88)
Bur Glenfield, North Shore City.		Bur Glenfield, North Shore City.

Mary was the daughter of William CLOSE and Elizabeth nee HARRISON.

Harry and Mary had four children named Athol, Eileen, Gilbert and Melva.

4th Generation	5th Generation	6th Generation	7th Generation
ATHOL WILFRED THOMAS b 7 December 1906 at New Lynn, Auckland. d 2 May 1996 (89) Cremated Albany, NSC. Urn of ashes placed in Clarkes family plot at Waikumete Cemetery. m 15 Nov 1933 ===== at Avondale, Auckland. **CLARA BEATRICE CLARKE** b 9 October 1909 at Dublin, Ireland. d 6 April 1953 (43) Bur Waikumete, A. (daughter of Henry Clarke and Kate Christina nee Willis) They had two children.	**BARRY LINDSAY THOMAS** b 3 December 1935 at Mt Albert, Auckland. m 26 Feb 1969 ====== at Murrumbeena, Melbourne, Australia. **DEANNA MAY SAULTRY** b 30 May 1941 at East Melbourne, Australia. (daughter of William Saultry and Thelma Irene nee Walters)	**MARK BARRY THOMAS** (a) b 2 January 1974 at Melbourne, Australia. **FIONA CATHERINE THOMAS** (a) b 1 August 1975 at Melbourne, Australia.	
	ELAINE JEAN THOMAS b 26 October 1940 at Avondale, Auckland. m 27 Oct 1973 ====== at Devonport, NSC. **JAMES RONALD TROUNSON** (Jim) b 29 May 1939 at Matamata. (son of Ronald Harris Trounson and Ruby Frances nee Watson)	**RONALD HARRIS TROUNSON** (Ronnie) b 7 May 1976 at Takapuna, NSC.	

EILEEN next page　　PATRICIA next page

HARRY continued

4th Generation	5th Generation	6th Generation	7th Generation
EILEEN RONA THOMAS b 26 March 1911 at Mt Albert, Auckland. m 1938 ========== at Devonport. NSC. **ERNEST COLIN LIGHT** b 1913 at Devonport, NSC. d 26 April 1970 (57) Cremated Waikumete, Auckland. (son of Leonard Douglas Light and nee They had 4 children.	**PATRICIA MARY LIGHT** b June 1939 at Auckland City. d 2 July 1939 (2 weeks) Bur Waikumete, Auckland.		
	LEONARD (Len) **DOUGLAS LIGHT** b 6 November 1940 at Auckland City. 1st m 18 May 1966==== at Auckland City. **JUDITH CLARE LIDDLE** b (ref 159) 1946 at Mt Eden, Auckland. d 10 December 1970 Cremated NSC. (daughter of Noma and Harry Liddle) : : : : : : : : : : : : : : : : :	Triplets **PENELOPE NOMA LIGHT** (triplet) b 10 December 1970 at Auckland City.	
		AMELIA JANICE LIGHT (triplet) b 10 December 1970 at Auckland City. m 28 January 1995==== at Devonport, NSC. **DONALD FREDRIK MAWHINNEY** b 6 January 1970 at Auckland City.	**BEN ROBERT MAWHINNEY** b 6 March 2000 at Auckland City.
		RACHEL (triplet) **PHILLIPA LIGHT** b 10 December 1970 at Auckland City. m 19 Dec 1998 ====== at Ponsonby, Auckland. **JOHN JAMES GILLESPIE** b 12 May 1963 at Auckland City.	**PATRICK MICHAEL GILLESPIE** b 28 November 1999 at Takapuna, NSC. **REBEKAH JUDITH GILLESPIE** b 30 April 2001 at Auckland City.
	KATHY next page	ARTHUR next page	

4th Generation	5th Generation	6th Generation	7th Generation
Eileen & Ernest continued	Len remarried… 2nd m 15 May 1980 == at Devonport, NSC. **KATHLEEN MARY GRAHAM** (Kathy) b 28 July 1952 at Christchurch. (daughter of Arthur Lorimar Graham and Margaret Ada nee Radford)	**ARTHUR LEONARD LIGHT** b 23 November 1983 at Takapuna, NSC. **PETER COLIN LIGHT** b 24 January 1984 at Takapuna, NSC. **RICHARD JOHN-PAUL LIGHT** b 13 July 1985 at Ashburton. **JOHN MAX LIGHT** b 24 July 1990 at Takapuna, NSC. **DAVID THOMAS LIGHT** b 13 November 1991 at Takapuna, NSC.	
	COLIN STANLEY LIGHT b 20 February 1943 at Auckland City. m 12 Feb 1972 ====== at Avondale, Auckland. **FRANCES ANN McCARTHY** b 27 November 1945 at Auckland City. (daughter of Francis Augustine McCarthy and Eileen Maud nee Seawright)	**MARITA ANNE LIGHT** b 18 March 1973 at Devonport, NSC. m 11 July 1998 at Taupo. **GARRY MARTIN STOUT** b 28 May 1972 at Takapuna, NSC. BRUCE next page	

228

4th Generation	5th Generation	6th Generation	7th Generation
Eileen & Ernest continued	Colin & Frances continued	**BRUCE FRANCIS LIGHT** b 19 November 1975 at Twizel, Canterbury.	
		SIMON ERNEST LIGHT b 19 April 1977 at Taupo.	
		ANTHONY COLIN LIGHT b 15 May 1980 at Tauranga.	
		GERARD JAMES LIGHT b 25 April 1982 at Tauranga.	
		MARK LEONARD LIGHT b 26 January 1984 at Tauranga.	
	JANICE MELVA LIGHT (Jan) b 27 November 1946 at Auckland City. m 1971== at Devonport, NSC. **LAWRENCE** (Laurie) **WILLIAM ERNEST HOVERD** b 23 April 1945 at Auckland City. (son of Arthur Duxbury Hoverd & Margaret Louise nee Roberts)	**AARON ARTHUR HOVERD** b 22 January 1975 at Hamilton.	
		JOY LOUISE HOVERD b 29 December 1976 at Tokoroa.	

4th Generation	5th Generation	6th Generation	7th Generation
GILBERT HENRY THOMAS (Bert) b 9 December 1916 at New Lynn, Auckland. d 26 July 1999 (83) Cremated, NSC. m 15 Aug 1942 ===== at Devonport, NSC. **AURIEL NINA WILSON** b 31 December 1917 at Christchurch. (daughter of William Wilson and Mary nee Morrison)	**MURRAY THOMAS** b 25 November 1946 at Castor Bay, NSC. m 7 April 1969 ====== at Deverport, NSC. **JULIA MARGARET ZUCCANI** b at (daughter of Zuccani and nee	**FIONA MARY THOMAS** b 17 October 1969 at Devonport, NSC.	
		COLLETTE JANE THOMAS b 23 September 1970 at Devonport, NSC.	
		DESMOND MARK THOMAS b 27 May 1974 at Devonport, NSC.	
	SHELLEY THOMAS b 24 July 1950 at Devonport, NSC. m 14 March 1969 ==== at Devonport, NSC. **JAMES MICHAEL STRONGMAN** b 31 July 1950 at Auckland City. (son of James Havelock Strongman and Shirley Delores nee Holden)	**TRACEY NICOLA STRONGMAN** b 1 August 1969 at Takapuna, NSC.	
MELVA JEAN THOMAS b 8 January 1919 at New Lynn, Auckland. m 18 June 1949 ===== at Auckland City. **TREVOR TORRINGTON MELVILLE COOKE** b 26 October 1918 at Feilding.	**GARY NORMAN COOKE** b 29 July 1953 at Devonport, NSC. m 18 March 1978 ==== at Devonport, NSC. **SUSANNE HELEN THOMS** b 3 August 1957 at Nelson. continued next page	**LEANNE HELEN COOKE** b 2 November 1982 at North Shore City.	
		MICHELLE DIANNE COOKE b 22 February 1986 at North Shore City.	

HARRY continued

4th Generation	5th Generation	6th Generation	7th Generation
Trevor T M Cooke was son of Charles Beval Melville and Vida Grace nee Simmons	Susanne was daughter of Bruce Thomas and Valmai nee Andrews)		
	LINDA MARY COOKE b 28 September 1956 at Devonport, NSC. m 2 June 1979 ====== at Belmont, NSC. **EDWIN JOHN MITCHELL** b 9 February 1953 at Newmarket, England. (son of William Charles Mitchell and Greta Edith nee Golden)	**CARL BRANDON MITCHELL** b 11 December 1979 at Takapuna, NSC. **STACEY BELINDA MITCHELL** b 5 August 1984 at Takapuna, NSC.	

CHAPTER NINE

7th Generation (3rd NZ)

MARY ANN (ANNIE) THOMAS

(1880-1967)

1880... BIRTH - AUCKLAND:
William and Eliza Thomas' fifth child was born 13 August 1880 at Waterview, Auckland. Registered as Mary Ann she was known as 'Annie'. Mary Ann is two words, and not hyphenated on her birth and marriage certificates.

1882... ASHBURTON: At the age of two years, Annie travelled with her family to live at Ashburton in the South Island.

1885... SCHOOL: **Ashburton.**
Four days after her fifth birthday on 17 August 1885, Annie's father enrolled her at the Ashburton Borough School, and she would have travelled there each day with her brothers Jack and Harry.

Annie left this school on 19 August 1887 *"to go to North Island"*. Soon after 7 September 1887 aged 7, Annie and her family travelled to the North Island and settled at Ngawapurua near Woodville.

Woodville.
Annie's brother Jack was enrolled by their father at the Woodville School on 30 January 1888, and we assume she was too. Her record just says *"Came from South Island."* We also assume she left the Woodville School around 1891 aged 11, when her brothers transferred to the Mangatainoka School. Did she go to this school too, or was her education finished at age 11 ?

1891 to 1898. There is nothing remembered of Annie's life between these years when aged 11 to 18. She must have worked in the district though, for she met, and agreed to marry Len Gardner of nearby Nikau. She gave her occupation on her marriage certificate as *"Domestic of Makomako"*.

1898... Annie's parents and her younger siblings shifted from Ngawapurua to live at New Lynn in Auckland late in 1898 when Annie was 18. At this time, she may have elected not to go to Auckland, but to live at Makomako and help her sister Eliza at 'Rosefarm'.

Also living at Nikau, 8 km away, was Annie's eldest sister Lizzie. Between these two Sowry farms was Gardner Road, and Andrew Gardner's farm where his son Len lived and worked. One can easily imagine these three families moving in similar circles, attending the same Church and shops, and a friendship growing between Annie and Len.

1904... MARRIAGE:

On 27 July 1904, Annie aged 23 married LEONARD ALFRED GARDNER, (Len) a 28 year old farmer, at his father's residence at Nikau. Samuel Barnett of the Primitive Methodist Church came out from Woodville to perform the service, and Louis and Harriett Gardner were the official witnesses. Annie's father was described as a 'carpenter'.

The GARDNER family.

Len Gardner was born at Foxhill near Nelson in the South Island on 11 August 1875, to farmer Andrew Gardner and his wife Keziah nee Hughes. Len had a brother Hal (was Gardner & Yeoman sawmillers of Pahiatua) and a sister who became Mrs Griffiths.

Andrew Gardner moved from Pahiatua to farm at Nikau about 1890. He was a deeply religious man and arranged for church services to be held in his house, with a Methodist minister coming out from Woodville once a month. From 1896 services were held in the school building every Sunday. (MC)

Andrew Gardner's dairy farm was about 100 acres. He employed Fred and Minnie Clark from 1926 to 1938 to milk his cows, daughter Grace advises.

OCCUPATION: After they married, Len and Annie lived and worked on his father's farm at Wakarara, some miles inland from Waipawa. (ND)
Ngara Battersby remembers Len and Annie lived at Woodville on the main Gorge Road for a while, and had a sawmill operating at the top of Saddle Hill, which felled and cut timber from her father's (Huia Houlbroooke) and two other nearby farms. The saw mills were always being moved as each lot of trees were removed.
When Len signed his Will, he gave his occupation as 'Benchman'. This referred to the specialised activity of operating the saw which turned trees into timber. (ND) Over the years we believe Len found work at two Gardner sawmilling businesses, brother Hal's mill at Pahiatua, and Charles Gardner, D. Brown and J. Tuck's mill at Eketahuna.

CHILDREN: Annie and Len Gardener had two children...
Dorothy May born 27 October 1908 at Pahiatua...
Phyllis Grace born 19 August 1912 at Eketahuna.
Grandchildren Ngaire and Myrle called Annie "My-My". (As little Ngaire couldn't get her tongue around 'Grandma'.) Len was known as 'Granddad'.

ANNIE and LEN GARDNER

PALMERSTON NORTH:

1930... For a while Annie and Len had a farm on the corner of Troup and Main Road, Woodville. Annie took care of the farm, milking ten or so cows by hand and tending a few sheep, while Len was away working at a sawmill.
Aged in their 50's, Annie and Len moved from Woodville to live at 56 Limbrick Street, Palmerston North, and from there Len worked at the Wakarara Sawmill, and was able to travel home only once a month. They lived there in retirement for the rest of their lives. (ND)

1933... Daughter Dorothy married Len Baker at Palmerston North.
1935... Len, aged 60 signed his Will 15 June at Palmerston North.
1935... First grandchild Ngaire, born 18 September at Palmerston North.
1938... Daughter Phyllis married Bob Waters at Palmerston North.

MEMORIES...
from Annie's grandchildren:

'My-My' would always have a full lolly jar, and when we visited her we loved to listen to stories about her days as a young girl.

Myrle always looked forward to Annie's brothers and sisters coming to stay with them, as 'they were such fun to be with'.

Ngaire recalls watching Annie boil up ingredients in the copper to make soap, and she used to help her cut up newspaper for toilet use.

Annie and Len always had a 10 gallon jar of ginger-beer at hand.

Annie was a very private person and lived for her family.

Every Sunday she lunched at daughter Dorothy's home, especially after Len died.

ANNIE GARDNER nee Thomas

Len loved to go for long walks, and spent a lot of time on his vegetable garden and with his fruit trees in Palmerston North.

Both Len and Annie could drive a car, and Len used to forward rock the car to make it go faster up a hill, to his granddaughter's delight.

Annie planted "Black-eyed Susie" flowers (orange with black centres) all the way down the centre of their driveway.

1948... LEN DIED:

Len passed away on 4 September 1948 aged 73 at the Palmerston North Hospital. His residential address was given as 56 Limbrick St, Palmerston North. He was buried at Kelvin Grove Cemetery, Palmerston North.

<u>Len's Will</u>. He left an estate of £ 1727.89 to his wife Annie, and his two trustees were Annie and his son-in-law Leonard James Baker, a factory hand of Palmerston North.

3 GENERATION PHOTO: Dorothy, Ngaire and Annie in 1955

1967... ANNIE DIED:

On 6 June 1967, at the age of 87, Annie died and was buried alongside Len at Kelvin Grove Cemetery, Block 13, Plots 44 and 46. Her death notice advises her final residence as 56 Limbrick Street, and that she was a member of the Fitzroy Street Gospel Chapel.

Annie's Will. Annie signed her Will soon after Len's death, and her estate was divided equally between her two daughters Dorothy and Phyllis. Her two son-in-laws were nominated as her trustees, but R. C. Waters died before her, and L. J. Baker became her sole trustee.

HEIRLOOMS... Granddaughter Ngaire has three items she treasures.........
A wine-coloured glass cup she received for her first birthday which is engraved *"From Gandma 1936"*.
Salt and pepper ducks, that were always on Annie's table.
One rose-coloured glass mug with a hand painted scene with a child, a souvenir Annie received on attending the *"Auckland Exhibition in 1899"*.

--oo0Ooo--

ANDREW GARDNER and wife KEZIAH nee HUGHES (ND)
On the back of this photo is written... (1886.   February 1-1893)
We have no idea what these dated imply.)

237

MARY-ANN (ANNIE) THOMAS FAMILY TREE:

3rd Generation

MARY-ANN THOMAS………… married…………..…... **LEONARD ALFRED GARDNER**

b 13 August 1880   27 July 1904   b 11 August 1875 (Len)

at Waterview, Auckland.   at Nikau, NZ.   at Foxhill, near Nelson.

d 6 June 1967   (87)   d 4 September 1948 (73)

Bur Kelvin Grove, Palmerston North.   Bur Kelvin Grove, Palmerston North.

Len was the son of ANDREW GARDNER and KEZIAH nee HUGHES

Annie and Len had two children they named Dorothy and Phyllis.

4th Generation	5th Generation	6th Generation	7th Generation
DOROTHY MAY GARDNER b 27 October 1908 at Pahiatua. d 7 January 1992 (83) Bur Palmerston North. m 27 Dec 1933 ===== at Palmerston North. **LEONARD JAMES BAKER** (Len) b 20 November 1901 at Ongaonga, Hawkes Bay. (son of John James Baker and Kate nee Sebley)	**NGAIRE JOY BAKER** b 18 September 1935 at Palmerston North. m 5 March 1955 ===== at Palmerston North. **WILLIAM HILTON MURRAY DITTMER** b 18 October 1933 at Otaki. (son of Frederick William Dittmer and Olive Minnie nee Hall)	**BARRY LEONARD WILLIAM DITTMER** b 5 March 1957 at Otaki. m 1 October 1977 ==== at Levin. **ELIZABETH RUTH BURTON** b 20 December 1958 at Wellington.	**KEREN ELIZABETH DITTMER** b 12 September 1978 at Wellington. m 16 December 2000 at Palmerston North. **JONATHAN CRAIG MARSHALL** b 16 August 1976 at Napier. **MICHAEL BARRY DITTMER** b 16 May 1980 at Auckland.
		KEVIN MURRAY DITTMER b 6 May 1960 at Otaki. m 22 January 1982 ==== at Paraparaumu. **JENNIFER ANGELA BISS** b 3 September 1959 at Wellington.	**JONATHAN MURRAY DITTMER** b 23 July 1984 at Wellington. **AMBER-JAY FLORA DITTMER** b 17 November 1985 at Napier.

GRANT next page

4th Generation	5th Generation	6th Generation	7th Generation
Dorothy & Len cont..	Ngaire & Murray cont..	**GRANT HILTON DITTMER** b 10 October 1963 at Otaki.	
		LYNETTE JOY DITTMER b 21 March 1966 at Otaki. m 16 May 1992 at ==== Groomsbridge, England. **STUART NORMAN LENNOX** b 12 June 1964 at Masterton.	**OLIVIA MARIE LENNOX** b 25 May 1996 at Hamilton. **JAMES STUART LENNOX** b 8 July 1999 at Hamilton.
	MYRLE MARY BAKER b 23 April 1940 at Palmerston North. m 4 Feb 1961 ====== at Palmerston North. **RODERICK (Rod) CAMPBELL WATT** b 23 December 1940 at Armadale, Island of Skye, Scotland. (Rod was the son of Robert Kirk Watt and Mary Anne nee Bell)	**PETER ROBERT JAMES WATT** b 11 March 1963 at Palmerston North. m 16 Dec 1983 ====== at Hastings. **BRONWYN ANN WHITFIELD** b 17 April 1964 at Hastings.	**JOSHUA ROBERT JAMES WATT** b 23 October 1985 at Hastings. d 8 January 1999 Bur Havelock North. **COREY DYLAN WATT** b 27 February 1988 at Hastings. d 8 January 1999 Bur Havelock North. **JADE ALANA WATT** b 9 May 1990 at Hastings. **TYLER CONNOR WATT** b 5 September 1993 at Hastings.

4th Generation	5th Generation	6th Generation	7th Generation
Dorothy & Len contin..	Myrle & Rod continue	**KAREN MYRLE WATT** b 13 November 1965 at Palmerston North. m 16 Nov 1985 ===== at Palmerston North. **MAXWELL JOHN HOUGHTON** (Max) b 18 August 1958 at Palmerston North.	**VICTORIA MYRLE HOUGHTON** b 20 July 1987 at Palmerston North. **JESSICA ELIZABETH HOUGHTON** b 10 March 1990 at Palmerston North. **BREANNA LEANNE HOUGHTON** b 6 December 1993 at Palmerston North.
PHYLLIS GRACE GARDNER b 19 August 1912 at Eketahuna. d 13 March 2001 (88) Bur Palmerston North. m 10 January 1938 at Palmerston North. **ROBERT CHARLES WATERS** (Bob) b 5 August 1892 at Palmerston North. d 18 April 1966 (73) Bur Palmerston North.			

CHAPTER TEN

7th Generation (3rd NZ)

ARTHUR GORDON THOMAS

(1882-1955)

1882... BIRTH - ASHBURTON:

Arthur Gordon Thomas was born on 29 December 1882 in Ashburton, New Zealand, the sixth child of William (carpenter) and Eliza Thomas.
We believe he received the 'Gordon' in memory of his great grandmother Isabel nee Gordon who brought his mother Eliza to New Zealand.

1888... SCHOOL: Woodville.

Arthur's family shifted to the North Island settlement of Ngawapurua, near Woodville late in 1877 when he was almost 5. There is an Arthur Thomas enrolled at this school 14 October 1889 but no other details have survived.

Mangatainoka.

1893... The Mangatainoka School Roll lists Arthur from 1893 to 1898, from age 10 to 15. Results of the 1893 exams... only comment *"been away from school"*. 1895 exams... he did not pass reading and spelling and was in the same class as brother Albert. 1896 exams... Arthur passed reading and arithmetic. 1897 exams... now 15, Arthur passed Standard 2 exams, had attended only 120 half days and it is noted he... *"did not learn his poetry"*.

1898... AUCKLAND:

Arthur's father again moved his family, this time to Auckland, where he purchased a large block of land and initially became a farmer. Now at the age of 16, Arthur worked for his father on this 88 acre property in New Lynn. He learnt farming skills and also took up carpentry like his father. He must have been involved in his father's brick-works from 1903 to 1908 and was probably doing some carpentry work near by.

After the brick-works closed Arthur is thought to have been employed more as a carpenter. He was aged 27, when in 1909 his father sold part of his farm to his brothers Jack, Harry and Albert. This was a year before Arthur married and he was probably doing carpentry work near New Plymouth.

Charles Wilmshurst's farm was situated near Stratford and the Kopokanui Cemetery. As a young man Arthur found employment on this farm and, while here, met his bride-to-be... Elsie. (FT+JG)

1910... MARRIAGE:
Arthur (27) was married to **ELSIE ROSE WILMSHURST** (21) on 29 September, by Rev. C. C. Harrison at the Kahouri Bridge Methodist Church near Stratford, Taranaki. (Elsie's father had donated the land to the Church.)
Arthur advised he was a 'carpenter' usually residing in Auckland.

The bridesmaids were Elsie's sister Ella and Arthur's sister Edie Thomas. Albert Thomas and Herbert Lidyard attended the groom. Witnesses who signed their marriage certificate were Arthur's brother, Albert Peter Thomas of Wanganui - Captain, Elsie's sister Ella Mildred Wilmshurst of Kahouri Bridge, and her father Charles Wilmshurst a 'farmer' of Kahouri.

A newspaper report of the occasion mentions... *"The Church decorations were tastefully placed, and a number of friends opened the service by singing the wedding hymn. The bride was dressed in cream voile, prettily tucked with cream lace insertion, and bore the usual long veil, wreath and bouquet."* When the day was complete Arthur and Elsie *"left by mail train for their future home in Auckland, via New Plymouth."*

Elsie was a daughter of Charles Wilmshurst and Caroline (Carrie) nee Lynyard. She was born 5 November 1888 in Featherstone, near Wellington, but lived most of her early life at Stratford.
Elsie was enrolled at Featherston School by her father on 29 January 1894 and at this time they lived at Fernside. Elsie left this school on 9 March 1897 *"to go to Normanby School"*. During 1895 the records show Elsie was in Primer 1 at the Featherston School, while her elder sister Mary was in Standard 1. (Nat Arch)
From the farm at Kahouri Bridge near Stratford, Elsie and her sisters had to walk 2-3 miles to Stratford School and then after school they were required to help their father hand milk the cows. (JG)
Her father Charles was most particular about how their surname was spelt, as with an H as in Whilmshurst it was the German way and that was not an acceptable relationship in the early 1900s. (PT)
A brief WILMSHURST Family Tree follows at the end of this chapter.

CHILDREN: Arthur and Elsie had three children........
    1911... FLOSSIE was born in Auckland.
    1915... GORDON was born in Auckland.
    1924... PERCY was born in New Plymouth.

1915... NZPO Directory:
Living in New Lynn, Auckland was...   *Arthur Thomas... Builder.* (33)

RIMU STREET: Like brother Harry, Arthur also lived in Rimu Street, New Lynn, close to his parents. In fact Arthur's family lived over the road, across the creek, and almost opposite brother Harry.

AUCKLAND: Land Sales.
Arthur was not part of his brothers Jack, Harry and Albert's 52 acre subdivision and sales activity of 1913-14.

Land Information title Vol 206/275 records father William selling to Arthur on 28 July 1913, a half acre part of Lot 20. (refer page 96)

Vol 210/111 and plan 11011, describes Arthur's subdivision into 4 pieces on 19 May 1916 and sale of Lot 1 to Ernest Bongard, Lot 2 to Robert Mayne and his discharging a mortgage held by his father.

TARANAKI:
Soon after these 1916 sales, Elsie must have had a desire to return to New Plymouth and be nearer to her family, because they were soon living in the Westown suburb of New Plymouth. From here they purchased a 100 acre farm on the corner of Great South Road and Koru Street, one mile from Oakura township and about 7 miles (14 km) south west of New Plymouth. They had a herd of milking cows. Whilst farming and living here, Arthur planted a double row of pine trees. (FT+PT)

The Oakura farmhouse. On the porch are Arthur's mother Eliza, wife Elsie and daughter Flossie. Arthur is standing in front.

1916... William's Will.

On 22 May 1916 Arthur's father William signed his Will. This recorded that William had lent Arthur £ 200 and held a mortgage but no detail is given of the security.   (Arthur paid off this debt two months after his father signed his Will. The loan probably enabled Arthur to buy the half acre of Lot 20.)

**THE FAMILY
1932.**

at back...
**Gordon and
Flossie**

at front...
**Elsie, Percy
and Arthur.**

1923... Arthur's father William Thomas died 22 February in Auckland.
William appointed wife Eliza and sons Arthur and Albert as his Executors. After Eliza died in 1935, Arthur was still signing land and mortgage papers as late as October 1937.

1933... Daughter Flossie recalls that Arthur's mother Eliza (then a widow) lived some months with them on the Oakura farm. Some notes we saw state......... *"On the 21st March 1933 Flossie left home to live with Queeny Plewes and Eliza used her bedroom. On the 17th July Arthur and Eliza made a trip to Auckland and returned to the farm on the 21st.*
On the 2nd April 1934 (Easter Monday) Arthur's sister Edie Dove collected Eliza and took her to live with them in Mt Albert, Auckland." (FT)

1934... Elsie's father Charles Wilmshurst (80) died on 10 June.
1935... Arthur's mother Eliza Thomas (83) died on 6 March in Auckland.

1937... The Oakura farm was sold and Arthur aged 55, Elsie and family moved into the New Plymouth suburb of Fitzroy.
Their last address was 17 Atiawa Street, New Plymouth. (PT)

MEMORIES:
Granddaughter Amy has fond memories of visits to see them. She recalls as a little girl she enjoyed sitting on granddad Arthur's knee and drinking the lovely carrot juice he made for them. She also remembers he had a large and fully equipped carpentry workshop and a very big vegetable garden that he

THE FAMILY 1947: at back Elsie and Percy.
at front are Arthur, Flossie and Gordon.

maintained at Fitzroy. At some point in his life, Arthur made a tall 'grandfather-clock' which stood in their home at Fitzroy. The clock passed to son Gordon. It has never broken down and in the future, will be handed down to Arthur's grandson Ron. (AT)

Amy recalls her grandma Elsie as a very religious lady who attended church two or three times a week. Every one had to sit about the house quietly and she would not allow visiting family to work, knit or play loudly on Sundays. She remembers always staying with them during school holidays and enjoyed the many trips her grandmother and aunty Floss took them on to Pukekura Park and nearby beaches. Amy says *'their house was big and posh with lovely flower gardens everywhere'*. Another memory was of grandma's baking, especially her pastry squares filled with raisins or sultanas, chopped fresh mint and sugar, and baked in the oven. (AT)

When Amy brought her English born children Maria and Michael to New Zealand, about 1975, her Grandma (86) was very frail but still insisted on cooking for them. This kind act is still remembered fondly by them today. At this stage of her life Elsie used to enjoy having Flossie play the piano and her great-grandchildren sing for her and other visitors. (AT)

1938... Elsie's mother Carrie Wilmshurst (84) died 6 October 1938.

1942... Son Gordon married Joan Ruby Taylor in Auckland.
1949... Son Percy married Noeleen Land in New Plymouth.

1955... ARTHUR DIED aged 72 on 5 November 1955 and
        was buried at the Te Henui Cemetery in Taranaki.
He could not have picked a worse day. It was his wife's 67th birthday.
Arthur had signed his Will 30 May 1949 and left all his Estate (under £ 600)
to his wife Elsie Rose Thomas. No special bequests were made.

1976... ELSIE DIED aged 87 on 15 April 1976 in New Plymouth and was
buried with Arthur at the Te Henui Cemetery, Taranaki.

--oo0Ooo--

The WILMSHURST family. (1909 to 1906)

**standing from left... ELLA, LILY, father CHARLES and ANNIE.
sitting from left... EDIE, mother CARRIE, EVA and ELSIE.** (JG)

The WILMSHURST Family Tree:

1st NZ Generation	**JOHN THOMAS WILMSHURST** lived in Pluckley, Kent, England and arrived on 22 May 1841 at Wellington, NZ, on the *"Lord William Bentnick"*. He married 30 August 1847 at St Pauls Church, Wellington, to **RACHEL ANN MUDGWAY** lived at Hollingbourne, Kent, England and arrived with her parents and family 11 June 1841 at Wellington, NZ, on the *"Catherine Stewart Forbes"*. They had eight children including... CHARLES WILMSHURST.

2nd NZ Generation	**CHARLES WILMSHURST** born 10 Nov 1853 at Johnsonville, Wellington, NZ. (Charles died 10 June 1934 and was buried at New Plymouth.) He first married on 27 May 1874 at Wanganui, New Zealand, to **ELIZABETH SPRY** born 12 March 1858 at Adelaide, Australia, to Thomas and Ann Spry (nee Pugsley), died 1883 at Johnsonville, NZ. They had six children.

CHARLES ALBERT WILMSHURST	b 1874	d 1951
HERBERT EDWARD WILSMHURST	b 1876	d 1942
HEDLEY OSCAR WILMSHURST	b 1878	d 1923
FREDERICK JAMES WILMSHURST	b 1879	d 1948
RACHEL ANN (Annie) WILMSHURST	b 1880	d 1955
GEORGE WILMSHURST	b 1881	d 1964

CHARLES WILMSHURST then married on 27 August 1884 at the Primitive Methodist Church, Webb St, Wellington, to **CAROLINE (Carrie) LINYARD** born 10 Oct 1854 at Birmingham, England. (Carrie died 6 October 1938 at Marton & buried at New Plymouth.) (Carrie's parents were **HENRY HUMPHREY LINYARD** and **MARY ANN** n **CULLF**. They lived in Birmingham and later moved to Keighley, Yorkshire.) Caroline came to NZ with her sister Mary Anne and her husband Anthony Emmett, arriving at Christchurch on the *"Lady Jocelyn"* in December 1882. Charles and Carrie had five daughters.

MARY EDITH (Edie) WILMSHURST	b 1885	d 1965
LILY WILMSHURST	b 1887	d 1930
ELSIE ROSE WILMSHURST	b 1888	d 1976
ELLA MILDRED WILMSHURST	b 1891	d 1971
IDA EVELYN (Eva) WILMSHURST	b 1893	d 1958

3rd NZ Generation	**ELSIE ROSE WILMSHURST** born 5 November 1888 at Featherston, Wellington. She married on 29 September 1910 at Stratford, New Zealand, to **ARTHUR GORDON THOMAS** born 29 December 1882 at Ashburton, NZ. They had three children...... Flossie, Gordon and Percy.

The Wilmshurst details were provided by Joy George, Cambridge, who has researched these families.

ARTHUR GORDON THOMAS FAMILY TREE:

3rd Generation
ARTHUR GORDON THOMAS... married.............................. **ELSIE ROSE WILMSHURST**

b 29 December 1882	29 September 1910	b 5 November 1888
at Ashburton. NZ.	at Stratford, NZ.	at Featherston, Wellington.
d 5 November 1955 (72)		d 15 April 1976 (87)
Bur Te Henui, New Plymouth.		Bur Te Henui, New Plymouth.

Elsie was the daughter of Charles WILMSHURST & Caroline (Carrie) nee LYNYARD.

Arthur and Elsie had three children named Flossie, Gordon and Percy.

4th Generation	5th Generation	6th Generation	7th Generation
FLOSSIE LURLINE THOMAS b 20 August 1911 at Auckland.			
GORDON CHARLES WILLIAM THOMAS b 2 August 1915 at Mt Eden, Auckland. d 20 November 1999 Cre Hawera.　(84) m 10 Oct 1942 ====== at Otahuhu, Auckland. **JOAN RUB Y TAYLOR** b 8 July 1924 at Keri Keri, Northland. They had 7 children. (She was daughter of Edwin Bishop Taylor b 5 Mar 1890, Hastings, England. Married Amy Fuller on 25 Aug 1923. Edwin d.. 11 Jan 1975 Bur Keri Keri. Amy died 9 Dec 1937, Bur Russell	**AMY WINIFRED THOMAS** b 31 January 1942 at Otahuhu, Auckalnd. 1st m 4 Oct 1965 ==== at St Pancras, London, England. **STAVROS** (Steve) **HADJI-MICHAEL TSANGARI** b 1 October 1944 at Cyprus. d 7 August 1972 Bur at Cypress. (son of Sotires Hadji Tsaggari & wife Maria.) : : : : : : : : : :	**MARIA JOAN TSANGARI** b 18 February 1964 at London, England. : : : Maria & Partner **NEIRMAL SINGH ==** b 16 February 1960 at Bristol, England. (son of Abtar Singh & wife. Both were born in Bombay, India) MICHAEL next page	**CHANTEL NATASHA AMY JOAN TSANGARI** b 22 June 1985 at Bristol, England. **CHANDANI SHAMINE MICHELLE KAUR** b 29 June 1991 at Bristol, England. **LUTCHAMY SEETA KAUR** b 27 February 1994 at Bristol, England. **KYE SINGH** b 5 June 1995 at Bristol, England. CIARIN next page

ARTHUR continued

4th Generation	5th Generation	6th Generation	7th Generation
Gordon & Joan continue	Amy & Steve continued : : : : : : : : 2nd m 23 Aug 1979 at Bristol, England. **CHWANG TAN** b 26 April 1939 at Singapore. d January 1999 (59) Burried Weston-Super- Mare, England.	**MICHAEL GORDON** **TSANGARI** b 29 July 1967 at London, England. m 12 April 1985 ===== at Bristol, England. **ANGELA GREEN** b 30 January 1967 at Bristol, England. (daughter of Angela & Richard Green) : 2nd m 30 June 2000 at Yate, England. **ALISON CLARE** **ROBINSON** b 1 April 1968 in England.	**CIARIN STEVEN** **TSANGARI** b 25 June 1985 at Bristol, England. **SIMON RICHARD** **TSANGARI** b 24 September 1986 at Bristol, England. **BERNADETTE** **MARIE TSANGARI** b 3 June 1987 at Bristol, England.
	DELCIE JOAN **THOMAS** b 18 May 1944 at Papakura, Auckland. m 16 Dec 1960 ====== at Hawera. **ROBERT** (Bob) **WALKINGTON** b 6 October 1937 at Waverley, Taranaki. (son of Bernard Walkington and Ada nee Sinclair)	**LYNETTE JOAN** **WALKINGTON** b 29 June 1961 at Patea, Taranaki. partner =========== **DAVID PACKER** b 1957 (ref 2087) at Patea, Taranaki. (son of Joe Packer and Pat nee Bud) : m 24 May 1986====== at Wanganui. **MURRAY MILNE** **GILL** b 2 January 1956 at Auckland City. (son of Milne Gill and Nessie Paykel nee Jack)	**DALE** **WALKINGTON** b 5 February 1980 at Patea, Taranaki. **EMILY JANE GILL** b 10 May 1991 at Wanganui. **MARK PATRICK** **GILL** b 16 February 1993 at Hastings.
		PAMELA next page	WADE next page

4th Generation	5th Generation	6th Generation	7th Generation
Gordon & Joan continue	Delcie & Bob continue	**PAMELA ANNE WALKINGTON** b 22 August 1962 at Patea, Taranaki, NZ. m 16 April 1982 at === Muchea, W Australia.	**WADE McKENZIE** b 8 May 1987 at Swan Dist.. Midlands, Western Australia.
		ALLAN DONALD McKENZIE b 3 February 1948 at Yallourn, Victoria, Australia. (son of Donald McKenzie and Roma Louie nee Tilley)	**LANE McKENZIE** b 20 July 1990 at Swan Dist.. Midlands, Western Australia.
		BRIAN JAMES WALKINGTON b 28 September 1966 at Patea, Taranaki. m 26 June 1993 at ==== Broome, West Australia.	**SARAH-JANE WALKINGTON** b 12 November 1992 at Derby, W Australia.
		DEANNE PRICE b 30 July 1966 at Perth, Australia. (daughter of Alan Graham Price and Cheryl-Ann nee Murray)	**SHERILYN GRACE WALKINGTON** b 8 November 1993 at Port Headland, West Australia.
			BEN WALKINGTON b 15 April 1999 at Port Headland, West Australia.
		BERNARD RAYMOND WALKINGTON b 13 September 1968 at Patea, Taranaki. m 6 Feb 1993======= at Hawera.	**HAYDEN ROBERT WALKINGTON** b 1 December 1995 at New Plymouth. SHAUN next page

ARTHUR continued

4th Generation	5th Generation	6th Generation	7th Generation
Gordon & Joan continue	Delcie & Bob continue	Bernard married.... **KIRSTY ANN BULMAN** b 25 November 1971 at Hawera. (dau. of Kerry Bulman & Christine nee Wells)	**SHAUN DAVID WALKINGTON & HUGH JAMES WALKINGTON** still born twins b 26 June 1997 at New Plymouth.
			JAMIE ELISE WALKINGTON b 11 March 1998 at New Plymouth.
	RONALD GORDON THOMAS (Ron) b 21 September 1945 at Otahuhu, Auckland. m 9 March 1968 ===== at Hawera. **LINDA WEST** b 24 December 1949 at Rotorua. (daughter of Raymond George West and Katie nee Wetini.)	**JANICE LINDA THOMAS** b 8 July 1969 at Hawera. m 15 Jan 1994 ====== at Hawera. **DERRICK CARL WILKIE** b 9 August 1961 at Gisborne. (son of David Robert Mervyn Wilkie and Lorraine Phoebe nee McFarlane)	**DYLAN TAMATI WILKIE** b 6 January 1995 at Kaitaia. Northland.
			TESSA BERNICE WILKIE b 25 December 1997 at New Plymouth.
		MICHELLE CAROL THOMAS b 26 January 1971 at Hawera. partner=========== **WILLIAM JAMES TOIMATA** (Willi) b 13 October 1963 at Wellington. (son of Hikitoa Toimata and Huia nee Rokena)	**HUIA TONI DANIELLE TOIMATA** b 21 June 1992 at Wellington.
			KARARAINA (Kara) AROHA TOIMATA b 22 August 1996 at Wellington.
		BERNICE next page	WAYNE next page

4th Generation	5th Generation	6th Generation	7th Generation
Gordon & Joan continue	Ron & Linda continue	**BERNICE FAYE THOMAS** b 16 September 1972 at Hawera. m 22 Dec 1990 ====== at Normanby, NZ. **CHRISTOPHER MAX MARINO** b 9 June 1970 at Rotorua. (son of Christopher Tamamutu Marino and Alice Te Whetu nee Gage)	**WAYNE MASON MARINO** b 9 February 1991 at New Plymouth. **NADINE LINDA TE WHETU MARINO** b 16 December 1992. at Taupo. **TAMAMUTU KAHUIARIKI REGAN MARINO** b 28 October 1995 at Rotorua.
		RONDA MAIRE THOMAS b 11 January 1974 at Hawera. partner=========== **JASON PAUL SYMES** b 10 December 1973 at New Plymouth. (son of Kevin Symes & Rosemary nee Moody : partner=========== **CRAIG PURSGLOVE** b 30 October 1971 at Porirua, Wellington. (son of Neil Pursglove & Joyce Ann nee Walker)	**JESSE RONALD THOMAS** b 23 January 1989 at Hawera. **ETHAN GLEN PURSGLOVE** b 7 April 1998 at Wellington. **MONIQUE BROOKE PURSGLOVE** b 19 July 1999 at Wellington.

4th Generation	5th Generation	6th Generation	7th Generation
Gordon & Joan continue	**MAUREEN DORIS THOMAS** b 10 October 1946 at Inglewood. m 23 Sept 1967 ====== at Hawera.	**WENDY KARIN MEYER** b 10 September 1968 at Patea, Taranaki. m 16 Jan 1988 ====== at Whenuakura.	**DANIEL PATRICK NIEDERBERGER** b 27 October 1988 at Wanganui.
	BRUCE MEYER b 25 April 1943 at Hawera, Taranaki. (Bruce was son of.... Ernest William Meyer b 26 Jan 1905, m 29 June 1937, Patea, d 15 Sept 1975 and Florance Mary nee Hotter b 23 Feb 1915 and d 28 April 1980)	**PETER EDWARD NIEDERBERGER** b 28 November 1957 at Hawera, Taranaki. (son of... Walter Niederberger and Marie Bertha nee Imboden)	**JENNA MARIE NIEDERBERGER** b 28 April 1990 at Hawera.
			SARAH JANE NIEDERBERGER b 8 June 1993 at New Plymouth.
			ANDREW GLENN NIEDERBERGER b 5 October 1995 at New Plymouth.
		MICHAEL GLENN MEYER b 3 September 1970 at Patea, Taranaki. m 12 Feb 1994 ====== at Kakaramea. NZ.	**LOGAN MICHAEL MEYER** b 22 May 1995 at New Plymouth.
		MICHELLE LEE WHITEMAN b 5 August 1969 at Patea, Taranaki. (Daughter of Selwyn Grant Whiteman and Janet Marie nee West)	**LIAM JARROD MEYER** b 29 November 1996 at New Plymouth.
	COLLEEN next page	SUZANNE next page	KAYLEIGH next page

4th Generation	5th Generation	6th Generation	7th Generation
Gordon & Joan continue	**COLLEEN JENNIFER THOMAS** b 4 May 1950 at Stratford. 1st m 21 Mar 1970===== at Hawera. **LESLIE PATRICK WHITE** b 17 March 1949 at Takapau, NZ. (son of Bernard Gerald White and Joyce nee	**SUZANNE JENNIFER WHITE** b 26 March 1971 at Patea. partner ============= **RODERICK MORGAN RYAN** b 14 September 1966 at Matamata. (son of Morgan Ryan and Valrae nee Bailey)	**KAYLEIGH JENNIFER RYAN** b 14 June 1997 at Hamilton. **DYLAN MORGAN RYAN** b 12 March 1999 at Hamilton.
	: : : : : : : : : : : : : : : : : :	**KAREN MARIE WHITE** b 10 August 1972 at Patea. partner ============= **ELLIOT MICHAEL WALSH** b 5 August 1969 at (son of Michael Walsh and Isabel Mary nee Brooks)	**JIM ELLIOT WALSH** b 5 July 1997 at Rotorua. **ADAM MICHAEL WALSH** b 1 January 1999 at Rotorua.
	Colleen 2nd married on 24 February 1996 at Kakaramea. **WILLIAM MICHAEL BUCKLEY** b 9 May 1943 at Hamilton. d 15 Sept 1997 (54) Cremated Rotorua.	**JEANETTE LESLEY WHITE** b 21 July 1973 at Patea, Taranaki. partner **ROWAN GREIG EDWARDS** b 12 December 1971 at Te Puke. (son of Larry Edwards and Gaile nee Johnstone)	
	CAROL next page		

4th Generation	5th Generation	6th Generation	7th Generation
Gordon & Joan continue	**CAROL RAEWYN THOMAS** b 9 December 1957 at Patea, Taranaki. m 14 July 1979 at Hawera. **WILLIAM JOHN GALLIERS** (Bill) b 16 July 1947 at Lower Hutt. (son of Henry William Galliers and Joyce Frances nee Ralph)		
	NYLA ELSIE THOMAS b 1 August 1959 at Patea, Taranaki.		
PERCY ALWYN THOMAS b 20 October 1924 at New Plymouth. m 16 April 1949 ===== at New Plymouth. **NOELINE WINSOME LAND** b 10 December 1928 at New Plymouth. (Daughter of Ernest John Henry Land and Ruby Isobel nee Rielly)	**LYNDA JUNE THOMAS** b 26 February 1950 at New Plymouth. m 17 May 1969 ===== at New Plymouth. **ROBERT CANICE GAGE** (Bob) b 14 February 1948 at Lower Hutt. (son of Alexander Mennie Gage and Eleanor May nee Scott)	**MICHAEL ROBERT GAGE** b 12 November 1969 at New Plymouth. partner ========== **LYNETTE GILL** b at	**COLE MICHAEL GAGE** b 25 May 1994 at Takapuna, NSC.
			RUA SAMUEL GAGE b 19 February 1997 at Sydney, Australia.
		KRISTINA MAREE GAGE b 7 February 1971 at Auckland City. m 16 March 1996 ==== at Devonport, NSC. **ROBERT WILLIAM GRIMSHAW** b 4 May 1970 at Takapuna, NSC.	**TYLER ROBERT GRIMSHAW** b 27 December 2000 at Takapuna, NSC.

4th Generation	5th Generation	6th Generation	7th Generation
Percy & Noeline contin..	Lynda & Bob continue	**STEFAN PETER GAGE** b 10 December 1973 at Devonport, NSC.	
		CATHRYN ANN GAGE b 15 March 1975 at Takapuna, NSC. partner============ **TIMOTHY JOSEPH O'KEEFFE** b 12 January 1974 at Tauranga. : Cathryn married on 7 Oct 2000======= at Devonport, NSC. **DARREN McKENZIE BRUCE** b 1 December 1969 at Auckland City.	**NATHAN ROBERT GAGE** b 25 August 1995 at Takapuna, NSC. **ARREN McKENZIE GAGE--BRUCE** b 31 May 1999 at Takapuna, NSC.
	MARY ISABELLA THOMAS b 27 June 1955 at New Plymouth. 1st m 6 March 1976=== at Takapuna, NSC. **GORDON MERVYN AUSTIN** b 14 January 1957 at Auckland City. (son of Molly and Mervyn Austin. Mervyn died and Molly married Peter Thompson) : 2nd m 18 Feb 1983=== at Birkenhead, NSC. **ANTHONY DARRYL GRANT** (Tony) continued	**KELLIE MAREE NOELINE (AUSTIN) GRANT** b 20 July 1978 at Auckland City. partner ========== **BRETT TENI PERENARA** b 7 October 1972 at Auckland City. **JOANNAH TRACEY GRANT** b 5 August 1980 at Takapuna, NSC.	**KERALEIGH TYKESHA MARY GRANT** b 19 January 2000 at Takapuna, NSC.

4th Generation	5th Generation	6th Generation	7th Generation
Percy & Noeline cont...	Tony was born on b 7 April 1957 at Auckland City. (A son of Melodyann Grant and Gordon Ernest Smith he was adopted by grandparents Lewis Claude Grant and Maude Emily nee Farrant)		
	PAUL ARTHUR ERNEST THOMAS b 28 March 1958 at New Plymouth. m 16 Aug 1980====== at Birkenhead, NSC. **DEBORAH MARY ROSSALL-BENNETT** b 6 August 1961 at Liverpool, England. (daughter of Bernard Bennett and Gail Mary nee Preston) Paul and Deborah seperated and Deborah now has two half-siblings for Sarah and Sean..... Allyson Elizabeth Jaques born 26 March 1997 and Glynn Edward Norman born 23 July 2001.	**SARAH MARY THOMAS** b 14 September 1981 at Auckland City. **SEAN PAUL THOMAS** b 6 July 1983 at Auckland City.	

CHAPTER ELEVEN

7th Generation (3rd NZ)

ALBERT PETER THOMAS

(1885-1963)

1885... BIRTH - ASHBURTON:

Albert Peter Thomas was William (carpenter) and Eliza Thomas' 7th child, born 23 March 1885 while the family was living in Allenton, Ashburton.

1887... NGAWAPURUA:

Soon after September 1887, when Albert was aged 2½, his family moved to the North Island to live in Ngawapurua near Woodville.

1890... SCHOOL: Woodville.

The Woodville School enrolment register states Albert started school on 21 September 1889 when aged 4½, and in 1891 he left *'to go to the Pahiatua'* school aged about 6. Nothing has been found of his attendance at Pahiatua.

Mangatainoka.

The Mangatainoka School records show Albert attended from 1893. There are no other comments for 1893, but he sat exams in 1895 and failed reading, spelling and arithmetic. In 1896 Albert passed arithmetic, and in 1897 he passed Standard 2 exams. In 1898 his Standard 3 exam records are blank. Aged 13, late in 1898, Albert, his brother Arthur and sisters Ethel and Rose left this school.

1898... AUCKLAND:

Albert's parents and some of his brothers and sisters left Ngawapurua and travelled to live on an 88 acre farm in New Lynn in Auckland. His schooling, considered to be completed, he worked with his father on this New Lynn property learning farming, carpentry, brick making and sailing.

1898 to 1912: Little is remembered of Albert's life from age 13 to 27, but he was involved with his father's brickworks (1903-8), was in charge of and sailed the scow which transported the bricks about the Auckland harbour.
Son Jim recalls a photograph of this two-masted boat hanging in their home.

In 1903, aged 18, Albert became part of his father's agreement to sell to his three sons, Jack, Harry and Albert, 52 acres of the New Lynn farm. (page 93) This land was registered in their names in October 1909, when Albert was 24, and he was involved in the initial subdivision sales during 1913/14. There were a great many land transfers between the brothers, and Albert left the scene early. However, we have found that he, with brother Arthur, held mortgages over various sections of the land until as late as 1937.

In September 1910 aged 25, at brother Arthur's wedding in Levin, Albert signed as a witness giving his occupation as 'Captain' and his address then as 'Wanganui'. Later, he moved to live on his parents farm in Auckland.

Before he married, Albert and his brother Harry played the violin for the Salvation Army band. When he married, Albert adopted the Open Brethren faith which Ethel's family followed. (RE)

1912... MARRIAGE:
Albert married ETHEL VIOLET LADBROOK at the Elim Hall in New Lynn on 9 October 1912. It was the first wedding to be held there.
Both gave their age as 27, but Ethel was actually a 29 year old 'Domestic' and Albert said he was a 'Builder'.
The officiating minister was H. L. Thatcher of the Open Brethren.
Witnesses were Albert's sister Edie and William Shadwick.
More LADBROOK detail follows at the end of this section.

CHILDREN:
Albert and Ethel had six children...   Cyril born 1913, Mary b1916, twins Jim and Martin b1918, Victor b1919 and Ruth b1923.
Their first grandchild Allan James England arrived in 1938.

1910... DAFFODILS:
"About 1910 Albert purchased a 30 acre farm in Atkinson Road, Titirangi from the original owner Mr O'Jier. Half the property was planted in daffodils and the balance was used for strawberries, and other flowers. The 1930's depression did not greatly effect the farm's output. This was probably because the Thomas family worked from 4am to after sunset every day. Albert farmed this land for 50 years before it was subdivided and sold in 1960." (WA) Son Jim advised that this comment in the book *"West Auckland Remembers"* was true. He recalls that he and his brothers would be picking daffodils by 6 am and sometimes it was dark. With breakfast eaten,

they then had to walk five miles to school every day. After school they had newspapers to deliver on foot, then more time to spend with the daffodils to complete the day. (WJT)

1912... Albert and Ethel, with Edie Thomas and William Shadwick.

Albert supplied daffodil bulbs every year to the 'Yates' organisation. (MW)

1918: ETHEL with 4 month old twins Martin and Jim.

Albert and Ethel's farm faced Atkinson Road, Titirangi and seems to have been purchased over a number of years.

The initial daffodil farm of about 8 acres was added to in August 1922, when Albert bought a next door block of 22 acres from J H Field. (Vol 328/64). Also, Land Information record Vol 1098 / 143 shows Albert still owned this land in 1954 when he signed survey plan DP39716 as owner, for further subdivision. Earlier records include Vol 294/125 of 1919 and there are others yet to find.

Albert used his carpentry skills to build a new home on the property. (WJT)

Ethel had a strong faith and walked to church twice a week from her home in Titirangi. Her children and church were her life. (ME)

1916... Mortgage. Albert had a mortgage with his father on the daffodil property, and another near the Whau River bridge. We have been unable to trace this but it is mentioned in his father's Will which was signed in 1916.

1923... Albert's father William Thomas died 25 February 1923 aged 74.
Albert's mother Eliza Thomas died 6 March 1935 aged 83.

1930's photo of Albert Thomas and family at the daffodil farm.
Number 1 is Albert, 2 Ethel, 3 Cyril, 4 unknown, 5 Jim, 6 Victor,
7 Martin, 8 Ruth. The other people are employees. (WJT)

1934... Albert and Ethel separated.

Although Albert remarried, Ethel did not. Albert stayed at the farm and with Cyril as Manager, continued growing daffodils there.

Ethel spent a few months with sister Edie Dove at her Mt Albert home, then found a rental house in New Lynn. The other five children joined her there. Her three sons found jobs to support them all.

World War II.

Ethel was in poor health most of her final years, which she spent alternately with daughter's Mary and Ruth and their families. When sons Jim, Martin and Victor went off to the War, she seemed to just hang on until they returned home to New Zealand safely, and then she passed away.

1946... ETHEL DIED:

On 12 May 1946, three days after her 63rd birthday, Ethel died in the front room of daughter Mary's home. She was buried at Waikumete Cemetery, Anglican section, Row 4, Plot 101.

1961... Albert travelled to Palmerston North for his niece Myrle's marriage to Rod Watt, and later he gave them a bed while they were on their honeymoon in Auckland. (MW)

1963... ALBERT DIED: Albert spent his final nine months in the home of son Jim and Lois. He died on his 78th birthday 23 March 1963. Described as a 'Retired Horticulturist' he was buried at Waikumete Cemetery, Protestant Lawn, Block C, Section 5, Plot 71. There is no headstone on his gravesite.

> Albert signed his Will on 23 August 1962 and instructed his executors, sons Victor and Jim, to divide his estate of under £ 8,000 equally between his six children.

--oo0Ooo--

The LADBROOK family.

1. <u>**William**</u> Ladbrook, born 18 April 1818 - died 24 April 1873 aged 55.
> (His father was William Ladbrook, a coachman.)

He married 29 August 1841 at Bitton, Gloucestershire, England, to Eliza (Tate) Day, born 7 April 1820 and died 1897 in New Zealand aged 77.

Her parents were George Day and Mary nee Ham of Somerset, England.

They arrived at Port Nicholson, New Zealand on the *"Birman"* in 1842.

They had seven children... Eliza b 1845, William Charles b1846, George Arthur b1849, John b1852, Henry Alfred b1856, <u>**James**</u> Adolphus b1858 and Selina Ann b1861.

----ooo00ooo----

2. James Adolphus Ladbrook, born 1858 Prebbleton, Christchurch and died 1889. James, a farmer, married in Christchurch, 5 June 1878 to Mary Maria Trivett/Trevitt born 9 October 1858 in Shropshire, England.

> Her parents were Thomas Trivett (as spelt on wedding certificate) and Jane nee Farmstone / Firmstone who arrived at Lyttleton, New Zealand, on the *"Metropolis"* 16 June 1863.

They had four children... Mabel Selina b1880, Herbert Aldolphis b1881, <u>**Ethel**</u> Violet b15 May 1883 at Cambridge Terrace, Christchurch, and Beatrice Maud b1885.

----ooo00ooo----

We thank Allan Ladbrook (2 Edwin St, Gore, Southland. NZ.) for sharing his research with us. Allan has many more details, including history of his family's early days in the Ladbrooks district, 12 miles south of Christchurch, where the family settled.

ALBERT PETER THOMAS FAMILY TREE:

3rd Generation

ALBERT PETER THOMAS....married.....................................**ETHEL VIOLET LADBROOK**

b 23 March 1885	9 October 1912	b 15 May 1883
at Ashburton, NZ.	at New Lynn, Auckland.	at Christchurch.
d 23 March 1963 (78)		d 12 May 1946 (62)
Bur Waikumete, Auckland.		Bur Waikumete, Auckland.

Ethel was a daughter of James Adolphus LADBROOK and Mary Maria nee TRIVETT

Albert and Ethel had six children named Cyril, Mary, James, Martin, Victor and Ruth.

4th Generation	5th Generation	6th Generation	7th Generation
CYRIL ALBERT THOMAS	**SHIRLEY WINIFRED THOMAS**	**STEVE CHARLES WAHAPU**	
b 1 April 1913 at	b 6 January 1940	b 29 April 1960	
New Lynn, Auckland.	at Auckland City.	at Auckland City.	
d 15 August 1981 (68)	d 16 Sept 1988 (48)		
Bur Waikumete, A.	Bur Cambridge.	**SHARON SHIRLEY WAHAPU**	**LANIA SHIRLEY TIA MARIE WAHAPU**
m 28 Aug 1937======	m 12 Dec 1959======	b 12 January 1966	b 9 June 1989
at Auckland City.	at Auckland City.	at Cambridge.	at Auckland City.
WINIFRED ENGLAND.	**CHARLES WAHAPU**	partner ============	
b 3 April 1916	b 26 September 1932	**KAPI LANSAIKI**	
at Rotorua.	at Pipiwhai, Northland.	b 5 December 1968	
d 22 October 1987 (71)	(son of Henare Maketu	at Auckland City.	**TIARE BILLIE-JEAN LANG**
Bur Waikumete, A.	Wahapu and Teangonui	:	b 29 April 1998
(Winifred was sister of	nee Wihongi)	Sharon married on	at Auckland City.
James who married		28 June 1997 ======	
Cyril's sister Mary, and		at Hamilton.	
daughter of Walter		**BRENT JOHN LANG**	**KIANA PHEONIX LANG**
Frederick England and		b 30 December 1971	b 8 June 1999
Lucy Alice nee Shaw)		at Te Kuiti.	at Auckland City.
They had 3 children.		(son of John Lang and	
		Lynne nee Greig)	
	DAVID CYRIL THOMAS (Dave)	**REBECCA JUNE THOMAS**	
	b 1 June 1949	b 12 November 1975	
	at Auckland City.	at Auckland City.	
	m 16 Sept 1972 =====	m 17 February 1996	
	at Auckland City.	at Auckland City.	
	ROBINA next page	COLIN next page	

4th Generation	5th Generation	6th Generation	7th Generation
Cyril & Winifred cont..	DAVE married **ROBINA SHIRLEY LOIS WEBBER** b 22 Sept 1949 at Auckland City. (daughter of Herbert Roy Webber and June nee Broomfield, known as Griffen)	REBECCA married **COLIN MICHAEL QUEDLEY** b 5 September 1976 at Auckland City. (son of Bruce Colin Quedley and Beverley Annette nee Thomas) **SHANNON STACEY THOMAS** b 9 January 1979 at Auckland City. m 13 November 1999 at Auckland City. **GRAEME MAURICE INGLIS** b 13 November 1975 at Auckland City. (son of John Gilmore Inglis and Maureen Carol nee Woodcock) **JUSTIN DAVID THOMAS** b 28 July 1982 at Auckland City.	
	KEVIN WALTER THOMAS b 9 July 1950 at Auckland City. m 31 Aug 1985====== at Hamilton. **FIONA ANNE HILTON** b 31 May 1960 at Hamilton. (daughter of Peter Graham Hilton and Noeline Betty nee Winchcombe)	**AMANDA HILARY THOMAS** b 23 October 1986 at Auckland City. **ELLICE MIRIAM THOMAS** b 24 November 1988 at Auckland City. **BENJAMIN KEVIN THOMAS** b 10 March 1994 at Auckland City.	

ALBERT continued

4th Generation	5th Generation	6th Generation	7th Generation
MARY ETHEL THOMAS b 13 June 1916 at New Lynn, Auckland. m 29 May 1937 ===== at New Lynn, Auckland. **JAMES ENGLAND** b 6 November 1915 at Rotorua. d 9 April 1992 (76) Bur Waikumete, A. (He was an elder brother of Winifred who married Cyril Thomas, and son of Walter Frederick England and Lucy Alice nee Shaw) They had 7 children.	**ALLAN JAMES ENGLAND** b 30 May 1938 at New Lynn, Auckland. m 26 March 1960 ==== at New Lynn, Auckland. **MAUREEN HAY** b 21 March 1942 at Albury, NSW, Australia. (daughter of Arthur Glen Hay and Erryl Eileen nee Hall)	**VERA LEIGH ENGLAND** b 6 October 1961 at Henderson. m 1981 =========== at Surfers Paradise. **STEVE CHAPMAN** b 14 February 1951 in Australia.	**MELISSA LANA CHAPMAN** b 12 September 1983 at Surfers Paradise, Queensland, Australia.
		MARTIN JAMES ENGLAND b 29 February 1964 at Henderson.	
		MARY JEAN ENGLAND b 11 September 1966 at Avondale, Auckland. m 27 January 1990 at Parnel, Auckland. **STEPHEN GLYNN GOODALL** b 8 December 1965 at Auckland City.	
	GORDON FREDERICK ENGLAND b 7 October 1939 at New Lynn, Auckland. m 25 May 1963 at ==== Onehunga, Auckland. **GAIL ELIZABETH JACKSON** b 1 September 1943 at Onehunga, Auckland. (daughter of Arthur Jackson & Nada Eileen nee Pople. Nada died 16-Sept-1988 Bur Mangere.)	**DEBORAH ANN ENGLAND** b 30 June 1965 at Grey Lynn, Auckland. m 5 May 1990 ====== at Orewa, Northland. **PHILLIP ANTHONY SIMS** b 24 July 1968 at Auckland City. (son of Anthony Sims & Maureen nee Hylton)	**NATHAN PHILLIP SIMS** b 14 October 1994 at Takapuna, NSC. **KIMBERLY MARY SIMS** b 28 August 1996 at Takapuna, NSC. **TODD LUKE SIMS** b 2 June 1998 at Takapuna, NSC.

4th Generation	5th Generation	6th Generation	7th Generation
Mary & James continue	Gordon & Gail continue	**NIGEL GORDON ENGLAND** b 4 October 1968 at Grey Lynn, Auckland. m 2 Feb 1993======= at Warkworth. **JOANNE IVY ENGLAND** b 28 April 1969 at Hamilton. (daughter of Lawrence and Cherril England)	**CAITLAIN TRESSIA ENGLAND** b 24 October 1994 at Warkworth.
		ELIZABETH DELWYN ENGLAND b 22 December 1972 at Grey Lynn, Auckland. m 4 April 1998 ====== at Orewa, Northland. **OWEN TREENCE PONTYNER** b 31 July 1973 at Whangarei.	**CORDEL PAUL PONTYNER** b 12 June 2000 at Takapuna, NSC.
	TREVOR MAURICE ENGLAND b 30 September 1946 at Glen Eden, Auckland. m 9 March 1968 ===== at New Lynn, Auckland. **PAMELA BETTINA BROWN** b 22 March 1946 at Auckland City. (daughter of James Fultcher Brown who died 7 September 1999 and Bettina Elsa nee Sherlock)	**ANTHONY TREVOR ENGLAND** b 20 July 1969 at Henderson, Auckland. partner =========== **TRACY POTTER** : : m 18 Oct 1997 ====== at Oratia, Auckland. **SALLY ANN HOLT** b 21 July 1973 at Helensville. (daughter of Dave Holt & Margaret nee Bisman)	**LIAM ANTHONY POTTER** b 23 March 1992 at Takapuna, NSC. **ISABELLA ANN ENGLAND** b 6 April 2001 at Waitakere, Auckland.
		DARREN next page	GESINA next page

ALBERT continued

4th Generation	5th Generation	6th Generation	7th Generation
Mary & James continue	Trevor & Pamela cont..	**DARREN JAMES ENGLAND** b 9 March 1971 at Henderson, Auckland. m 15 Feb 1997 ====== at Auckland City.	**GESINA CHRISTINE ENGLAND** b 18 December 1997 at Waitakere, Auckland.
		LISA CHRISTINE FARMER b 30 August 1972 at Helensville. (daughter of Lou Farmer Frances nee Kistenmaker)	**JAKE JAMES ENGLAND** b 17 June 1999 at Waitakere, Auckland.
		CRAIG MARK ENGLAND b 19 December 1974 at Henderson, Auckland. m 27 August 2000 at Fiji. **FIONA MARIE FULLER** b 16 April 1975 at Auckland City. (daughter of Don Fuller & June Gregory nee Day)	
		TIMOTHY BRETT ENGLAND b 10 February 1981 at Western Springs, Auckland.	
(Sorry! Lucy is third child... and should be before brother Trevor.)	**LUCY ETHEL ENGLAND** b 20 March 1945 at New Lynn, Auckland. m 13 March 1965 ==== at New Lynn, Auckland. **NEIL ARTHUR CREMER** continued next page	**GARY LEONARD CREMER** b 15 October 1968 at Howick, Auckland. m 6 April 1991 ====== at Manukau, Auckland. **NICOLA MARIANNE JONES** continued next page	**MITCHELL DEAN CREMER** b 5 June 1999 at Auckland City.

ALBERT continued

4th Generation	5th Generation	6th Generation	7th Generation
Mary & James continue	Neil was born b 24 February 1944 at Auckland City. (son of Cyril Leonard Cremer and Doris Isabel nee Skelton)	Nicola was born b 26 September 1969 at Whangarei. (daughter of Murray Jones and Marianne nee Clarke)	
		ALAN NEIL CREMER b 17 June 1971 at Howick, Auckland.	
		ANGELA FAYE CREMER b 8 December 1974 at Howick, Auckland. m 19 January 2001 at Howick, Auckland. **JASON DAVID O'HEARN** b 6 April 1974 at Howick, Auckland. (son of Lennard Andrew O'Hearn and Joan Hollie Luanna nee Moir)	
	RUSSELL NOEL ENGLAND b 22 January 1950 at New Lynn, Auckland. m 15 May 1971 ===== at New Lynn, Auckland. **MARGARET ANNE CORNALL** b 10 August 1950 at New Lynn, Auckland. (Margaret was daughter of James Allan Cornall (died 31 Aug 1933) & Claire Emily nee Brown)	**RACHAEL MARGARET ENGLAND** b 31 August 1974 at Sydney, Australia. **SHANE RUSSELL ENGLAND** b 17 September 1975 at Waitakere, Auckland. **KARENA CLAIRE ENGLAND** b 23 April 1978 at Hellensville.	

4th Generation	5th Generation	6th Generation	7th Generation
Mary & James continue	Russell & Margaret cont.	**LEON JAMES ENGLAND** b 24 February 1980 at Hellensville.	
	BETTY JEANETTE ENGLAND b 21 November 1952 at Glen Eden, Auckland. m 2 May 1970 ====== at New Lynn, Auckland. **MAURICE JOHN BARTON** b 31 January 1950 at Castor Bay, NSC. (son of Victor Johnston Barton and Beryl Violet nee Marden)	**MICHAEL JOHN BARTON** b 17 January 1973 at Auckland City. m 3 Oct 1992 ======= at Auckland City. **NICCOLE KAY MILLAR** b 2 October 1971 at Mt Albert, Auckland.	**JAMES VICTOR PHILIP BARTON** b 18 February 1991 at Papatoetoe, Auckland. **JESSICA TEGAN MARIA BARTON** b 10 February 1995 at Howick, Auckland. **TONY NIGEL HOWARD BARTON** b 23 April 1996 at Howick, Auckland.
		ALASTER JAMES BARTON b 6 June 1975 at Mt Albert, Auckland. m 20 November 1999 at Auckland City. **CAROLYN ANN PEAKE** b 23 October 1979 at Christchurch.	
	CAROL JEAN ENGLAND b 25 February 1954 at Pt Chevelier, Auckland. m 6 May 1972======= at New Lynn, Auckland. IAN next page	**CATHERINE LOUISE DAWSON** b 14 May 1974 at St Helens, Auckland.	

4th Generation	5th Generation	6th Generation	7th Generation
Mary & James continue	Carol married **IAN THOMAS DAWSON** b 28 November 1948 at Ashburton. (Son of Harry Thomas Dawson and June Patricia nee Gallagher)	**HOWARD THOMAS DAWSON** b 23 June 1976 at St Helens, Auckland.	
WALTER JAMES THOMAS (Jim) b 19 April 1918.. *twin* at Auckland City. m 5 Feb 1949 ====== at Auckland City. **LOIS MAY SHAW** b 13 December 1928 at Auckland City. (daughter of Fredrick Herbert Shaw and Hazel Lilian nee Tarlin) They had 3 children.	**WARREN JAMES THOMAS** b 26 April 1951 at Auckland City. m 20 May 1972 ===== at Morrinsville. **LYNNE LESLEY BRYANT** b 28 December 1953 at Morrinsville, Waikato. (daughter of Ena and Douglas Bryant) : : : : : : : : : : : : : : : :	**GAVIN JAMES THOMAS** b 23 June 1974 at Auckland City. m 22 April 1995 ==== at Kumeu, Auckland. **KRISTAL MARGARET STEVENS** b 26 May 1970 at Kaikohe, Northland. (Daughter of Barry Stevens and Francine nee Clarke) **KERRY ALLAN THOMAS** b 2 March 1976 at Auckland City. **TIMOTHY ANDREW THOMAS** b 2 March 1980 at Auckland City. **SHALAGH MARIE THOMAS** b 6 May 1983 at Auckland City.	**DANIEL JAMES THOMAS** b 12 January 2002 at North Shore Hospital

4th Generation	5th Generation	6th Generation	7th Generation
Jim & Lois continue	Warren & Lynne cont == : 2nd m 24 March 1995 **JAYNE WATSON** (daughter of Veronica and Fred Watson)	**ERIN JANE THOMAS** b 24 December 1985 at Auckland City.	
	NOELINE LOIS THOMAS b 11 February 1954 at Auckland City. m 17 Aug 1974====== at Auckland City. **ROBERT ANDREW CRAWFORD** b 12 July 1954 at Hamilton. (son of Robert Crawford and Dorothy nee Currie)	**JASON ROBERT CRAWFORD** b 4 July 1979 at Auckland City.	
		MICHELLE LOIS CRAWFORD b 24 March 1982 at Auckland City. Solo parent ========	**CAITLYN LOIS CRAWFORD** b 13 April 2000 at Henderson, Auckland.
		FIONA LEANNE CRAWFORD b 10 November 1983 at Auckland City.	
	BARRY FREDERICK THOMAS b 20 September 1957 at Henderson, Auckland. m 9 April 1977 ====== at Auckland City. **PAULINE JOAN BULT** b 29 November 1957 at Auckland City. (daughter of Leo Peter Bult and Joukje Yvonne nee Witteveen)	**CARLEEN MARGARET THOMAS** b 10 May 1981 at Auckland City. **STEPHEN JAMES THOMAS** b 23 November 1983 at Auckland City. **SOPHIE NICOLE THOMAS** b 14 October 1988 at Auckland City.	

4th Generation	5th Generation	6th Generation	7th Generation
MARTIN WILLIAM THOMAS b 19 April 1918..*twin* at Auckland City. d 27 October 1977 (59) Bur Auckland. m 18 February 1950=== at Auckland. **JOYCE ADELINE HARVEY** b 19 March 1926 at Auckland City. (daughter of John Harvey and Annie Victoria nee Sidwell) They had 3 children.	**ROBIN MARTIN THOMAS** b 1 August 1953 at New Lynn, Auckland. partner =========== **ANDRENA SCROGIE** b 6 April 1955 at Buckingham, England. (daughter of William John Scrogie and Betty nee Clemmit) : m 3 April 1976 ====== at Titirangi, Auckland. **DENISE FAY HART** b 2 May 1957 at Auckland City. (dau of Brian Bernard Hart & Joy Rita nee Howarth) : partner =========== **CORALIE DAWN McIAY** b 2 January 1955 at Palmerston North. (daughter of Francis Desmond Price and Eila May nee Perry)	**JASON MARTIN THOMAS** b 5 February 1971 at Henderson, Auckland. m 10 July 1999 at Oratia, Auckland. **JO-ANN FRANCINA van KUIJK** b 19 January 1974 at Auckland City. **BENJAMIN** (Ben) **MARTIN THOMAS** b 6 April 1979 at Mt Albert, Auckland. **JAMES JOSHUA THOMAS** b 4 June 1984 at Henderson, Auckland.	
	JODY LESLEY THOMAS b 26 August 1955 at New Lynn, Auckland. m 27 Nov 1975====== at Oratia, Auckland. **SIDNEY GORDON JUDD** b 20 December 1953 at Swanson, Auckland.	**JEREMY WILLIAM JUDD** b 17 July 1977 at Mt Albert, Auckland. **BRYCE SYDNEY JUDD** b 7 June 1979 at Dargaville, Northland.	

ALBERT continued

4th Generation	5th Generation	6th Generation	7th Generation
Martin & Joyce continue	(Sidney was son of Harry Wallace Judd and Hetty Maria nee Bellamy)	**KATIE MARIA JUDD** b 5 September 1980 at Dargaville, Northland.	
	KIM ERIN THOMAS b 20 October 1959 at Avondale, Auckland. m 20 May 1977 ===== at Auckland City. **BARRY WILLIAM LYSAGHT** b 24 July 1957 at Auckland City. (son of William Stanley Lysaght and Reta nee Cook)	**JERRARD WILLIAM LYSAGHT** b 3 November 1978 at Henderson, Auckland. **ADAM BARRY LYSAGHT** b 13 October 1980 at Henderson, Auckland. **BRIDGET JOYCE LYSAGHT** b 5 July 1982 at Henderson, Auckland.	
VICTOR DOUGLAS THOMAS b 21 December 1919 at New Lynn, Auckland. d 27 Sept 1994 (75) Bur R.S.A, Hastings. m 10 Oct 1945===== at Hastings. **DORIS HELEN WIRE** b 10 August 1921 at Feilding. d 18 April 1999 (77) Bur R.S.A, Hastings. (dau of Alfred James Wire and Katherine Amelia nee Brungar) They had 3 children.	**BRIAN DOUGLAS THOMAS** b 3 February 1947 at Hastings. m 7 Aug 1971 ===== at Hastings. **CAROL McALPINE** b 3 November 1947 at Hastings. (daughter of John McAlpine and Pearl nee Beckett)	**AMANDA JANE THOMAS** (Mandy) b 4 July 1967 (a) at Hastings. m 10 October 1992 at Hastings. **IAN DUMBLETON** born at Wellington. : partner =========== **KEVIN MURRAY KNOX** b 27 June 1967 at Christchurch.	**ZACHARRY ADEN KNOX** b 10 February 1992 at Hastings.
		PAUL next page	ANTHONY next page

4th Generation	5th Generation	6th Generation	7th Generation
Victor & Doris continue	Brian & Carol continue	**PAUL JOHN THOMAS** b 16 July 1972 at Hastings. partner =========== **FREDA WILAMENA KIRE** b 15 April 1970 at Hastings.	**ANTHONY MAU MAHARATIA KIRE THOMAS** b 1 February 1992 at Hastings.
			MISTIQUE TE AORANGI KIRE THOMAS b 16 August 1996 at Hastings.
			PAORA JOHN THOMAS b 26 March 1998 at Hastings.
	BARRY PETER THOMAS b 5 January 1958 (a) at Napier.		
	SHARYON ANNETTE THOMAS b 11 March 1964 (a) at Hastings. m 9 Feb 1985 at ===== Eskdale, Hawkes Bay. **GEOFFREY JAMES NEVERMAN** b 17 July 1961 at Napier. (son of Richard Allan Neverman & Valmai Joan nee Campbell)	**ANDREW JAMES NEVERMAN** b 14 November 1990 at Hastings.	
		MICHELLE NICOLA NEVERMAN b 9 January 1993 at Hastings.	

RUTH next page

ALBERT continued

4th Generation	5th Generation	6th Generation	7th Generation
RUTH EUPHEMIA THOMAS b 23 January 1923 at Auckland City. m 17 June 1944 at === New Lynn, Auckland. **BASIL <u>ARNOT</u> HARRIS EDWARDS** b 22 May 1916 at Upper Hutt. d 26 Sept 1993 (77) Bur Crow's Nest, Queensland, Australia. (son of Stanley Arnot Edwards and Bernice Mary nee Humphries) They had 8 children.	**DOREEN RUTH EDWARDS** (by deed poll... **DEE**) b 9 July 1945 at Te Kopuru, Northland. 1st m 25 Jan 1964==== at Wanganui, NZ. **JOHN DENNIS CAVE** b 19 April 1941 at Wanganui, NZ. (son of Jack Cave and Nan nee Houghton) : : : : : : : : : : : :	**DARREN JOHN CAVE** b 23 October 1964 at Wanganui, NZ. m 27 Dec 1987 ====== at Sydney, Australia. **KARYL MIRAM SANCHEZ** b 15 December 1963 at Uruguary.	**JAKE ANDREW CAVE** b 25 March 1994 at Wollongong, NSW, Australia.
			JAY JACINTA CAVE b 20 February 1997 at Sydney, Australia.
		MICHELLE CAROLYN CAVE (became HILTON) b 16 April 1967 at Wanganui, NZ. m 2 Nov 1996 ====== at Sydney, Australia. **TIMOTHY ADRIAN FISHWICK** b 2 October 1973 at Perth, Australia.	**HOLLY DEE FISHWICK** b 6 September 1997 at Sydney, Australia.
	2nd m 4 Sept 1978 === at Wollongong, Australia **ANDREW HILTON** b 15 November 1953 at Sydney, Australia. (son of Emil Hilton and Theresa nee Katz)	**JAMIE STEPHEN HILTON** b 30 March 1979 at Wollongong, NSW, Australia.	
		MELANIE RUTH HILTON b 24 March 1982 at Sydney, NSW, Australia.	(Melanie died 12 Sept 2002 in a car crash (20)
	STANLEY ARNOT EDWARDS b 18 October 1946 at Dargaville, Northland NZ continued next page	**ADAM LINDSAY EDWARDS** b 8 June 1972 at Caringbah NSW, Australia. continued next page	

ALBERT continued

4th Generation	5th Generation	6th Generation	7th Generation
Ruth & Arnot continue	Stanley married m 16 Aug 1968====== at Caringbah, NSW, Australia. **ELISABETH JEAN** **PORTER** b 23 August 1948 at Kasaji, Belgian Congo. (ELISABETH was daughter of missionaries Dr Ronald Ernest Porter and Lillian Rosa nee Beamish)	Adam married m 5 December 1992 at Crow's Nest, Queensland, Australia. **KATHRYN** **ELIZABETH** **PROTHEROE** b 29 December 1973 at Brisbane, Queensland, Australia.	
		JASON KARL **EDWARDS** b 13 February 1974 at Takapuna, NSC, NZ. 1st m 11 Dec 1993 at Toowoomba, Queensland, Australia. **SUSAN JAYNE KEMP** : 2nd m March 1998 === **EDWINA LINDSAY** **HOOPER** b 30 March 1971 at Laidley, Q, Australia.	**INDIA TAYLOR** **EDWARDS** b 16 February 1999 at Toowoomba, Brisbane, Australia.
	IRENE ETHEL **EDWARDS** b 8 July 1949 at Dargaville, Northland. m 8 March 1969 ===== at Caringbah, NSW, Australia. **WESLEY EARL** **ELPHICK** b 17 May 1947 at Junee, NSW, Australia. (son of Edward Benjamin Elphick and Florence Ruby nee George)	**NATASHA LEIGH** **ELPHICK** b 16 February 1973 at Sydney, Australia. m 18 Dec 1993 ====== at Crow's Nest, Queensland, Australia. **JASON IVAN SMITH** b 1 June 1973 at Crow's Nest, Queensland, Australia. GARTH next page	**JOSHUA DAVID** **SMITH** b 21 October 2000 at Toowoomba, Queensland, Australia.

4th Generation	5th Generation	6th Generation	7th Generation
Ruth & Arnot continue	Irene & Wesley continue	**GARTH WESLEY ELPHICK** b 13 December 1975 at Mt Albert, Auckland. m 30 June 2001 at Darwin, N.T, Australia. **ILYSE MAGDALENE TURNBULL** b 20 December 1979 at Darwin, Northern Territory, Australia.	
		VANESSA JOY ELPHICK b 5 March 1982 at Mt Albert, Auckland.	
		NADINE SHEREE ELPHICK b 30 March 1984 at Toowoomba, Queensland, Australia.	
	ALLAN JOHN EDWARDS b 7 August 1950 at Wanganui, NZ. d 6 March 1951 (7 mth) Bur Akatarawa, Wgtn.		
	GLENYS JOY EDWARDS b 25 March 1952 at Wanganui, NZ. 1st m 20 March 1971== at Miranda, Sydney, A.	**JUSTINE SYMONNE FRAZER** b 5 July 1974 at Sydney, NSW, Australia.	
	WARREN MATTHEW FRAZER continued next page	**BIANCA BENICE FRAZER** continued next page	**CALEB ASHLEY JOHANSEN** continued next page

ALBERT continued

4th Generation	5th Generation	6th Generation	7th Generation
Ruth & Arnot continue	Warren was born b 22 June 1950 at Crows Nest, NSW, Australia. (son of Kevin Matthew Frazer and Lola May nee Hunter) : 2nd m 26 August 1983 at Auckland. **RICHARD DANA LAMBERT** b 20 August 1953 at Wanganui.	Bianca was born b 2 April 1976 at Sydney, Australia. m 21 Dec 1996 ====== at Auckland. **DAVID WILLIAM** **JOHN JOHANSEN** b 20 December 1975 at Wellington, NZ.	Caleb was born b 17 September 1995 at Auckland. NZ.
	LOIS BERNICE **EDWARDS** b 21 June 1953 at Wanganui, NZ. 1st m 31 March 1973== at Sydney, Australia. **JAMES ERNEST** **HUDSON** b 2 April 1950 at Birmingham, England. (son of Howard Hudson and Betty nee Hawkswood) : : : : : 2nd m 11 Feb 1984 === at Sydney, Australia. **KYM ROBERT** **NELSON** changed by deed poll to **HUDSON** b 25 April 1955 at Sydney, Australia. (son of Ronald Nelson and Ellie nee Stewart)	**SHAYLAH LEE** **HUDSON** b 25 September 1975 at Auckland City. m 4 November 2000 at Wollongong, NSW, Australia. **LEE DOUGLAS** **SULLIVAN** b 19 April 1981 at Port Kembla, Australia. **BENJAMIN TODD** **HUDSON** b 26 February 1978 at Auckland City. **CHLOE KYM HUDSON** b 24 June 1984 at Sydney, Australia. **BRENT ROBERT** **HUDSON** b 29 July 1986 at Sydney, Australia.	

4th Generation	5th Generation	6th Generation	7th Generation
Ruth & Arnot continue	**KAREN JUDITH EDWARDS** b 7 August 1958 at Wanganui, NZ. m 31 Jan 1976 ====== at Whenuapai, Auckland **JOHN ALAN BARTLETT** b 29 July 1956 at Hamilton. (son of Alan Bartlett and Doreen nee Dinan)	**SAMUEL JOHN BARTLETT** b 27 February 1979 at Auckland, NZ. m 10 July 1999 at Lismore, NSW, Australia. **CHRISTINE ANNE SOUTHWELL** b 1 June 1979 at Sydney, NSW, Australia.	
		KATRINA ANNE BARTLETT b 21 May 1980 at Sydney, Australia. m 29 September 2001 at Ravensbourn, Queensland, Australia. **PETER EDWIN RUMBALL** b 15 May 1979 at Clifton, Queensland, Australia.	
	ROBYN BERYL EDWARDS b 26 May 1960 at Wanganui, NZ. m 15 March 1980 at == Dunmore, NSW, Aust.. **NATHAN MARK KEMP** b 12 April 1960 at Takapuna, NSC, NZ. (son of Roderick Kemp & Sharon nee Galagher)	**AARON NATHAN KEMP** b 23 June 1987 at Sydney, Australia. **JASMINE SHEREE KEMP** b 26 August 1989 at Sydney, Australia.	

L to R: *back*, **Jim Thomas, HARRY DOVE & ROSE**, Ethel Thomas. *front*, **Rene, Ivy, Gwen, Edna & Rolly.**

CHAPTER TWELVE

7th Generation (3rd NZ)

E. ROSE B. THOMAS

(1887-1967)

1887... BIRTH - ASHBURTON:
William and Eliza's eighth child was born 22 January 1887 in Ashburton, in the South Island of New Zealand. She was registered as Eleanor Rose Beatrice Thomas but was known to everyone as Rose.

Late in 1887, Rose, not yet one year old, left Ashburton and travelled with her family to live in Ngawapurua, near Woodville in the North Island.

SCHOOL: In February 1892 when Rose was 5, William and Eliza were living in Ngawapurua and their older children were attending Woodville School. Existing records show Rose started there on 28 March 1894 and also note she was staying with Mrs Sowry (Eliza) until 22 June 1894. About this time all the children transferred to the Mangatainoka School. The school's records show Rose, aged 8 attended in 1895 and, aged 11 in 1898 having passed her Standard 2 exam. William and Eliza and their younger children moved to live in Auckland late in 1898. Rose stayed and lived with sister Lizzie Sowry, and aged 13 attended the Nikau School in 1900 from that address. Here she passed reading, writing, spelling and composition but only gained 2 out of 5 for arithmetic.

1898... AUCKLAND.
It is not known when Rose moved to Auckland, and there is no record of her attending the New Lynn School where her younger siblings attended.

1911... ELECTION:
When aged 24, the 1911 Electoral Rolls listed Rose Thomas as 'Spinster' and misspelt her first name as 'Helen'.

1913... MARRIAGE:
On her 26th birthday, 22 January 1913, Rose married **HARRY DOVE** aged 29 at Elm's Hall in New Lynn, Auckland. Attending Rose were sister Ethel, brother Jim, and the first five children of brother Jack. (See photo page 281.)
Rose's sister Edith, later married Harry's brother Arthur Dove.

Jack Thomas' 1912 wedding day.
L to R at back... **Harry Dove with Rose and Jack Thomas.**
in front............ **Jack's second wife Violet and her sister Gertie Earl.**

Harry Dove emigrated to New Zealand on the *SS Corinthian* in 1911 at the age of 25. Most of his family joined him in Auckland in 1914.

The **Dove family history** is covered in more detail in Edith's chapter and is complete with a 9 generation family tree starting on page 304.

CHILDREN: Rose and Harry had four daughters named, Gladys, Leonie, Iris and Olive. Details of descendants follow later in this chapter.

Harry's mother Emma lived with them for a while.

1929... COUNCILLOR:

At the Henderson Public Library we found the undated advertisement or household-flyer. (page 284) Harry served on the council from 1929 to 1931.

A May 1929 photo in the New Lynn Borough Council's Jubilee booklet, shows members of its first Council. Mayor Charles Fisher Gardner and councillors Harry Dove, George Lawson, John Worthington, William (Billy) Platt, Stanley J. James, Chas. A. Stanley and Town Clerk J. R. Reich.

Granddaughter Geraldine Anderson from California wrote that 'Harry was a Councillor in Auckland, a concert violinist and conductor of the Auckland Philharmonic, a lawn bowls champion, a magnificent artist in every conceivable medium... and a womaniser.' (GA)

1929... GENERAL STORE:

The photograph included here of Harry Dove's store on Great North Road, New Lynn shows all the family and employees at that time. Of the 12 people visible, we have identified Olive as the smallest in a white frock with Leonie on her left and Gladys to her right. Also included are Harry, Rose and the office lady. We wonder if the older lady is Harry's mother Emma Dove?

Ted Scott recorded this same photo in his book *'Through the Lens'* and said *"You could buy virtually anything at Dove's Store... it had plenty of character."* The front of the shop advertised that available are.... coal, timber, posts, concrete blocks, new and used furniture, scoria, sand, cement, lime, tar and shingle. There are three trucks lined up to carry the goods to wherever needed and two *Plume* petrol bowsers out in front of the shop. Visible also is the brand-new concreted roadway, and the building behind the store is the then recently completed Delta Theatre.

Harry and Rose lived behind their general store. Some years later he opened a Drapery Shop for Rose.

Dove's Store, New Lynn

1936... PARTING:

Around 1936 Rose and Harry separated and were later divorced.

Rose remained single.

Harry remarried to Violet Amy Ganderton on 30 November 1947 in New Lynn, Auckland. Violet died 26 April 1966 aged 77.

Daughter Olive recalls that Rose and Harry had a 're-meeting' around 1966 and had a pleasant time discussing their lives, together and after the parting.

1944... IRIS:

The *Mt Albert Observer* gave Rose moments of pride when reporting her daughter Iris's wedding. They described Iris as New Zealand Women's Table Tennis Singles Champion, (she was for three years in a row) and her husband Sergeant RM Rowntree as an Army Cricket Representative. (SH)

USA visits.

Rose made many trips to California to visit her daughter Leonie and family. *The Mt Albert Observer* noted Rose (67) left on her fourth visit on 30 June 1954. When they interviewed her, she stated she could remember the days when there were only a few houses scattered here and there amongst the scrub. There were only two trains a day from town and horse drawn cabs were the transport to her father's property at Kelston. The paper said Rose was equally well known in New Lynn, Avondale and Mt Albert for she conducted business in all three suburbs and she now lived in New North Road, Mt Albert in a most modern house built to her own design. (SH)

Leonie's daughter Geraldine, called Rose 'Grandma' but with her American accent it sounded more like 'Grandmaaaaar' to Rose. They often laughed about this. Leonie and Geraldine visited Auckland after WWII and the New Zealand family came to meet them and listen to the 'little yank' talk. (GA) Grandson Richard Rowntree recalls calling Rose 'Nana Rose'.

EMMA: Geraldine also met Emma Dove, Harry's mother, and recalls *'she was stone deaf but the day my mother (Leonie) was born she heard her cry and her voice was the only sound she ever heard and she could hear her from that day on... but nothing else.'* (GA)
Emma Dove died 19 August 1948 in Auckland aged 86.

1967... DEATH:
The year of 1967 started badly for this Dove family.
On 7 January **Harry Dove** died aged 81 whilst living at 26 Rainford Street, Mt Roskill, Auckland. Harry's Will has not survived to the year 2000.

On 12 March **Rose Dove** died aged 80 whilst living at Glamis Hospital on New North Rd, Auckland where she had been living for the past two years. Rose signed her Will 29 June 1954 and after paying all debts the balance was equally divided between her children. There were no special bequests.

ROSE: Geraldine Anderson writes of her grandma Rose......
'Rose was strong and courageous, she was awe-inspiring ...
and could have been the prototype of today's self-made success...
... She faced adversity with strength and conviction.'

Harry and Rose, although not living together for many years, were buried side by side at Waikumete Cemetery, Protestant Lawn, Block C, Section 8, Plots 96 and 98, by their children and William Morrison, Funeral Directors.

Rose's plaque carries the message...
"A much loved and devoted mother."

E. ROSE B. THOMAS FAMILY TREE:

3rd Generation

ELEANOR ROSE BEATRICE THOMAS married……… **HARRY DOVE**

b 22 January 1887 (ROSE)	22 January 1913	b 2 June 1885
at Ashburton, Canterbury, NZ	at New Lynn,	at Shoreham by Sea, Brighton, Englanc
d 12 March 1967 (80)	Auckand.	d 7 January 1967 (81)
Bur Waikumete, Auckland.		Bur Waikumete, Auckland.

> Harry was the son of HENRY GEORGE DOVE and EMMA nee SMITH.
>
> Rose's sister Edith married Harry's brother Arthur Dove.
>
> Rose and Harry had four daughters they named Gladys, Leonie, Iris and Olive.
>
> Harry's 2nd marriage, Violet Amy Ganderton 30 Nov 1963 at New Lynn Auckland. No issue.

4th Generation	5th Generation	6th Generation	7th Generation
GLADYS ROSE DOVE b 22 April 1914 at New Lynn, Auckland. d 9 August 1997 (83) Bur Auckland. m 26 Oct 1936 ====== at Auckland. **CECIL OWEN WILSON** (Ces) b 7 July 1913 at Auckland. d 22 April 1980 (66) Bur Auckland. (son of Thomas Wilson and Annie nee)	**ROBYN OLIVE WILSON** b 20 July 1944 at Auckland. m 11 July 1967 ====== at Auckland. **ROBERT GEORGE WANNAN** b 24 July 1943 at Auckland. (son of John Wannan and Alice nee Childs)	**GLENN ROBERT WANNAN** b 6 February 1969 at Auckland. m 26 Feb 1994 ====== at Auckland. **NGAIRE JEAN SIMPSON** b 18 February 1969 at Auckland.	**TODD GRAHAM WANNAN** b 15 July 1998 at Auckland. **NICOLE ASHLEIGH WANNAN** b 20 August 2000 at Auckland.
		KARL DAVID WANNAN b 9 February 1971 at Auckland. m 8 Nov 1997 ====== at Auckland. **LARA JANE NUTTALL** b 24 October 1973 at Auckland.	**MIKAYLA LOUISE WANNAN** b 3 January 2000 at Auckland.
		MARK BRENT WANNAN b 15 March 1974 at Auckland. m 20 February 1999 at Auckland. MICHELLE next page	

4th Generation	5th Generation	6th Generation	7th Generation
Gladys & Ces continue	Robyn & Robert cont..	Mark married **MICHELLE LINDA** **BARKER** b at Auckland.	
LEONIE GRACE **DOVE** b 28 March 1917 at New Lynn, Auckland. d 23 January 1982 (64) Burried at Haywood, California, U.S.A. m 24 July 1939 ====== at Oakland, California. **CLARENCE ERVIN** **ANDERSON** b 22 June 1905 at Ogden, Utah, U.S.A. d 26 Nov 1992 (87) Burried at Haywood, California, U.S.A. (son of Eva and William Ervin Anderson)	**GERALDINE OLIVE** **ANDERSON** (Gerri) b 30 May 1941 at Oakland, California, U.S.A.		
IRIS MAY **DOVE** b 28 October 1918 at New Lynn, Auckland. d 8 April 2000 Bur Waikumete, A. m 15 January 1944 === at Mt Albert, Auckland. **MALCOLM** **RICHARD** **ROWNTREE** b 15 March 1919 at Auckland City.	**RICHARD JOHN** **ROWNTREE** b 25 February 1950 at Mt Albert, Auckland. m 23 Oct 1971 ====== at Auckland City. **JULIE GLEN** **SCRIMGEOUR** b 8 November 1950 at Auckland City. (daughter of Alan Scrimgeour and Glenn nee Daysh)	**DION RICHARD** **ROWNTREE** b 24 February 1978 at Mt Albert, Auckland. **RYANNE GLEN** **ROWNTREE** b 18 December 1980 at Mt Albert, Auckland.	
MALCOLM continues	GERALDINE next page	MONIQUE next page	

ROSE continued

4th Generation	5th Generation	6th Generation	7th Generation
Iris & Malcolm continue (Malcolm was the son of Richard William Rowntree and Lillian nee Howard)	**GERALDINE IRIS ROWNTREE** b 6 December 1951 at Mt Albert, Auckland. m 10 June 1972 ===== at Mt Albert, Auckland. **ROBERT JAMES RAE** b 22 April 1950 at Mt Eden, Auckland. (son of Cyril Ian Dalrymple Rae and Ellen Mary nee Breen)	**DARRYN IAN RAE** b 29 April 1976 at Mt Albert, Auckland. **MONIQUE KYLIE RAE** b 17 June 1978 at Mt Albert, Auckland.	
OLIVE MAVIS DOVE b 14 August 1924 at New Lynn, Auckland. m 3 December 1949 at Mt Albert, Auckland. **NEVILLE GEORGE ALFRED PERKINS** b 7 July 1927 at Pt Chevelier, Auckland. (son of Alfred William Perkins and Winifred Blanche nee Dutton)			

CHAPTER THIRTEEN

7th Generation (3rd NZ)

ETHEL ISABEL THOMAS

(1888-1942)

1888... BIRTH - WOODVILLE:

At Woodville on October 1, Ethel Isabel Thomas was born, the 9th child of William and Eliza Thomas. Her middle name was registered by her mother as Isabel but the Family Bible records it as 'Isabella'.

She signed her marriage certificate in full... Ethel Isabel Thomas.

Ethel's great-grandmother on her mother's side was Isabel Gordon from Scotland, and we feel Ethel was named after her.

Father William was a 'carpenter' aged 40 and Eliza was aged 37.

1893... SCHOOL: While living at Ngawapurua Ethel turned five and her father enrolled her at the Woodville School on 20 November 1893.

This year had been a busy year for the family. Ethel's sister Alice was born, Jane Thomas, her grandmother, died in Auckland and eldest sister Lizzie married. Ethel left the Woodville school 3 May 1894 and transferred to the Mangatainoka School with her brothers and sisters. She passed both exams... Standard 1 in 1897 and Standard 2 1898, while at Mangatainoka.

1898... AUCKLAND:

Late in 1898 Ethel's parents moved to Auckland where her father bought land at New Lynn. The New Lynn School records for **1899** show Ethel in Standard 3, attended 235 half days out of the 390 half days the school was open. On 22 September she was tested on reading, spelling and dictation, writing, drawing, arithmetic, composition and geography. She gained a pass.

1900... Standard 4 and another pass. **1901...** Standard 5 and another pass and in this exam on 23 September she spelt these words... enough, suppose, floating, fearless, empty, honour, mowers, surface and Christmas. Two arithmetic items were... How far does a horse go in 18 hours at the rate of 9 mile an hour? and... $\{(27-6x3) \text{ div } 4\} x3 +5 -4 = ?$

1902... Standard 6, Ethel now nearly 14, gained the maximum grade of 6 for reading, spelling, writing, geography and drawing and 5's for composition and arithmetic. This is the last record that has survived the years.

1905... WORK: In the mid 1900's Ethel left Auckland and travelled south.

Seeking employment Ethel spent time in Otorohanga where she did some waitressing. In Hunterville she met a girl named Sarah who became her life-long friend. Sarah shifted to Wanganui when she married Arthur Pepper. About this time Ethel moved to Nikau. Mavis Houlbrooke advised Sid Hawken that his mother went to work on her sister Lizzie's farm at Nikau.

1913... BRIDESMAID:

Rose Thomas married in January 1913 and her wedding photo (page 281) shows her being attended by sister Ethel (aged 24), brother Jim and brother Jack's children.

1918... WOODVILLE:

As a young soldier, Laurie Hawken returned from WWI to his family at Woodville and soon noticed Ethel Thomas. The Hawken and Walker families were early settlers in the district and two of Ethel's elder sisters, Lizzie and Eliza married two sons of another prominent Woodville settler family named Sowry.

ETHEL as a young lady. (RJS)

1921... MARRIAGE:

Ethel aged 32, married **ERNEST LORENZO HAWKEN**. He was known as Laurie and then aged 28. They were wed on 6 August 1921 at the Taihape Methodist Church by the Rev. William Lea. Official witnesses were C. G. Hawken a newsagent of Rangataua and J. H. Thorpe a carpenter of Lower Hutt. Ethel gave her profession as 'dressmaker' and Laurie described himself as 'sawmill yardman'. Neither had been married before. Ethel states she was born at Mangatainoka but her mother registered her birth as born at Woodville. Ethel's father William was recorded as 'retired', then aged 72.

Laurie's parents were Ernest and Maggie Hawken.

Laurie was enrolled at Petone Central School 10 April 1905 and he left that school on 25 November 1907 to 'go to work.'

Laurie told his son Sid, he received the middle name of Lorenzo because soon after his birth his father was impressed by a newspaper article about a famous Lion Tamer named Lorenzo.

Ethel and Laurie had two children known as Sid and Nita.

A full list of their descendants follows.

TIMBER:

Saw-milling became a major part of Ethel and Laurie's life, as they moved about the North Island following available work.

Laurie worked for some time in the King Country for Len Gardner, (he had married Annie Thomas, another of Ethel's sisters).

Then they moved to Horopito for some time, then to Turangarere 12 km north of Taihape.

About **1926** they moved to Tawa Flat, north of

ETHEL and LAURIE wedding day 1921

Wellington. Here Laurie found work at Tawa Timber Co. They settled here and in latter years Laurie became Managing Director of that company.

1922... SIDNEY:

Ethel and Laurie's first child, a son they named Sidney, was born 3 April 1922 at Taihape while the family were living at Turangarere.

> (We are grateful to Sid for the many hours he has spent assisting us with this historical section of Ethel's life. T.)

1924... NITA:

Nita was Ethel and Laurie's second child, born 22 October 1924 at Taihape.

1929... NZ DEPRESSION:

During the Depression years 1929-31, Ethel played an active part in the community of Tawa Flat. She was on the local Relief Committee and son Sid has memories of her arranging supplies of meat etc for delivery to local families. Whenever a 'swagger' walked up to Ethel's home, he was always sure of a good meal, sitting on the back steps to enjoy it.

Husband Laurie was quite happy with the situation, and fully supported Ethel's feeding of those people in need. Later, after Ethel had died, one of those 'needy ladies' phoned Sid at work and told him how grateful she was to receive his mother's help and aid, those many years earlier.

1931... CLUBS:

Sid advises that about 1931 Ethel was a foundation member of the Tawa branches of the Plunket Society and of the Women's Institute, and that she remained an active member for many years. She had a lot of interests and often acted as Treasurer or Secretary. Ethel joined the Tawa Drama Club and both Sid and Nita have fond recollections of seeing her in numerous skits and plays. There are some excellent examples of Ethel's artistic ability too, through a few items she made. There is a brass spark-guard and Sid has some pine-needle trays and sewing boxes.

ETHEL at Tawa Flat. (RJS)

Ethel often travelled great distances to demonstrate and pass on her art and craft skills.

ENTERTAINING: Sid recalls their home always full of visitors, especially at weekends. He and Nita would hang over the gate, admiring and counting the cars parked there. Ethel loved cooking and was adept at numerous goodies including lamingtons, pikelets, meringues, scones, etc but often had to place orders with the local pastry cook.

1937... SID:

The poliomyelitis epidemic struck the family in April and Sid (15) lost most of the use of both legs. His life continued in callipers and on crutches and this must have put a tremendous strain on the whole family. Ethel died five years after this event and her sister Rose helped Sid over the following years.

1942... ETHEL DIED:

While the family lived at Tawa Flat, Ethel died at home aged 53. On June 13, Sid (20) was returning home with the groceries and, making his way up the steps heard a heavy thud from inside. He searched the house for his mother, finding her dead on her bedroom floor, a vase of her beloved flowers scattered beside her. Sid continues... *"When she suddenly collapsed and died the whole district mourned. The long stretched out procession of cars were crammed full of her friends and acquaintances, as she was transported to Porirua. She had been greatly loved and respected by all whom she came in contact."* Of the effect Ethel had on Sid he says, *"She was one of the sweetest most caring and dearest Mothers any child*

LAURIE, ETHEL, NITA, SID & 'Lady'   Tawa Flat 1939

could have. She was always at hand in case I needed help during my rehabilitation. Due to her wonderful love, understanding and foresight, I learned to be strong and to cope with my paralysis. Memory of her guiding influence and love, will always succour me and give me strength."
Ethel was buried at Porirua because there was no cemetery at Tawa Flat.

MEMORIES of TAWA FLAT: Sid has fond memories as a lad of being with his mother and Nita, shopping at the big stores of Wellington, of riding an elephant, seeing other Zoo animals and feeding pigeons in Courtney Place. The whole family spent many hours together at the beaches near Tawa. Sid recalls cousin Mavis Houlbrooke telling them how beautiful they all thought Ethel was when she lived with them on the farm at Nikau, and how they loved her ready smile.
After Ethel died Laurie stayed on working at Tawa Flat.
Nita married Don Nairn at Petone in 1944.
Sid joined Ethel's sister Rose Dove's family in Auckland and attended University, gained his B. Com. Sid married Faith Collins in 1949.

Heirlooms... **CLOCK:** The mantle clock that rested above the fireplace in their Tawa Flat home is now in the care of Sid and has been promised to eldest grandson Russell, who will care for it for future generations.
      SPARK GUARD: Sid's daughter Elvin is the proud holder of a brass spark-guard made by her grand-mother Ethel. It depicts an old sailing ship and was worked by Ethel at an evening class.

LAURIE enjoyed tennis, swimming, picnics, tramping, fishing etc and a good joke and was a good boxer in his younger days. He is also remembered as being extremely good at training Alsatian dogs, and the family owned one for many years named 'Lady'. Earlier he had entered an Alsatian named 'Materlink Nada' in the New Zealand Field Trial Championship in Wellington and an English judge awarded the dog 98 out of 100. The dog's photograph even appeared in *The Dominion* newspaper. Laurie mastered shorthand and was also a very capable Maori linguist, often in demand. (SH)

1982... LAURIE DIED, on 20 June (89), his ashes were scattered at Karori.

Sid wishes to record these words about his mother........
"Her spirit lives on in the minds of all who knew and loved her…
relatives and friends all sampled her love and empathy."

The HAWKEN family

The WALKER family

<table>
<tr><td valign="top" width="50%">

1st Generation

SAMUEL JOLL born c1806 Cornwall, England.
   (Farmer and Blacksmith.)
married in Cornwall, England.
ELIZABETH TRELNING b. c1809 Cornwall
   = 5 children, Ann, Samuel, Sarah, John & Eliza.
   All chidren were born in Cornwall, England.
   emigrated to NZ on *'Timondra'* 2 Nov 1841
   arriving New Plymouth 23 February 1842.

</td><td valign="top" width="50%">

1st Generation

ENOCH WALKER born Masham, Yorkshire.
   (occupation ?)
married est Masham, Yorkshire, England.
ESTHER MARSDEN b Masham, Yorkshire.
   = 4 children, Thomas, Mary, Margaret, Enoch.
   All children thought to be born at Masham.

</td></tr>
<tr><td valign="top">

2nd Generation

HENRY HAWKEN b1836 Penzance, Cornwall.
   (Blacksmith.) d 11 Feb 1913 Woodville, NZ.
married 26 Feb 1862, New Plymouth, NZ.
ELIZA JOLL b c1840, Galstock, Cornwall.
        died 24 Nov 1909 Woodville, NZ.
   = 4 children, dau, dau, Ernest & Harry (d 28)
   (at present have no idea how Henry Hawken
    and Eliza Joll got to New Zealand.)

</td><td valign="top">

2nd Generation

ENOCH WALKER b 5 June 1840 Yorkshire.
   (Bootmaker) d 11 Sept 1907 Woodville, NZ.
married 1865 at Lancashire, England.
JAN GREENHALGH b Ainsworth, England.
        d 1879, Woodville, NZ.
   = 7 children, Thomas, Enoch, Esther, Emily,
   Margaret, James and Florence.
   Enoch and Jane emigrated to NZ in 1865 on
   the *'Berar'* arriving at Wellington.
   They lived at Greytown and Woodville, NZ.
ENOCH remarried to **ELIZA GROVES**
   = 11 children, William, Edward, Alice,
   Leonard, Roland, Frederick, Ivy, Eric,
   Charles, Hector and Albert.

</td></tr>
</table>

3rd Generation

ERNEST REDSTONE HAWKEN (Blacksmith) born 1872 West Clive, Hawkes Bay, NZ.
married 28 Sept 1892 at Woodville, New Zealand.
MARGARET (Maggie) ISABEL WALKER born 1872 at Wellington, New Zealand.
   Ernest died 31 August 1960, Petone, NZ.   Maggie died 8 August 1958, Petone, NZ.
Ernest and Maggie had 5 children. Ernest b1892 (Laurie), Cecil b1896, Violet b1900, Myrtle b1904,
   and Gwen b1907. The family were living at McLean St, Woodville when Laurie was born.

4th Generation

ERNEST (Laurie) LORENZO HAWKEN
   married
ETHEL ISABEL THOMAS.
   see Chapter Thirteen in this book for details of their lives
   and see following pages for details of their descendants to Easter 2001.
       (All these details received with thanks from Mark Prentice, via Sid Hawken.)

ETHEL ISABEL THOMAS FAMILY TREE:

3rd Generation

ETHEL ISABEL THOMAS...... married.............. **ERNEST LORENZO HAWKEN**

b 1 October 1888	6 August 1921	b 11 July 1893 (Laurie)
at Woodville, NZ.	at Taihape, NZ.	at Woodville, NZ.
d 13 June 1942 (53)		d 20 June 1982 (88)
Bur Porirua, Wellington.		Cremated, Ashes scattered at Karori, Wgtn.

Laurie, son of Ernest Redstone HAWKEN & Margaret (Maggie) Isabel nee WALKER.

Ethel and Laurie had two children they named Sidney and Nita.

4th Generation	5th Generation	6th Generation	7th Generation
SIDNEY (Sid) **LAWRENCE HAWKEN** b 3 April 1922 at Taihape. m 5 Jan 1949 ======= at Birkdale, NSC. **FAITH ROSEMARY COLLINS** b 25 February 1924 at Auckland City. (daughter of Gilbert Wentworth Collins and Ida Mary nee Lock)	**RUSSELL SIDNEY HAWKEN** b 9 January 1951 at Hawera. m 24 June 1978 ===== at Auckland City. **CHRISTINE MARIE SHAW** b 27 July 1951 at Auckland City. (daughter of Ronald Shaw and Marie Maureen nee Duggan)	**SEBASTIAN TATE HAWKEN** b 31 July 1981 at Napier.	
		MADELEINE JANE HAWKEN b 22 November 1983 at Napier.	
	ELVIN ROSEMARY HAWKEN b 29 March 1954 at Wellington. m 23 Oct 1976 ====== at Hamilton. **EDWARD LESLIE CHEESEMAN** b 13 August 1952 at Kawakawa, Northland. (son of Leslie Henry Walter Cheeseman and Jean Agnes nee Young)	**AARON JULIAN CHEESEMAN** b 5 July 1980 at Melbourne, Australia.	
		DREW DOUGAL CHEESEMAN b 28 December 1981 at Perth, Australia.	
		YANA JOY CHEESEMAN b 21 March 1984 at Takapuna, NSC.	
		BEVAN next page	

4th Generation	5th Generation	6th Generation	7th Generation
Sid and Faith continue	Elvin & Edward continue	**BEVAN LESLIE CHEESEMAN** b 7 February 1987 at Takapuna, NSC.	
		TEGAN ROSE CHEESEMAN b 21 July 1990 at Takapuna, NSC.	
	JILLIAN ETHEL HAWKEN (Jill) b 23 April 1957 at Hamilton. m 24 April 1982 ===== at Whangmata, NZ. **HORACE JOHN SPEAKE** b 20 December 1947 at Cambridge, NZ. (son of Cyril Arthur Speake and Ina Thora nee Christianson)	**DAVID JOHN SPEAKE** b 27 March 1983 at Hamilton.	
		TOMOTHY LUKE SPEAKE b 5 June 1985 at Auckland City.	
		LISA JOY SPEAKE b 14 April 1987 at Hamilton.	
		BEN DANIEL SPEAKE b 16 October 1990 at Hamilton.	
		SAMUEL JOSHUA SPEAKE b 15 September 1997 at Tauranga.	
	LANCE next page	CALLUM next page	

ETHEL continued

4th Generation	5th Generation	6th Generation	7th Generation
Sid and Faith continued	**LANCE JOHN HAWKEN** Surname changed by deed poll to **Gallagher--Hawken** b 24 March 1958 at Hamilton. m 22 Sept 1989 ===== at Auckland City. **KRIS MICHELE GALLAGHER** b 7 February 1963 at Nelson, NZ. (Daughter of Peter Gerald Gallagher and Margaret Patricia nee Hibberd)	**CALLUM TIMOTHY GALLAGHER-HAWKEN** b 1 February 1988 at Gold Coast, Queensland, Australia. **BRITTANY JANE GALLAGHER-HAWKEN** b 7 April 1990 at Takapuna, NSC.	
NITA EUPHEMIA HAWKEN b 22 October 1923 at Taihape. d 21 Oct 1996 (73) Ashes scattered at Te Anau. m 1 Jan 1944 ======= at Petone, Wellington. **DONALD JAMES HENRY NAIRN** (Don) b 10 March 1920 at Wellington. (son of Lionel Douglas Nairn and Grace Alice nee Henry)	**ROSLYN JOY NAIRN** b 25 December 1946 at Lower Hutt, Wgtn. m 11 Nov 1978 ===== at Dunedin. **GRAHAME CHARLES SYDNEY** b 23 May 1948 at Dunedin. (son of Jack Sydney and Elizabeth (Betty) nee Anderson)	**MELISSA KATE SYDNEY** b 17 May 1979 at Cromwell, Otago. **NICHOLAS GRAHAME SYDNEY** b 12 July 1981 at Cromwell, Otago.	
	GAIL MARIE NAIRN b 8 December 1951 at Wellington. m 15 Jan 1977 ====== at Queenstown, NZ. **GARY NEVIN KIRKMAN** b 11 October 1951 at Timaru. (son of Nevin John Kirkman and Margaret Mary nee Farquhar, who died 30 April 1998 & burried Timaru)	**DANIEL JAMES KIRKMAN** b 3 May 1980 at Balclutha. Otago. **ZOE MIRANDA ROSE KIRKMAN** b 8 July 1991 at Invercargill.	

CHAPTER FOURTEEN

7th Generation (3rd NZ)

EDITH MAY THOMAS

(1892-1978)

1892... BIRTH - PAHIATUA:

William and Eliza's eleventh child was born 25 February at Pahiatua, a few miles south of Ngawapurua where the family were living.

SCHOOL:

1897... The family were still living at Ngawapurua when in February, Edith turned 5. Her first school may have been at Maungatainoka where at this date her elder siblings were attending, however no record has been found.

1898... AUCKLAND:

Edith was now known as Edie, and aged 6 she travelled from Ngawapurua, to the family's new home at 16 Rata Street, New Lynn, Auckland.

SCHOOL:

1899... The first school record we have found for Edie, was at the New Lynn School on Examination Day 22 September 1899, when Edie was aged 7. In Primer 2 Class, she did not have to sit any exams.

1901... Now in Standard 1, Edie had a good attendance record of 329 out of 399 half days. In the exam she had to spell these words... leather, thrown, catching, fault, reading, heard, guard, teach and chains. There were 7 maths questions too which included... How many inches in 4 foot 2 inches? John had four pockets in his coat and 34 marbles in each. How many marbles all together? Edie had to add... 916 +8 +70 +121 +16 = ?

1903... Edie in Standard 3 had attended 318 half days.

1905... Edie attended Class 4 on 269 half days.

1906... Edie now in Standard 5, aged 14, attended 281 half days and this was the final record. Many records have not survived the years.

1907... AFTER SCHOOL:

Edie was employed as a dressmaker during the years before her marriage.

She met Arthur and soon after they became engaged Arthur volunteered for service in World War 1 but his false eye caused him to be rejected, even though he looked good and was very fit.

1916... MARRIAGE:

On 18 April 1916 Edie married **ARTHUR DOVE** at the Congregational Hall in New Lynn, Auckland. Arthur was a 'Storeman' aged 23. Arthur's parents were listed as Henry George Dove a 'Sea Captain', and Emma nee Smith. Witnesses to the wedding were Edie's father William Thomas, her brother Jim Thomas and Arthur's sister Emily Kate Dove. The Rev. W.H.A. Vickery performed the ceremony.

> **ARTHUR DOVE.** Arthur was born 16 December 1892 at Beckington House at Kingston-by-Sea in Sussex, England.
> We have been unable to locate a record of Arthur's baptism.

Arthur's younger brother William was 3 years 7 months when he was killed. He used to go to meet Arthur after school. On 24 October 1898 Arthur was holding his hand, when a loud noise from a steam roller frightened a horse pulling a covered wagon, just as it was passing them. It shied and bolted. The dray wheels went over William's body. Arthur not yet 6 years old, tried to pull him away. A witness said that action saved the wheels from going over his head. Arthur died aged 90 and never forgot the horror of those moments. (DT)

> On 18 September 1914, Arthur aged 21, left Tilbury, London by '*SS Ionic*' to emigrate to New Zealand. He reached Wellington on 6 November. Some relations in New Zealand knew Arthur as 'Tubby'.

Some Dove family history and a brief nine generation tree from 1640, starts on page 304 and was willingly supplied by Brian Arthur Dove of England, grandson of Arthur's brother Alfred George Dove, who remained to live in England.

CHILDREN: Edie and Arthur had two children they named Hector and Delcie. At Easter 2001 Edie and Arthur had seven grandchildren and fourteen great-grandchildren and their details follow later in this chapter.

The DOVE family... Arthur, Delcie, Hector and Edie about 1945.

HOME:
Edie and Arthur initially lived in New Lynn and soon after Delcie was born, they purchased a home at 53 Mt Albert Road, Mt Albert, Auckland which they owned for the rest of their lives.
Edie's father William Thomas died in February 1923, and Edie and family moved into her parents' 16 (today 26) Rata Street, New Lynn home to take care of her mother Eliza. For about eleven years they rented out their Mt Albert house, and about 1934 moved back into it taking Eliza now aged 82 with them. Here Eliza spent her final years. She passed away in March 1935.

OCCUPATION: Edie was fully occupied meeting her children's and the Rata Street house needs. Arthur gained employment soon after arriving in New Zealand. After marrying, he continued at Thompson Hills jam factory in Nelson Street, Auckland City as their 'Storeman' and finally retired from there aged 70, after giving them 49 years of loyal and reliable service. The company was bought out and, had he managed to work the full 50 years, he would have received a gold watch. In his early days there, he suffered the loss of his right eye in an accident. A small chip flew from a piece of steel he was hammering. For the rest of his life he wore a very realistic glass eye.

1976 DIAMOND WEDDING:
On 18 April 1976 Edie and Arthur celebrated 60 years of marriage and received four telegrams bringing warmest congratulations from The Queen at Buckingham Palace, Denis Blundell New Zealand Governor General, Allan Highet New Zealand Minister of Internal Affairs, and Mrs and Prime Minister R D Muldoon. During that day the Mt Albert Mayor and Mayoress called to 53 Mt Albert Road to offer their congratulations too. (DT)

HOBBY: Arthur became very good at repairing shoes for his family.
For many years in England Arthur played soccer at a senior level, and in the season 1912-13 he played for the Southwick Football Club when they won the Senior Cup. He received a medal to commemorate this event.
In retirement he took up bowls at which he became quite proficient. (DT)

GENERAL:
Edie and Arthur's daughter Delcie proudly retains a black crocheted scarf, afternoon-tea cloths and an old boar's tusk brooch, belonging to her mother.
Delcie has two saws used by her grandfather William. (page 82)
Their grandchildren knew Edie and Arthur as 'Grandma' and 'Granddad'.
Over many years Delcie has researched her New Zealand, English and Scottish families and has provided lots of the information in this book through certificates and photographs.   (Thank you Delcie. T)

1978... Edie died on 5 April 1978 aged 86. She left her mahogany bedroom suite and eagle ornament to daughter Delcie, and son Hector received the grandfather clock plus two boy and girl ornaments she treasured.

1983... Arthur lived his last 2½ years with daughter Delcie and died on 5 August 1983 aged 90 years. He was buried with Edie at Waikumete Cemetery, Protestant Berm Block A, Section 18, Plot 67. Battersley were their funeral directors. Arthur left his estate equally to his two children.
Edie and Arthur's headstone has the notation...   *"Sadly Missed"*

The DOVE Family.

On page 306 is a brief nine generation Dove family tree,
followed by descendants of Edie and Arthur Dove.

Captain HENRY GEORGE DOVE and wife EMMA nee SMITH

Henry George Dove and wife Emma Smith married on 2 September 1884 at the Registry Office in Brighton, Sussex, England. The first house Henry and Emma lived in was 'Malthouse Cottage' attached to the brewery nearby. Emma's family were Maltsters. They were still there during the 1891 Census. It is believed the family moved to *'Beckington House'* just before son Arthur was born in December 1892. Henry G Dove named his family home *'Beckington'* after the small village near Frome in Somerset, where he was born and raised. This house at Kingston-by-Sea (today absorbed by Shoreham-by-Sea) was sited over the road from the old Shoreham harbour's lighthouse, and still stands in the year 2000. (BD)

Henry and Emma had six children…. five sons, then a daughter.
Emma was born 6 February 1862 at St Johns Clayton in Sussex, to George and Martha Smith. After her husband Henry George Dove died aged 49 in 1909, and was buried at St Julian's parish Church, Kingston-by-Sea, Emma joined her family and emigrated to New Zealand. (BD)

Captain Henry George Dove sailed passenger boats *'Brighton'*, *'Princess May'* and *'Sussex Belle'* in the English Channel to the Isle of Wight and toured the Belgium coast for two years and on occasions carried a Royal person.

Henry must have been held in high regard by his employers...
The Waverly Shipping Group... as he received an inscribed gold watch from them when he married Emma.

The house on the left is **BECKINGTON HOUSE** the Sussex home of Henry & Emma Dove.

He was already a Captain at the early age of 24.

When Henry was aged 22, he was awarded the Humane Society's Certificate for diving off the bridge of a boat to save the life of one of his crew who could not swim. The chap had thrown a bucket overboard to get water. It was attached to a rope and with the boat moving, it pulled him into the sea.

The Captain's 'spyglass', passenger counter, whistle, coin case, cigar holder and the gold watch, are treasured heirlooms held by granddaughter Delcie.

Arthur's grandfather Henry Dove was the first policeman in Bristol and later at Beckington. He wore the number 129 and became a Sergeant. (BD & DT)

Arthur's eldest brother Harry emigrated to New Zealand in 1911. Arthur (21), his mother Emma 50, sister Emily 14, brother Frank 23 with his wife Elsie 27 and their son William (Bill) aged 1, travelled on the *'SS Ionic'* to join Harry in Auckland, just before the War started in 1914. (BD)

--oo0Ooo--

305

The DOVE FAMILY brief tree.

1st Generation **PETER DOVE** b1640,   married 1669   **DOROTHY   ?   ?**
                                           lived Wincanton, Somerset, England.
          3 children, Mary b1670, Peter b1673, Martha b1676.

2nd Generation **PETER DOVE** b1673   married 1695   **FRANCES STONE**
                                           lived Wincanton, Somerset, England.
          1 child Peter b1697   Peter and second wife Grace Clement = 13 children..

3rd Generation **PETER DOVE** b1697   married 1748   **ELIZABETH FARRINGDON**
                                           lived Wincanton, Somerset, England.
          7 children, John b1748, Sarah b1752, Elizabeth d1753, Elizabeth d1757,
                     Peter d1757, Martha b1760 and Benjamin d1767.

4th Generation **JOHN DOVE** b1748   married 1768   **ELIZABETH ATKINS** b1748
                                           lived Wincanton, Somerset, England.
          4 children, Elizabeth b1768, Morgan b1769, William b1777, Benjamin b1780.
   (Probable above, definite below. Yet to prove 100%, Morgan is son of John & Elizabeth. BD)

5th Generation **MORGAN DOVE** b1769   married 1801   **MARY LONGMAN** b1768
                                           lived Wincanton, Somerset, England.
          4 children, Jemima b1803, William b1805, Peter b1906, Benjamin b1811.

6th Generation **WILLIAM DOVE** b1805   married 1830   **MARY ANN HOSKINS** b1809
                                           lived Wincanton, Somerset, England.
          9 children, Henry b1832, William b1835, Ann b1836, ---b/d1839, Emily b1840,
                     ---b/d1844, ---b/d1846, John b1848, Alfred b1850.

7th Generation **HENRY DOVE** b1832   married 1856   **DINAH WELCH** b1834
                                           lived at Bristol and at Beckington, Somerset, England.
          3 children, Emma b1857, Kate b1858, Henry George b1860.   Henry died 1863. (31)
                                           Dinah remarried to William Riddle, no children.

8th Generation **HENRY GEORGE DOVE** b1860 married 1884   **EMMA SMITH** b1862
                                           lived at Shoreham-by-sea, Sussex, England.
          6 children, Harry b1885, Alfred George b1887, Frank b1890, Arthur b1892,
                     William b1895-d1898, Emily Kate b1900.
          Henry died 1909. (49)   Emma emigrated to New Zealand to be with her children.
          Harry arrived New Zealand in 1911 settling in Auckland. His mother Emma with Arthur,
          Emily and Frank, and Frank's wife Elsie and son William came to New Zealand in 1914.
          Alfred and family remained to live in England and Shoreham-by-sea in Sussex.

9th Generation Brothers **HARRY & ARTHUR DOVE** married sisters **ROSE & EDITH THOMAS**
          (see chapters twelve and fourteen for Harry and Arthur's New Zealand family detail.)

For more Dove information refer Brian Dove... dove@intradco.co.uk or www.badove@supanet.com

EDITH MAY THOMAS FAMILY TREE:

3rd Generation

EDITH MAY THOMAS............ married................**ARTHUR DOVE**

b 25 February 1892 (Edie)	18 April 1916	b 16 December 1892
at Woodville, NZ.	at New Lynn,	at Kingston-by-Sea, Brighton, England
d 5 April 1978 (86)	Auckland.	d 5 August 1983 (90)
Bur Waikumete, Auckland.		Bur Waikumete, Auckland.

      Arthur was the son of HENRY GEORGE DOVE and EMMA nee SMITH.

      Edith's sister Rose married Arthur Dove's brother Harry.

      Edith and Arthur had two children they named Hector and Delcie.

4th Generation	5th Generation	6th Generation	7th Generation
ARTHUR HECTOR JAMES DOVE b 7 June 1917 at New Lynn, Auckland. m 12 Feb 1949 ====== at Mt Roskill, Auckland. **CHARLOTTE MAUDE ALEXANDER** b 8 September 1927 at Allabab, India. (daughter of Robert John Alexander and Jessie nee Richie)	**CAROL EVELYN DOVE** b 13 January 1950 at Auckland City. m 8 Nov 1975 ====== at Mt Roskill, Auckland. **RICHARD PAUL RYE** b 14 April 1945 at Matamata. (son of Lionel Douglas Rye and Noeline Valma nee Jenkins)	**KEVIN WAYNE RYE** b 19 August 1975 at Auckland City. m 12 September 1998 at Mt Roskill, Auckland. **TRACIE MICHELLE GRIBBLE** b 28 July 1978 at Auckland City. **GLENN ANDREW RYE** b 21 October 1979 at Auckland City.	
	CHRISTINE DOVE b 27 August 1953 *twin* at Auckland City. m 17 Feb 1979 ====== at Mt Roskill, Auckland. **MICHAEL CLOW GALLAGHER** b 16 February 1950 at Hamilton. (son of Royden Morris Gallagher and Mavis Beatrice nee Laird)	**SARAH JAYNE GALLAGHER** b 7 January 1980 at Auckland City. m 28 October 2000 at Mt Roskill, Auckland. **ROBERT COLIN LYNNE** b 6 May 1980 at Auckland City. SHARON next page	

4th Generation	5th Generation	6th Generation	7th Generation
Hector and Charlotte continue	Christine and Michael continue	**SHARON LORETTA GALLAGHER** b 30 October 1981 at Auckland City.	
		BRETT MICHAEL GALLAGHER b 28 October 1985 at Auckland City.	
		DAVID ROYDON GALLAGHER b 28 September 1987 at Auckland City.	
	NOELINE DOVE b 27 August 1953 *twin* at Auckland City. m 30 Oct 1976 ====== at Mt Roskill, Auckland. **KEVIN ANTHONY EDWARDS** (Tony) b 5 July 1954 at Wellington. (son of Kevin Edwards & Colleen nee Minehan)	**MICHAEL ANDREW EDWARDS** b 20 July 1978 at Auckland City.	
		AMY JOANNE EDWARDS b 15 June 1982 at Auckland City.	
	JULIE MAY DOVE b 6 May 1962 at Auckland City. m 19 March 1983 ==== at Mt Roskill, Auckland. **COLIN HENRY LA PERE** b 15 January 1961 at Auckland City. (son of Robert Jurt La Pere & Patricia nee McDonald)	**JODINE RACHEL LA PERE** b 31 January 1986 at Auckland City.	
		DAVID ANDREW LA PERE b 9 June 1988 at Auckland City.	

4th Generation	5th Generation	6th Generation	7th Generation
Hector and Charlotte continue	**JOHN RAYMOND DOVE** b 7 August 1969 at Auckland City.		
DELCIE EVELYN DOVE b 27 July 1919 at New Lynn, Auckland. m 15 March 1947 ==== at Auckland City. **JOSEPH** (Bill) **TWIZELL** b 14 March 1921 at Kawa Kawa, Northland. d 13 Dec 1974 (53) Bur Schnapper Rock, North Shore City. (son of Joseph Twizell & Margaret nee Robson)	**RODNEY JAMES TWIZELL** b 11 September 1951 at Devonport, NSC. m 12 Nov 1981====== at Pakuranga, Auckland. **JANE LINDA GOSLING** b 24 December 1954 at Auckland City. (daughter of Fernly Charles Arthur Gosling and Audrey Elaine nee Levick)	**AMY KRISTIN TWIZELL** b 2 December 1983 at Mt Albert, Auckland. **DANIEL JAMES TWIZELL** b 26 May 1987 at Greenlane, Auckland.	
	LYNNE KAREN TWIZELL b 23 September 1955 at Narrowneck, NSC. m 8 May 1976 ====== at Takapuna, NSC. **RONALD MERVYN FINDLAY** b 29 December 1950 at Herne Bay, Auckland. (son of Mervyn Ronald Findlay and Rose nee Whitingham)	**KELLY ANN FINDLAY** b 6 February 1983 at Greenlane, Auckland. **JEFFREY IAN FINDLAY** b 14 December 1985 at Greenlane, Auckland.	

CHAPTER FIFTEEN

7th Generation (3rd NZ)

WALTER JAMES THOMAS

(1894-1917)

1894... BIRTH - NGAWAPURUA:

Walter James Thomas was known as 'Jim' and was the 13th child of William and Eliza Thomas. He was born at Ngawapurua on 8 November 1894.

1898... AUCKLAND: Jim was 4 when his parents moved to New Lynn.

1900... SCHOOL:

We believe Jim may have started school at New Lynn at the beginning of 1900. The records for 1900/1/2 have not survived to the present day.

In 1903, when nearly aged 9, Jim was in Primer 3 and the 2 September report shows he attended 297 and a half days. Year 1904 records are lost.

In 1905, Jim nearly aged 11 had progressed to Standard 1.

On 24 August 1906, Jim now nearly 12 was in Standard 2 and had a better attendance of 357 half days. 1907 records lost.

On 14 December 1908, Jim was 14 and in Standard 3. His exam results show 12/20 for reading, 28/40 spelling, 13/20 comprehension, 15/25 arithmetic. Jim's class mates were mostly aged 10 and 11. The report advises he received a 'conditional promotion to Standard 4' for 1909.

He lived with his parents at Rata Street, until he died.

CRAFTS:

Jim enjoyed working with his hands, and one item to survive the years is a wooden tea-tray he made and carved. Delcie Twizell treasures it.

1913... BEST MAN:

On 22 January 1913 Jim, aged 18, was Best Man for Harry Dove when Harry married Jim's sister Rose. A wedding group photo is on page 281.

On 18 April 1916 Jim, aged 21, was Best Man also for the wedding of his sister Edie to Arthur Dove and his signature appears on the certificate as a witness.

1917... ACCIDENT:

On the morning of 19 June 1917, Jim went to work at Messrs Parker and Lamb's timber mills in Fanshaw Street, Auckland. Shortly before 9am he was admitted to the Auckland District Hospital with serious injuries. The *New Zealand Herald* reports on the 20th *"..he was caught in a shafting belt..., During the afternoon it was found necessary to amputate one of his legs and it is thought that it will be necessary to remove an arm. At a late hour last evening he was reported to be in a low state."*

JIM DIED 27 June 1917, single and aged 22.

A report of the Coroner's enquiry into the 'Sawmill Fatality' appeared in the *New Zealand Herald* 30 June 1917. The Coroner Mr E. C. Cutten, S.M. found... *"Death was due to shock, caused by severe wounds and septic infection. The deceased was employed in a timber mill and while putting a rope around a revolving shaft, his apron became entangled. Deceased was caught up and carried around the shaft several times, receiving injuries which led to his death. The deceased was endeavouring to make an improper use of the revolving shaft in putting a rope around it, and his action was the sole cause of the accident. The shaft is not in an unsafe position and no blame is attachable to any other person."*

Sid Hawken recalls Jim's brave and realistic humour when he visited Jim in hospital. He writes that Jim told him... *"I shall pass through New Lynn once more, but I won't hear the whistle blow."*

Jim's cortege left his parents' home for the Waikumete Cemetery and he was buried in 'Presbyterian Block D, Section 6, Plot 27'.

ACKNOWLEDGEMENTS

OTHER WRITINGS and SOURCES.

Gazetteer of the British Isles 1887.   William White's Devon of 1850.
Family History Centre, Takapuna, Auckland................. for Devon, England, Old Parish Records.
Wises N.Z.P.O. Directory.   NZ Electoral Rolls.
The Auckland Directory 1873.   Chapman's New Zealand Almanac of 1862
Land Information, Auckland & Wellington.   Cyclopedia of NZ 1904.
National Archives Offices at Auckland, Wellington and Christchurch.
Public Library staff at Takapuna, Auckland, Woodville and Ashburton: Auckland Museum Library.
New Zealand Society of Genealogists.   Justice Department of NZ....Births, Deaths & Marriages.
John Barr.   "The City of Auckland"   J. T. Diamond. (OTW2) "Once the Wilderness"
Anthony G Flude.   "Henderson's Mill"   D. N. Hawkins.   "Rangiora"
A. M. Latta.   "Meeting of the Waters"   H. C. M. Norris.   "Armed Settlers"
J. R. McCorquindale. "The History of New Lynn"   Dick Scott.   "Fire on the Clay"
Ted Scott.   "Through the Lens"   W. H. Scotter. "A History of Canterbury, Vol 3"
A.H.Walker.   "The Story of Point Chevalier 1861-1961"   "Woodville 1875 - 1975"
(WA) West Auckland Historical Society.   "West Auckland Remembers" (Part 1 & 2)
(M) "Mangamaire..... A Century of Change 1897 - 1997".   (MC) Makomako Church 50th Anniversary.
Newspapers... The New Zealand Herald, The Auckland Star, The New Zealand Spectator & Cook Strait
Guardian, The Weekly News, Daily Southern Cross, The NZ Methodist Times, The Nokomai Herald,
The Ashburton Guardian, The Woodville Examiner, The Pahiatua Herald, The Pahiatua Bush Telegraph.

SPECIAL THANKS.

Alice Gillespie for original William Thomas knowledge.
Delcie Twizzel for sharing her Thomas, Carrie, McKay and Dove research.
Flossie Thomas for most of the photographs used in this book.
John Longhurst of the Ilfracombe Museum.
May Verney for assistance with Thomas family in Devon.
Violet and George Wright for Jack Thomas knowledge.
To Family historians...   Brian Dove (Dove),   Sid Hawken (Hawken),
Allan Ladbrook (Ladbrook),   Betty & Athol Sowry (Sowry),   Joy George (Wilmshurst).

VERY SPECIAL THANKS to all the grandchildren of William and Eliza Thomas.

Christine and Mary-Ann Attree and Kiri Price, for their valuable proof reading skills.
My wife Jill for showing great patience and the willingness to travel all over new Zealand and England in
research for this book.

Thank you to the contributors whose names are not mentioned in full, but by initials only....

AG = Alice Gillespie	FT = Flossie Thomas	ME = Mary England	OH = Olwen Hammond
AH = Anita Houlbrooke	GA = Gerri Anderson	MG = Marjory Gatfield	PT = Percy Thomas
ANT = Auriel Thomas	GC = Gary Cooke	M+TC = Melva and	RE = Ruth Edwards
AS and B +AS =	GW = George Wright	Trevor Cooke	RH = Ray Haslam
Betty and Athol Sowry	JCET = John Thomas	M MacD = Margert	RJS = Roslyn Sydney
AT = Amy Tan	JG = Joy George	MacDonald	SH = Sid Hawken
AWT = Athol Thomas	JR = June Roy	MW = Myrle Watt	TS = Trevor Sowry
BD = Brian Dove	JS = Jessie Sowry	NB = Ngara Battersby	VW = Violet Wright
BF = Betty Flexman	KA-R Keri Ashton-Reid	ND = Ngaire Dittmer	WJT = Jim Thomas
DT = Delcie Twizell	LA = Leon Ansin	NS = Neville Sowry	ZK = Zita Kay

Brent Robert 279
Chloe Kym 279
Howard 279
James Ernest 279
Kym Robert 279
Shaylah Lee 279

HUGHES Keziah 238

HULL Eunice 212

HUMPHRIES
Bernice Mary 276

HUNTER Lola May 279

HUTCHINSON
Sharron Dale 208

HYLTON Maureen 266

IMBODEN Marie B 253

INGLIS
Graeme Maurice 265
John Gilmore 265

INGRAM Hazel 147

JACK Nessie Paykel 249

JACKSON
Arthur 266
Gail Elizabeth 266
Katherine Elizabeth 213

JAMES
Alice Mary 193
Emma Kate 119
Jane 209
Rebecca Rose 119
Tony Richard 119

JARVIS Charlotte M 166

JENKINS
Noeline Valma 307

JENSEN Christine M 171

JOBE
Augustus Edward 138
Charee Frances 138
David Leslie 138
Denise Valerie 138
Royce Leslie 138

JOHANSEN
Caleb Ashley 278
David William John 279

JOHNSON Leslie 121

JOHNSTONE Gaile 254

JONES Murray 269
Nicola Marianne 268
Sarah Grace 123
Timothy Pryce 123
Warwick (Rick) 123

JUDD
Bryce Sydney 273

Harry Wallace 274
Jeremy William 273
Katie Maria 274
Sidney Gordon 273

KARL
Brian Robert 195
Darryn Robert 195
Steven Joseph 195

KATZ Theresa 276

KAUR
Chandani Shamine M. 248
Lutchamy Seeta 248

KAVANAGH
Raewyn Gail 120

KAY
Anya Zita 195
Bryce Robert 195
Denis Bernard 195
Gordon David 195
Leanne Raewyn 195
Robert 195
Sharon Angela 195

KEATS Naida 163

KEENE Alice 135

KELLY Lavina Joyce 210

KEMP
Aaron Nathan 280
Jasmine Sheree 280
Nathan Mark 280
Roderick 280
Susan Jayne 277

KENNEDY
Alan Frederick 205
Holly Rose Louvaine 205
Mary 116
Samuel Brian 205

KENNERLEY
Arnold 147
Bruce Arnold 147
David Michael 147
John Bruce 146
Lisa Jane 147

KERESOMA
Cheyne Hake 213
Gututala Hake 213
June Nofo 213
Karl Gututala 213
Nofoagamata 213

KING
Annie Grace 124
Brian Newton 163
Claudia Nicole 123
Dennis John 123
Fraser Alexander 123
Frederick Joseph 124
Heather Margaret 124
Joseph John 123
Marilyn Joy 163
Perry Joseph 124
Thomas 123

KIRE Freda Wilamena 275

KIRK
Rosalie Ann 164
Sarah 205

KIRKMAN
Daniel James 299
Gary Nevin 299
Neville John 299
Zoe Miranda Rose 299

KISTENMAKER
Frances 268

KITCHING Agnes 139
John 139

KNOX
Kevin Murray 274
Zacharry Aden 274

LA PERE
Colin Henry 308
David Andrew 308
Jodine Rachel 308
Robert Jurt 308

LAIRD Mavis B 307

LAMBERT
Richard Dana 279

LAND
Ernest John Henry 255
Noeline Winsome 255

LANG
Brent John 264
John 264
Kiana Pheonix 264
Tiare Billie-Jean 264

LANSAIKI Kapi 264

LARCOMBE Lillian 132

LASKEY
Diane Marie 162
Kenneth Maxwell 162

LAWTON Sally 128

LEAMAN
Bethany Skye 127
Mark James 127

LEMON
Joan Isobel 207
Major Alfred 207

LENNOX
James Stuart 239
Olivia Marie 239
Stuart Norman 239

LENSSEN
Barbara Theresa Mary 138

LEVICK
Audrey Elaine 309

LEVITT Florence J 216

LEWIS
Gordon 147
Ian Norman 147

LEWIS-ROBERTS
Simon Gary 141

LEYLANDER
Aaron Frank 175
Frank Roy Sowry 175

LIDDELL Patricia 120

LIDDLE Harry 227
Judith Clare 227
Mrs Noma 227

LIGHT
Amelia Janice 227
Anthony Colin 229
Arthur Leonard 228
Bruce Francis 229
Colin Stanley 228
David Thomas 228
Ernest Colin 227
Gerard James 229
Janice Melva 229
John Max 228
Leonard Douglas 227
Len Douglas (II) 227
Marita Anne 228
Mark Leonard 229
Patricia Mary 227
Penelope Noma 227
Peter Colin 228
Rachael Phillipa 227
Richard John-Paul 228
Simon Ernest 229

LINYARD Carrie 247/8

LOCK Ida Mary 297

LOIRING
Florence Beatrice 208

LONG Janine Marie 134

LOOKER Gladys 118

LOUGHLAN
Kathleen 149

LUNDIE
Margaret McKenzie 150

LYNNE Robert Colin 307

LYSAGHT
Adam Barry 274
Barry William 274
Bridget Joyce 274
Jerrard William 274
William Stanley 274

MacDONALD
Andrea Katherine 140
Claire Laura 140
Diane Margaret 140
Judith Anne 140
Kathryn Patricia 139
Michelle Elizabeth 140
Paul Charles 140

Percy William 139
Ron Charles 139

MacGREGOR
David 209
Taylor Ogilvy 209

McALPINE
Carol 274
John 274

McCALLISTER
Cyril Raymond 213

McCARTHY
Bruce Leslie 128
Frances Ann 228
Francis Augustine 228
Stacy Ann 128

McDONALD
Patricia 308

McERLAIN
Kelsie Anne 161
Tiffany May 161
Trevor John 161

McFARLANE
Lorraine Phoebe 251

McGIVERN
Wendy Frances 195

McGLONE Susan 117

McIAY Coralie Dawn 273

McINTYRE
Andrew Stewart 160
Luke Arthur Jackson 160
Rebecca Alice 160
Thomas Stewart Glynn 160

McKELVEY
Frederick George 165/9
Josephine Marjorie 165

McKENZIE
Alan Donald 250
Donald 250
Lane 250
Wade 250

McLEAVEY
Alfred 160
Marjorie 160

McLEOD
Alan William 215
Alma Margaret 150
Dianna Rose 215
Harry Benjamin 215
James 208
Joan Nancy 208
Ross Alan 215
Samuel John 215

McMILLAM
Adele Jane 141
Craig John 202
Denis Ritchie 202
Hayden Craig 142

Scott Wayne 202
Stuart Craig 141
Tara Maree 141

McQUILKIN
Abby Elizabeth 204
Ben Jonathan Thomas 205
Briar Kate Lillian 205
Colin James 204
Erin Christina 204
Laura Jayne 204

McSWEENEY
Elsie Marion 205

McWILLIAM
Brett John 173
Coral Rose 173
Ernest 173
Glenn Roy 174
John Ernest 173

MACDONALD
Stuart John 143

MACPHERSON
Colin Peter 176
Leslie Norman James 176
Peter Leslie 176
Wendy Ann 176

MAHER Peter George 137

MAIN Annette Kay 130

MAITLAND Eileen P 215

MALCOLM
Alexander Lumsden 134/7
Jessie Annie 137
Marjorie Flora 134

MANGAN Melissa L 195

MARCHANT
Eleanor Harriet 171

MARDEN Beryl V 270

MARINO
Christopher Max 252
Christopher Tamamutu 252
Nadine Linda 252
Tamamutu K. R. 252
Wayne Mason 252

MARSHALL
Alexander Gary 206
Bettina Joy 203
Craig Andrew 206
Gary Ross 206
Glenn David 206
John Boyd 204
Jonathan Craig 238
Keith Thomas 206
Lionel 204
Michael James 206
Scott Thomas 206
Zelma Rose 204

MARTIN
Aaron Charles 138
Ella Dawn 138

Kerry Charles 138

MASON
Keith 195
Reginald William 195
Trevor 195

MAWHINNEY
Ben Robert 227
Donald Fredrik 227

MAY Norma 196

MEADES
David John 135
Michael James 136
Julie Anne 136
Paul William 135
Sandra Beth 135
William Alec 135
William George 135

MELVILLE
Charles Beval 231

MEYER Bruce 253
Ernest William 253
Liam Jarrod 253
Logan Michael 253
Michael Glenn 253
Wendy Karin 253

MILES Leonard 171
Millicent Agnes E. 171

MILLAR Niccole K 270

MILLER Treena L 149

MILNE
Andrew Colin 172
Andrew Malcolm 172
Colin Bruce 172
Sheryl Rose 172
Wendy Anne 172

MINEHAN Colleen 308

MINIFIE Mabel 170

MINSON Pamela R 147

MITCHELL
Carl Brandon 231
Edwin John 231
Stacey Belinda 231
William Charles 231

MITTEN
Angela Anne 148

MOIR
Joan Hollie Luanna 269

MONTESANTO
Giampaolo 132

MOODY Rosemary 252

MOORECOCK
Valma Amelia 162

MOORMAN Joy P 125

MOOSMAN
Delma Iris 145

MORAN
John Charles 169
Sandra Janice 169

MORRIS
Janice Lynn 167

MORRISON
Cameron Gordon 145
Gordon Raymond 146
Mary 230

MOSS
Adam 199
Billy-Joe Kevin 196
David 199
Debra Helen 198
Dianne Carol 197
Evelyn Pearl 198
Gary 199
George Albert 196/198
Haylee Louise 199
Janet 199
Joelene Ellen 196
John Robert Hamilton 196
Kara Jeanne 199
Kenneth George 198
Kevin John 196
Lorna 207
Margaret 200
Mary-De Susan 196
Michael 200
Stephen James 196
Tania Ann 199
Timothy Lawrence J. 196

MOUNT
Roseana Ngarie Joyce 166

MUDGWAY
Jessica Priscilla 164
Jordan Keith 164
Keith Rua 164

MURRAY
Cheryl-Ann 250
Dian 145
Henry David 145

MURRIE James 128
Teresa Elizabeth 128

MYERS Bingley 122
Elizabeth (Betty) Jean 122

NAGEL Adrianna 143
Alan Ian 143
Betty Margaret 164
Carolyn Lee 145
Casey Larisa 144
Daryl John 144
Fiona Kim 145
Frederick 143
Graeme Anthony 144
Hayden Ian 144
Ian Frederick 143
Jade Daryl 144
Judith Merle 143
Kelly Ann 144
Kerrie Alana 144

Luke Anthony 144
Marc Kenneth 143
Maree Robyn 143
Matthew Graeme 144
Timothy 143
Tyrone 143
William Henry 164

NAIRN
Don James Henry 299
Gail Marie 299
Lionel Douglas 299
Roslyn Joy 299

NEAL
Andrew Michael 212
Gordon 212
Murray Denis 212
Rebecca Jayde 212
Stella Diana 119

NEEDHAM
Carlene Joanne 197
Lisa Alice 116

NEILSEN Carol A 162

NELSON
Kym Robert 279
Ronald 279

NEVERMAN
Andrew James 275
Geoffrey James 275
Michelle Nicola 275
Richard Allan 275

NEWBY
Robert Donald 146
Charlee Dian B-N 146

NEWING Linda Jean 207

NEWINGTON
Duncan 133

NICHO
Akeshia Crystal 170
Carlos Jared 169
Robert Samuel 170

NICHOLSON
Frederick 196
Pearle Eileen 196

NIEDERBERGER
Andrew Glenn 253
Daniel Patrick 253
Jenna Marie 253
Peter Edward 253
Sarah Jane 253
Walter 253

NIXON
Charles 149
Claudia Holly 149
Courtney Samantha 149
Georgia Monique H. 149
Kim Margaret 149
Lance Andrew 149
Raymond Charles 149
Wayne Raymond 149

NOMM Winifred 193

NORTON Elsie 137

NUTTALL Lara Jane 287

O'HARA Lynne Mary 118

O'HEARN
Jason David 269
Leonard Andrew 269

O'KEEFE Timothy J 256

O'REILLY Jerard 173
Hayden Ben 173
Luke Adam 173
Myles John 173
Vicky Jewelle 174

OGILVIE Noeline 177

OLIVER
Kaye Rosemary 212
Trevor 212

OLSEN Glenda Joy 197

ORAMS Alma J 138/140

OVERALL
Janine Marie 164
Kevin William 164

PACKER David 249
Joe 249

PAINTER
Elizabeth Sandra 217
Michelle Anne Marie 217

PALLANT Isobel 128

PARATA
Makareta Parks 214

PARKES David V 139

PARKINSON
Gethin Alan 213
James Douglas 165
Ryan James 165

PARNELL
Carl William 215
Hannah Elise 216
Kate Victoria 215
Kenneth John 216

PEAKE Carolyn Ann 270

PEARCE Janice 211

PERENARA Brett T 256

PERKINS
Alfred William 289
Neville George Alfred 289

PERRY
Anna Rachel 169
Brendon John 169
Douglas Craig 169